Camelot

A Role Playing Simulation

of Political Decision Making

Camelot

A Role Playing Simulation

of Political Decision Making

Fifth Edition

JAMES R. WOODWORTH

Miami University

W. ROBERT GUMP

Miami University

JAMES R. FORRESTER

West Liberty State College

 **WADSWORTH**
CENGAGE Learning‍

Australia • Brazil • Japan • Korea • Mexico • Singapore • Spain • United Kingdom • United States

Camelot: A Role Playing Simulation of Political Decision Making, Fifth Edition
James R. Woodworth, W. Robert Gump, and James R. Forrester

Publisher: Clark Baxter

Executive Editor: David Tatom

Development Editor: Stacey Sims

Assistant Editor: Rebecca Green

Editorial Assistant: Cheryl Lee

Technology Project Manager: Michelle Vardeman

Senior Marketing Manager: Janise Fry

Marketing Assistant: Teresa Jessen

Marketing Communications Manager: Kelley McAllister

Senior Project Manager, Editorial Production: Kimberly Adams

Executive Art Director: Maria Epes

Print Buyer: Barbara Britton

Permissions Editor: Stephanie Lee

Production Service: G & S Book Services

Copy Editor: Michele Chancellor

Cover Designer: The ArtWorks

Cover Image: Patrick Clark/Getty Images, Rubberball/Getty Images

Compositor: International Typesetting and Composition

For product information and technology assistance, contact us at
Cengage Learning Customer & Sales Support, 1-800-354-9706
For permission to use material from this text or product, submit all requests online at **www.cengage.com/permissions**
Further permissions questions can be emailed to
permissionrequest@cengage.com

Library of Congress Control Number: 2005926183

ISBN-13: 978-0-534-60279-6

ISBN-10: 0-534-60279-7

Wadsworth
20 Davis Drive
Boston, MA 02210
USA

Cengage Learning is a leading provider of customized learning solutions with office locations around the globe, including Singapore, the United Kingdom, Australia, Mexico, Brazil, and Japan. Locate your local office at **www.cengage.com/global**

Cengage Learning products are represented in Canada by Nelson Education, Ltd.

To learn more about Wadsworth, visit **www.cengage.com/wadsworth**

Purchase any of our products at your local college store or at our preferred online store **www.cengagebrain.com**

Printed in the United States of America
5 6 7 8 9   17 16 15 14 13

To those who brought Camelot to our lives
as we sought to create Camelot *for others:*

Marilyn, Deborah, and Victoria
Patricia, David, Laurie, and Timothy
Carolyn, Suzanne, Kimberly, and Carrie

About the Authors

James R. Woodworth has been a member of the Department of Political Science at Miami University (Ohio) since 1948. He received a Ph.D. in political science from Harvard University and had a postdoctoral fellowship at the University of Minnesota. He has served in several administrative positions at Miami University, including the chair of the Department of Political Science and associate dean of the College of Arts and Science.

Dr. Woodworth has been a member of the Oxford City Council, chaired the Oxford Charter Commission, and served as a trustee for a local hospital and as a consultant to the Fairfield (Ohio) Charter Commission. His publications include *Atlantis: Role-Playing Simulations for the Study of American Politics* (with W. Robert Gump), *Parliamentary Procedure,* and many articles.

W. Robert Gump has been a member of the Department of Political Science at Miami University (Ohio) since 1962. He received a Ph.D. in political science from the Ohio State University and a J.D. from the University of Michigan. He was admitted to practice at the Ohio Bar in 1952.

Dr. Gump has served as chairman of the Oxford City Planning Commission, as a trustee for a local hospital, and as a consultant to the Charles F. Kettering foundation, the City of Dayton Charter Review Committee, the City of Middletown Charter Review Committee, and the City of Hamilton Charter

Review Committee. His publications include *Atlantis: Role-Playing Simulations for the Study of American Politics* (with James R. Woodworth), and many articles.

James R. Forrester has been a faculty member of the Department of Social and Behavioral Sciences at West Liberty State College (West Virginia) since 1969. He received his Ph.D. in political science from West Virginia University in 1979.

He is a member of the Bethany Town Council in West Virginia and has been a presidential election consultant for WTOV–Channel 9, Steubenville/ Wheeling. His publications include *Government and Politics in West Virginia: Readings, Cases and Commentaries,* Fifth Edition, and many articles.

Contents

I UNDERSTANDING POLITICAL DECISION MAKING   1

Introduction   1

1 LOCAL GOVERNMENT: WHY STUDY IT?   5

Governments and Communities   5

Two Meanings of Community   5

The Organized Local Community   9

2 WHO GOVERNS, AND TO WHAT ENDS?   12

Politics, Government, and Democracy   12

Power or Resources?   14

What Is the Degree of Structuring in Community Decision Making?   15

Evolution of Community Power Patterns   16

Who Governs in Cities Today?   19

What Can We Conclude?   21

**3   THE LEGAL AUTHORITY OF CITIES:
     CONSTRAINTS AND POWERS   24**

Land-Use Control   27

Choosing the Form of Local Government   29

Housekeeping Functions   29

The Newer Uses of Eminent Domain   30

The Impact of Federal and State Regulation on Cities   33

**4   SOURCES OF LOCAL GOVERNMENT REVENUES
     AND THEIR CONSTRAINTS   36**

Revenue Sources   37

   Property Tax   37

   "Income" Tax   37

   Sales Tax   38

   User Fees   39

   Miscellaneous Fees   39

   Intergovernmental Transfers   39

   Borrowing   40

   Gambling and Lotteries   40

Taxation Problems for Municipal Decision Makers   41

   The Fairness Problem   42

   The Competition Problem   43

   The Enforcement Feasibility Problem   44

   The Problem of Earmarking   45

   The Problem of Preemption and Mandates   45

   The Problem of Terms and Conditions of Grants   46

   Other Administrative Costs   46

**5   ORGANIZED INTERESTS IN THE DECISION-MAKING
     PROCESS   48**

What Are Organized Interests?   48

Organized Interests Operations   49

   Institutional Groups   50

   Economic Interest Groups   50

Ad Hoc Groups   51

Culture War Issues   52

6 IMPLEMENTING DEMOCRACY   54

Policy Initiation   54

Citizen-Initiated Policy Proposals   55

Administration-Initiated Policy Proposals   55

Agenda Setting and the Policy Process   57

Political Recruitment   59

Who Runs?   59

How Are They Selected?   61

Local Government Issues   63

Two Types of Issues   63

The Scale of Issues   64

The Stakes of Issues   64

Citizen Access to Decision Makers   65

Responsiveness of Decision Makers   66

Redistributive Policies   66

Conclusion   67

7 FORMS OF LOCAL GOVERNMENT   68

Weak-Mayor and Council Form   70

Strong-Mayor and Council Form   72

Commission Form   73

Council-Manager Form   74

The Strong-Mayor and Council Form versus
the Council-Manager Form   75

8 LAND USE PLANNING, PLANNING DEPARTMENTS, AND PLANNING COMMISSIONS   79

Land Use Planning   80

Planning Department   80

Zoning   81

Planning Commission   82

Zoning Enforcement and Change   83

II SIMULATING POLITICAL DECISION MAKING 85

Welcome to Camelot 85

9 INTRODUCTION TO SIMULATION 87

Why a Simulation? 87

What to Look For 89

Other Things to Keep in Mind 90

10 STARTING THE SIMULATION 91

How to Use the Materials 91

How to Begin 92

The *Camelot Daily News* 92

Simulation Time and Real Time 93

The Order of Business in a Sample City Council Meeting 94

Council Meeting: First Session of Simulation, Agenda 94

Planning Commission Meeting: First Session of Simulation, Agenda 95

Council Meeting: Second Session of Simulation, Agenda 95

Planning Commission Meeting: Second Session of Simulation, Agenda 95

How to Run a Meeting 96

Rules of Parliamentary Procedure 96

How to Put a Motion on the Floor 97

How to Get to the Vote on Any Debatable Motion 97

11 ISSUES 100

Introduction 100

Resolution of Sympathy 101

The Fairness in Housing and Employment Issue 102

The Officer Protection Program Issue 102

Background Information 103

The Beauty Salon Zone Variance Issue 105

The Downtown Hotel Plaza Issue 106

The Budget Issue 110

The Massage Therapy Facility Issue   120

The Smoking Ban Issue   120

The "Obscene Photographs" Issue   121

The Strip Mall Development Issue   123

The Home for Unmarried Pregnant Teenagers Issue   127

The Topless Bar and Grill Issue   128

The Fire Hose Issue   131

The Noise Ordinance Issue   132

The Eminent Domain Issue   136

The Drug Testing Issue   138

The USA Patriot Act Issue   139

Setting   140

The Wildflowers Issue   142

The Private Use of Public Space Issue   143

Background   144

The Simulation   144

The Issues   145

The Couches in the Yards and on the Porches Issue   146

The Curfew Issue   148

The Rights of a Home Owner Issue: Home Decorations   149

Zoning Appeals Board Issues   152

Issue 1: The Carport Variance Request   152

Issue 2: The Art Sale from the R-2 Zone Home Variance Request   152

Issue 3: "The Sideyard or Backyard?"   153

12 REFERENCE MATERIALS   155

Camelot: Basic Data   155

Population   155

Economics in Camelot   156

Camelot: Area Descriptions   156

Camelot Heights   156

The Central Business District (CBD)   157

College Town   157

Crown Knolls   157

Forest Acres   158

Madisonville   158

North Madisonville   158

River Town   159

University Park   159

Camelot Acres   159

South Ridge   159

The Charter   160

Zoning Regulations and Land Use   166

The "Sunshine Law"   169

13 ELECTIONS   171

Election Procedures—City of Camelot   171

City of Camelot Sample Nominating Petition   172

14 ROLE DESCRIPTIONS, SETTINGS, AND LISTS OF DUTIES   174

How to Use the Role Descriptions   174

Camelot City Government and Lists of Duties of Some of Its Officers   174

The Mayor   175

The Council, City Manager, and Assistant Manager   175

The Planning Commission   180

The Newspaper Roles   183

Involved Citizens   184

Role Request   195

City of Camelot Nominating Petition   196

Your Evaluation of *Camelot*   197

City of Camelot Initiative Petition   198

TOPICAL BIBLIOGRAPHIES   199

INDEX   203

QUICK REFERENCE PAGE   216

MAP OF CAMELOT INSIDE FRONT AND BACK COVERS

List of Figures

Figure 1-1   The Community
Figure 6-1   Forming Public Policy
Figure 7-1   Forms of Government
Figure 11-1   The Downtown Hotel Plaza Issue Map
Figure 11-2   Camelot Fire Department Station Map
Figure 11-3   The Sideyard or Backyard Issue Map

Preface

Camelot was created as a response to student concerns that our urban politics course readings provided theory and background understanding but gave the students little feel for how politics really work. In natural science courses, students use laboratories to test theory. Simulations provide laboratories for political science. *Camelot* is a *role playing* simulation of political decision making in a medium-size city that uses the council-manager form of government. As one reviewer commented, *Camelot* is unique; there is nothing else like it on the market today.

CAMELOT'S OBJECTIVES

Students often look upon the outcomes of political decision making as predictable or predetermined, perhaps even rigged in some cases. *Camelot* introduces them to a world of contending—and sometimes contentious—groups and people, whose values and goals range from extreme liberal to extreme conservative. That world includes a rich diversity of viewpoints—on appropriate means for pursuing equality of opportunity, on right to life, on defense of freedom of expression, on affirmative action, on defense of property rights and gay rights, and more. Students learn quickly that this competition among

interests and viewpoints, with their varying degrees of organization and cohe-
siveness, makes political decision making both complex and time consuming.

A second assumption widely held (at least implicitly) among students is that
most urban problems could be solved if only they were in charge or if those in
charge would listen to them. That is where a simulation is most instructive, for
it is a controlled reality that creates situations like those encountered in the real
world. Students discover that their viewpoints and their solutions may not be
widely shared, that other citizen-students (playing their roles) may vigorously
disagree. In order to make any decision, some degree of agreement must be
obtained, and in order to gain agreement broad enough to include a majority,
some compromise usually is necessary. Yet if decision makers compromise their
principles in order to gain majority support, some of the citizens who elected
them may feel betrayed and angry. Because *Camelot* includes an election, lessons learned may involve the pain of defeat.

For both the students and the instructor, a simulation provides a change of
pace. From its inception more than twenty-five years ago *Camelot* has been a
popular experience for students. Again and again, student evaluations have
praised it as a great learning experience. It is not merely a game intended to
identify "winners and losers"; the variety of issues and the complexities and
ambiguities of motives and behaviors prevent that in the simulation, as in life.
It is a role playing simulation with twenty-four different issues from which the
instructor can choose those that most reinforce the objectives of the course.
Though it may seem hyperbole to a reader of this preface, in years of experience we have found that, if students play their roles, then Camelot becomes a
real city to them. The debriefing and critique session (discussed later in detail),
scheduled at the end of the simulation, gives the instructor an opportunity to
make sure that the lessons of the simulation are brought home to the students
through their own observations and comments.

CAMELOT'S FEATURES

The Roles

While *Camelot* can be, and has been, run with as few as fifteen students, a total
of seventy-six roles are provided. The students are expected to play particular
roles as realistically as possible. Each key role is provided with a rather detailed
description of who the individual is and what his or her values are. The following is only a *sampling* of the roles.

Decision Makers

City Council, including a mayor chosen by council from among its members
Planning Commission

City Manager

Zoning Appeals Board (optional)

City Solicitor (attorney)

Organized Interests

Developers

Entrepreneurs (for example, a massage therapy operator, a beauty salon owner, and owners of small and large businesses)

Media (a reporter and the editor of the *Camelot Daily News*)

Religious Groups (for example, representatives of main-line and minority churches and fundamentalism)

Moral Conservatives (for example, proponents of rights to life, anti-obscenity)

Moral Liberals (for example, proponents of freedom of choice and freedom of expression)

Institutional Groups (for example, police and public health officials)

Others

Clerk of Council

Chief of Fire Department

Chief of Police

Director of Homeland Security

Attorneys (three)

ACLU Representative

NAACP, Head of Local Chapter

Retired Professional Football Player

High School Teacher

President, League of Women Voters

Student Body Vice President, Camelot State University

(*These are just some of the roles.*)

The Issues

The instructor may choose from twenty-four different issues in *Camelot* that involve budgets, revenues (including possible tax increases), moral questions, zoning, house color, and more. Some examples follow.

Budget

Resources are always scarce. Students must choose whether to provide funds for the police (new weapons, drug enforcement), health protection programs (women's health programs, Planned Parenthood), and revitalization of decaying areas in order to provide jobs and increased revenues. In order to pay for any or all of these, taxes must be increased, which in turn may incur citizen anger and cause defeat at the next election.

Moral Issues

Shall Council continue to fund a publicly supported art museum that displays photographs viewed by some critics as obscene?

Shall there be a ban of upper-body nudity in public places, specifically a topless bar?

Shall zoning laws be revised to allow the establishment of a home for unmarried pregnant teenagers?

Regulatory Issues

What decibel levels should be permitted for automobile stereos, or for noise from residential properties? How should the restraints be enforced, and what should the penalties be?

Zoning Issues

Should the maximum height section of the zoning laws be changed to permit the construction of a downtown hotel? The hotel and its plaza would revitalize one square block of a decaying downtown, cost the city nothing, and provide jobs and increased revenues. It would also require that a historic church and cemetery be moved and the sacrifice of one-seventh of the only park in downtown Camelot.

Should an exception be made to permit a beauty salon to operate in a residential area?

Should developers be permitted to build a strip mall in an area of single-family dwellings on land zoned for senior citizen housing?

(*This is only a sample of the issues.*)

The Election

Camelot provides all the information that students need to carry out the election. A nomination petition is included in the book, as is a sample ballot. All the instructor should have to do is remind the Clerk of Council to prepare the ballot(s) in advance of election day.

CAMELOT'S ORGANIZATION

Part One: Understanding Political Decision Making

Part One provides students with the necessary background information to participate in the simulation.

Chapter 1 explores the several meanings of the word *community*, focusing particularly on the separation of community from what we call "government."

Chapter 2 emphasizes the relationship between political resources and political influence. It also calls attention to the writings of Paul Peterson and Clarence Stone who, despite significant areas of disagreement, emphasize the convergence of interests of entrepreneurs with those of elected officials, the former for profits, the latter for tax revenues, to pay for citizen demands for city services.

Chapters 3 and 4, respectively, deal with the legal authority of cities in policy-making endeavors and with constraints imposed by the types and amounts of revenue available to local government. In this fifth edition, Chapter 3 has some discussion of more recent uses of eminent domain. On the topic of revenues, Chapter 4 calls attention to revenue sources for cities, especially riverboat and casino gambling.

Chapters 5, 6, 7, and 8 focus on organizing and operating local government decision making, including such topics as the involvement of organized interests (Chapter 5), how policy and recruitment choices are made (Chapter 6), local governmental and electoral forms and procedures (Chapter 7), and land-use planning (Chapter 8).

Part Two: Simulating Political Decision Making

Chapter 9 is an introduction to simulation for the student. It reviews the purpose of a simulation and instructs students on what to look for during the simulation.

Chapter 10 explains how to start the simulation and how to use the materials. A sample role request form is provided. So that everyone knows what has happened recently, students can (and should) read "Yesterday's Edition" of the *Camelot Daily News*.

Other helpful materials included in Chapter 10 are:

Council proceedings: a sample meeting

- How to run a meeting and the rank order of commonly used motions (a parliamentary procedure guide)
- Agendas for the first two council sessions
- Agendas for the first two planning commission meetings

Chapter 11 provides descriptions of the twenty-four issues, and additional supporting information has been provided in the fifth edition for some issues. Five of the issues are new for this edition:

- Fairness in Housing and Employment
- Smoking Ban
- Eminent Domain
- Fire Hose
- USA Patriot Act

Many of the other issues have been extensively revised to bring them up to date.

Chapter 12 includes a collection of helpful (and in a few cases essential) reference materials:

- A very brief description of the city of Camelot.

- A description of each of the neighborhoods of Camelot.

- The Charter of the city of Camelot. This is based on a real charter, modified slightly to fit the needs of the simulation. Although many of the students will not read most of the charter, it can be a very useful tool for the more alert and energetic students who choose to explore its provisions. Two of its features can be important—those relating to restrictions on the behavior of members of council (for example, attendance) and those that explain the procedure for initiative, referendum, and recall.

- Zoning Regulations. Students often find it necessary to refer to these regulations. They are based on an actual zoning code but are presented in a compact outline form.

- A description of the "Sunshine Law." This includes the standard wording that requires all meetings of public bodies to be open to the public (with exceptions listed). Often, this law comes as a surprise to students, and Camelot officials may find it stressful.

Chapter 13 takes students and the instructor through an election. The election is one of the highlights of the simulation and becomes a rich source for discussion during the debriefing and critique session. (See the discussion that follows on the debriefing and critique session.)

Chapter 14 provides descriptions of the roles. Though sometimes there is a correlation between the amount of detail in a role description and the importance of that role in the simulation, the correlations may be only partial. And there is NOT a reliable correlation between the importance or status of a role in real life and the importance of that role to the simulation. Instructors will see that some humble roles are very important to certain issues in the simulation, while other roles that appear to be high status have relatively little impact on any issue. For example, the university president has, at most, only modest involvement in a few issues (with the exception of the Fire Hose Issue), but a beautician has a central role in a zoning issue.

Inside the front and back covers of *Camelot* is a map of the city of Camelot. It shows the locations of the various neighborhoods and the zoning of each one.

SUPPLEMENTARY MATERIALS: THE INSTRUCTOR'S MANUAL

There is an Instructor's Manual of some sixty pages, available to instructors who have adopted the fifth edition of *Camelot*.

A FINAL NOTE

There is a student evaluation sheet at the end of *Camelot,* located just before the Topical Bibliographies. We ask students to fill in this sheet each time *Camelot* is used. We urge you to do the same. Not only has it been gratifying to read how most students enjoyed the experience, but it is equally reassuring to discover what they believe they learned.

Though assistance received from others is routinely acknowledged within the world of publishing, the quality and value of help given us by an array of friends and colleagues extends far beyond routine. We wish to recognize West Liberty State College student Andrew Cunningham, who is both the Web master and a photographer with the Wheeling (West Virginia) Fire Department, for his help in developing the new fire chief role. And it gives great pleasure to again record indebtedness to our good friend, excellent colleague, and superb secretary, Dotti Pierson, for her indispensable contributions to a new edition.

PART I

Understanding Political Decision Making

INTRODUCTION

Camelot was created to simulate for students what they might expect to experience as members of a city council or planning commission, or as citizens dealing with those bodies. It was believed that you, the student, would find these simulated city council and city planning commission sessions both enlightening and just plain fun. Nearly three decades of "living" in and with our imaginary city has justified these hopes. Yet somewhere along the way, Camelot changed—not so much in what it did or what its player-citizens did, but rather in what it conveyed to students and what they learned. *Camelot* is more than it appears to be.

Without emphasizing the point, *Camelot* introduces you to decision making and, by extension, to the policy process. To reword that sentence in nonjargon terms, the simulation reveals that the adoption of a city ordinance (whether it be a budget, a zoning land-use issue, or a value-laden issue such as the Wildflowers Issue) is not a simple matter. You will discover that other people may not agree with you on many of the issues—there is conflict over values. As with many truisms, these are truths we accept in the abstract as needing no discussion. Yet such truths can yield painful experiences when one has to deal with them.

Moreover, you will find that there are many stages to decision making: from the earliest beginnings of an idea or proposal, to its inclusion on some public body's agenda, to its adoption, and finally, to its implementation. This is what is meant by the term *policy process.*

As soon as one views *Camelot* as an illustration of the complexities of decision making in the policy process, it becomes apparent that some interesting parallels exist. Urban politics, at least when decision making is involved, is in some ways like national politics. Our attention tends to focus on the uniqueness of each of the levels of politics, however, so we fail to see the similarities because the names and titles of the actors and the scale of the activity are different.

The policy process invariably involves a struggle among conflicting values and groups; inevitably, the conflict widens as coalitions form. Sometimes, the values are so deeply felt that a solution is impossible and deadlock occurs. Fortunately, on most issues, however, the hard bargaining leads to compromise and resolution. You will find, perhaps to your surprise, that the underlying lessons of *Camelot* are applicable to all levels of the policy process. The primary objective of *Camelot* is to give you a "hands on" experience in the form of a simulation; however, it is important that the simulation experience be viewed within a social science context that introduces you to problems of human choice and interaction.

The stark facts of historical change are clear. For many thousands of years, our ancestors lived as hunters and gatherers of food, a way of life that under most circumstances restricted the size of a group to perhaps fifteen or twenty persons. Today, the majority of Americans live in metropolitan areas having more than a million residents. Extraordinary changes have occurred in the pattern of human existence over the past ten to twenty thousand years; at first exclusively hunters and gatherers, humans later became principally farmers and herdsmen; then, the past two centuries alone have seen the emergence of factory workers, railroaders, truck drivers, auto mechanics, television technicians, pilots, astronauts, Internet providers and patrons, and designers of computer chips that are almost too small to see. Most recently, we have witnessed the rapid development of the service sector of our economy, driven especially by the many companies furnishing telecommunications, software, and Web sites for the Internet, to this nation and others. We remind ourselves that 95 percent of the nation's labor force was engaged in farming and husbandry when the U.S. Constitution was adopted, and the major cities of the land—New York, Philadelphia, and Boston— had populations hardly sufficient to constitute a suburb today.

Perhaps we can recognize in our prehistoric ancestors clustered in small groups the rudimentary form of what today we call a *community.* Later, over millenia, the smaller groups (troops, tribes, clans, etc.) grew to ever larger groupings, each of which may be termed a community. But the term *community* does not have the meaning today that it had as recently as several centuries ago. In the next chapter, we will examine the way the meaning of *community* has changed in the past century.

A second term warranting consideration is *government*. Most of us take for granted the existence of some form of government, even though the hunters and gatherers just described had nothing we would recognize today as a government unless the concept is stretched beyond what most of us would accept. Nevertheless, the word *government* has been with us for many centuries, even though its meaning has varied from time to time and place to place. More often than not, the term has referred to a command system headed by an authoritarian ruler or ruling clique. But at other times, such as in the Athens of Socrates and Plato, or in the United States and certain other industrial democracies during the past century or so, the structure and processes of government have been called *democratic*.

Chapter 1 of this book considers the difference between government and community. Chapter 2 then turns to the questions: What is meant by democracy? How can a government (particularly a city government) be made democratic or kept democratic? Is it important to know *who* governs?

Subsequent chapters pursue the theme of local democracy by examining legal and fiscal constraints on the citizenry's capacity for self-determination in U.S. cities (Chapters 3 and 4), by discussing the relationship between democracy and the local activities of organized interests (Chapter 5), by examining the implementation of mechanisms and procedures that sustain democracy (Chapter 6), and by surveying the structures (or forms) of local government, differentiated according to the relationship between the chief executive officer and the council (Chapter 7).

Let us turn now to an examination of the meaning or, more accurately, meanings of the term *community*.

1

Local Government:
Why Study It?

GOVERNMENTS AND COMMUNITIES

Today, if we wish to have a good understanding of cities, it is not enough to regard the city simply as a component of that larger government, the nation-state. Cities are in part governments, but often they are referred to as communities, as well. Government is only one facet of that complex entity we call *city*. A city may be viewed as a community, or perhaps a cluster of communities, and so we turn now to an examination of the term *community* so that we may have a better foundation for understanding Camelot.

TWO MEANINGS OF COMMUNITY[1]

Probably nobody knows the total number of definitions of the term *community*. A sociologist friend of the authors quit counting after collecting sixty-five. This section of *Camelot* limits its attention to only two meanings of *community*, but those two meanings offer us a pair of very important definitions that, taken together, substantially increase our understanding of urban processes and change.

---

1. The following discussion relies heavily on the very thoughtful discussion by Scott Greer in *The Emerging City* (New York: Free Press of Glencoe, 1962).

The first way of understanding the meaning of *community* is to define it in terms of the perceptions of its members. In this view *community* is defined as a group of persons having a sense of shared (or common) destiny. The members of the community have an awareness that they are all "in the same lifeboat together." Defined in this fashion, the members of a community usually share a geographic location as well as a destiny. It is the awareness of shared destiny that distinguishes this definition of *community* from such phrases as "community of scholars" or the "Italian-American community in New Haven." In the latter two instances, the notions of shared *values* and shared *interests* are emphasized, but the notion of shared *destiny* becomes less prominent, perhaps even insignificant. And it is the sense of shared destiny that is critical for our discussion here. Awareness of shared destiny, rather than the more limited awareness of shared values or interests, furnishes the basis for common endeavors in village, town, or city.

Five hundred years ago, the people of an English village or town could be expected to have a strong sense of common destiny. Their lands were part of the fiefdom of the local baron, to whom they owed allegiance that included payment of taxes and specified labor on the roads each year. In return, the baron owed them justice and protection against predations by outsiders. They shared the risks of hazards such as drought, storm, crop failure, plague, epidemic, pestilence, and the danger of being caught in the middle of a conflict between rival lords. Today, the hazards are different, but the geographic scope of our personal notion of *community* is still relatively small. We may live in the Chicago metropolitan area, but identification of our community is likely to be more specific, such as Wilmette, Western Springs, or Homewood. We may live in the Dallas–Fort Worth metropolitan area, but if we live in one of the suburbs—such as Arlington, Irving, or Plano—our community identification is almost certain to be with that suburb.

The second way to understand the meaning of *community* begins again with an examination of life in that English village or town of five centuries ago. Each person needed food, clothing, and shelter. Because humans are social beings, each person also needed some companionship, usually including a spouse in adulthood. Each villager or town resident also needed to pay or exchange something for the necessities of life. That something might be labor, an item of handicraft, agricultural produce, or an animal. (Only the well-to-do were likely to have many coins to use as a medium of exchange.) To phrase the matter more analytically, the *functions* of providing food, shelter, clothing, companionship, and so on were performed by the population of the town and the surrounding farms and forests. Commodities, services, friendships, kinship, entertainment, the consolations of religion—all these were available (if at all) within the town or its immediate vicinity. If a need or want could not be satisfied within a radius of, say, ten miles (a half-day journey, one way), people did without it. Thus, when

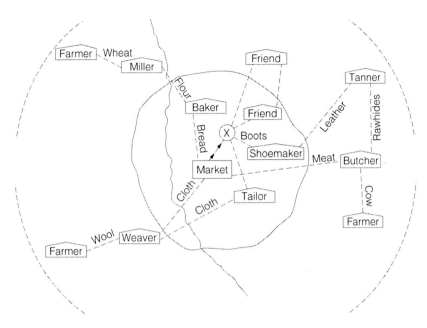

FIGURE 1-1 The Community

we define that English community in terms of its *performance of functions* for the population, we find that the geographic extent of the community was about the same as the geographic extent of the community previously defined by a sense of shared destiny.

We can illustrate this point by having you, the reader, imagine that you lived in that town five centuries ago. Imagine yourself living at some point, call it "X," within the town. Now imagine a map of the town and the countryside that locates your home, point X. (See Figure 1-1.) Imagine further that the map locates suppliers important to you, such as the shoemaker, the butcher, and the baker. Imagine still further that the map also locates those persons who supply your suppliers. Thus the shoemaker receives cured hides from the tanner, the tanner receives the uncured hides from the slaughterhouse that is operated by the butcher, the butcher receives the cattle and hogs for slaughter from the farmers. Another example is the baker, who receives flour from the miller, who receives wheat and oats from the farmers in the area. Draw on the map all of the lines connecting these people (and the many others that also will occur to you), and you have sketched the approximate geographic extent of the *community* showing the *interdependence* of these people on one another for performing the *functions* that meet their needs, wants, and desires in life. These lines of *functional interdependence* can be used to outline the boundaries and define the community in one way just as the awareness of a *shared destiny* can be used to outline the boundaries and define the community in another way.

Five centuries ago, the community defined by these lines of functional interdependence had approximately the same geographic boundaries as did the community defined by a sense of shared destiny. Each type of community reinforced the other, for their boundaries coincided. But what has happened today? The two communities have been wrenched apart by technological change. Not only have the connecting lines lengthened dramatically in many instances, but those lines no longer stop at the same outer boundary. Some connecting lines extend across the ocean—witness the introduction of the Beatles to the United States in the 1960s, or American rock groups to Japan today, or the internationalization of classical music via compact discs that bring orchestras and soloists from all the industrialized nations together in an international record market. The list goes on and on.

And let us not overlook the communication of information. The social impact of television cameras and broadcast stations linked together by a satellite twenty-two thousand miles above the earth's surface almost defies description, especially in this era of increasing use of e-mail and the World Wide Web.

Some needs still are fulfilled relatively close to one's home. Bricks for a new house have low cost and substantial weight, a combination not conducive to marketing across a large region or nation, let alone overseas. Potato chips and deli salads also tend to be produced locally—chips because they do not hold up well in shipping, salads because they are easily subject to spoilage. Procter & Gamble's development of Pringles, which are uniform in size and shape, is an attempt to use technology to solve the shipping problem of potato chips and thus eliminate the necessity to produce them locally.

Social relationships present a more complicated picture. Although they are no longer confined to the small locality of five centuries ago—many or most of us have friends in other communities, other states, and perhaps other nations— the majority of those social relationships are still located within an area that seems relatively small by today's standards, even if relatively large by the standards of earlier centuries.

To summarize, the two communities that once reinforced each other have been wrenched apart by change, and the boundary of the community defined by functional interdependence has become blurred and impossible to discern for two reasons. First, the impact of tremendous increases in the *speed* with which goods, people, and information are transported today has permitted the development of regional, national, and international trade on a vast scale. Second, extraordinary decreases in the *costs* of transportation have made these extensions of markets economically feasible.

This, then, is the setting in which U.S. cities must be understood today. A city today is psychologically less significant to its citizens than in the past. While it remains functionally significant in *some* very important respects, it also is true that the city is functionally important in *somewhat fewer* respects than was its predecessor. For example, the city continues to be extremely important for providing services such as water, electricity, sewerage, and safety protection. However, we can see its diminished importance as a focus of employment, of social life, and of civic participation when we compare the attitudes and behaviors of persons born prior to the end of World War II (1945) to those of persons born later. The important result, for our purposes here, has been change in our understanding of a community when it is defined by functional interdependencies, for the changes described have caused such a community to disappear. The community of functional interdependencies has been supplanted by what is now called *the organized local community,* most of which is governmental, and it includes neighborhoods, villages, suburbs, and cities.

THE ORGANIZED LOCAL COMMUNITY

The title of this section needs modifiers in front of the word *community.* It is no longer accurate to use the word *community* by itself. We live in a world of *communities,* meaning that we create, make use of, work with, play with, or do many other things with many different groups of people who as collectives perform particular functions, whether for social, business, governmental, or other purposes.

It has been noted that the community of functional interdependencies has disappeared. One consequence is the increase in the number of choices for the individual at the local level. Two hundred years ago, the local community defined the choices for the individual. For example, a boy visiting his grandfather's farm many years ago would find water supplied by the well for the house and the spring for the livestock; the privy and a dry well eliminated the need for a waste collection system; a good part of the food was produced on the farm; and a collie dog and shotgun provided the police protection. It is a rare person today who can provide any of these functions unaided by others. Most people recognize immediately the need for collective action to provide a safe water supply, adequate police and fire protection, and a waste and trash collection service.

Regulatory functions are a second example of the need for collective action and they are a consequence of the growth of larger populated areas. Although *Camelot* is intended to provide an experience of how a medium-sized city operates, the urban reality is one of an extensive center of population made up of dozens, perhaps hundreds, of cities and suburbs. Some of the problems created by these masses of population require regional, or even national, regulation to protect the health and/or safety of the population. Thus pollution controls are ineffective if limited to one municipal corporation, and the creation and disposal of hazardous waste is of immediate concern to a large population.

The need for public convenience provides another example of collective action in the form of engineering required for highway construction, traffic control mechanisms, the creation of left-turn lanes or center-turn lanes, and left- or right-turn highway arrows—all of which are instances of public support for collective action, in this case regulatory functions involving highways.

The preceding paragraphs suggest that though communities may exist at the local level, they are likely to be quite fragmented and often issue specific; they also may lack an ability to sustain public support over time. If one type of choice involves collective action to obtain services, create regulations, and generate finances for publicly perceived conveniences, then another type of choice might be categorized as *lifestyle*. The term *lifestyle* has come to be associated in popular language with such topics as sexual behavior, sexual preferences, or family size and living arrangements. However, long before these particular subjects became prominent in public agendas and discussion, many other examples existed of what we call *lifestyle preferences*, some of which were established by governmental action, others by non-governmental action. For example, the public may have wished to regulate how land was used in a particular local community, or there may have been a desire to preserve historic structures, or property owners may have wished to require that grass and weeds be cut on all land at certain times each year. To be effective, zoning, historic preservation, and weed control require collective action by a local government. These objectives may or may not be essential, but they quite clearly are actions that reflect public lifestyle preferences as opposed to *public needs*.

Other lifestyle topics do not require governmental action, but they too reflect local public preferences. Local service clubs may decide to support sports programs or flower gardens. One of the latest examples is the "adopt-a-highway" program, in which various service organizations (Girl Scouts, Boy Scouts, college fraternities or sororities, or other private organizations) undertake to clean up the litter along a specified section of a public highway. Groups of individuals will at times organize a neighborhood effort to discourage the sale of drugs, or clean up trash, or perform crime-watch services. Noisy teenagers, abortion clinics, and adult video stores and bookstores have experienced organized, nongovernmental efforts to enforce community expectations that go beyond governmental regulation and perhaps go beyond the capacity of government to regulate.

To sum up, this chapter began with a question: Why study local government? The discussion then described briefly the changes that have occurred in the meaning of the word *community*. At one time it was assumed that *community* and *village*, or *community* and *town*, had similar meanings. The residents of a place shared the same values, interests, and sense of goals or destiny. No longer do we assume that the city in which we live is *our community*, a place of shared values, interests, and destiny.

A second change occurred as a result of the changes in what is referred to as functional interdependence, meaning the extent to which the services and the goods we need or want are provided from within our local community. The essentials of modern living—fuel, electricity, food, water, fire and police protection, food safety, and so on—are delivered locally but originate in distant places. If one adds information to the list of essentials, the concept of a functionally interdependent community is stretched beyond recognition. For example, anyone today with a home computer and a modem can, by way of the Internet, access a library in Berlin to see if that library's holdings include a needed document or book title.

Thus, the word *community* today requires a modifier. We speak of religious communities, educational communities, or (to choose the example of particular interest to Camelot's citizens) "the organized local community." These communities may choose to encourage or promote functions (activities) that require local government to develop some collective action, whether it be a zoning restriction, the preservation of a historic landmark, an attempt to get everyone to cut their grass or pull their weeds, or enforcement of a particular code of behavior. Local government touches our lives every day in a very direct way, which is one of the main reasons we study it. And it is on this aspect of local government that *Camelot* will focus.

2

Who Governs,
and to What Ends?

POLITICS, GOVERNMENT,
AND DEMOCRACY

Chapter 1 examined the term *community* and described the increasing separation between two of that term's important meanings. The first meaning of community was defined by the awareness of citizens that their individual destinies are to some degree tied to the destiny of the community—the members of the community have a sense of shared destiny—and the second meaning of community was defined by the lengthening radii of functional interdependence. Chapter 2 examines the community's politics and government, focusing especially on the question of whether democracy can be found there and, if so, under what circumstances.

First, it will be useful to clarify several terms: *politics, government,* and *democracy.* David Easton's definition of *politics* as *the authoritative allocation of values for a society,*[1] perhaps the most widely used of all definitions in political science, is the starting point. The values belong to the citizens, both individually and collectively, and the chief instrument for allocating those values authoritatively is government

---

1. David Easton, *The Political System: An Inquiry into the State of Political Science* (New York: Alfred A. Knopf, 1953).

(the city government for our purposes in *Camelot*). *Government* is an instrument, or tool, used by the community to help in making political decisions.

Candidates for local office often invoke the concept of democracy and talk about their vision of how the community can become more democratic. This has appeal, for the words *community* and *democratic* suggest something desirable and valuable. Each word tends to evoke a warm feeling, a favorable response, in the listener. But on reflection, it appears that democracy is a trait of government rather than a trait of a community. Thus, we can describe a city government as democratic, undemocratic, or somewhat democratic, as the case may be; and we can say that a community has a democratic government; but it would be misleading to attribute the quality of being "democratic" to a community itself rather than to the government of the community.

Definitions and descriptions of democracy abound. A general description is that *democracy is a way of choosing who shall rule and, broadly, to what ends.* That description, while accurate as far as it goes, does not give an adequate basis for differentiating democratic from non-democratic, nor does it distinguish more democratic from less democratic. To do that, one must specify criteria by which democracy can be identified. The two criteria of democracy we use are:

1. A pattern of accountability of the rulers to the ruled, usually sought via competitive elections and supplemented by such techniques as interest group activity, court challenges to officials (in the United States), and the spotlight of discussion and publicity played on issues and on actions of officials, both elected and appointed, during the intervals between elections.

2. The free play of ideas in the formation of public policy (i.e., freedom of expression).

Thus, the working definition of democracy used in *Camelot* is that *democracy is a way of choosing who shall rule and, broadly, to what ends, by pursuing accountability of the rulers to the ruled through competitive elections and freedom of expression.*

The difficulty with definitions is that, while they can tell you what to look for, they cannot tell you what you will find when you look. If you examine the governmental structure and processes of your hometown, will you find a democracy? Until you or someone you trust has made such an examination, the answer may be unclear. You may hope to find a democracy but find instead a city dominated by a crime syndicate. You may look for the "democratically elected representatives of the people" and find instead a "political machine." Often, political machines have been associated with corruption at the ballot box, in hiring and firing employees, and in contracting for public works, but does such corruption indicate that democracy is not present? Or may democracy sometimes coexist with corruption? Does more democracy necessarily produce better government and wiser public policy outcomes?

Consider this: some mayors have earned enviable reputations as policy entrepreneurs who set forth an agenda of progress and economic development for their cities. Tom Johnson in Cleveland in the early 1900s, Richard Lee in New Haven during the 1950s, Ivan Allen in Atlanta during the 1950s, and William H. Hudnut in Indianapolis in the 1980s come to mind as examples. But some other mayors have chosen the role of ideological demagogue until removed by disappointed and angry voters. Within the past three decades, Dennis Kucinich in Cleveland and Frank Rizzo in Philadelphia manifested this type of divisive approach to mayoral leadership, and most commentators judged it counterproductive. Are only the first four officials illustrative of democracy, or are all six consistent with local-level democracy? The election of a demagogue, followed by his removal by voters at another election, may well be evidence that democracy is alive and well. No one claims that voters always make the best choices, but it is essential to the maintenance of a democracy that voters be allowed to make such choices, whether wise or unwise.

The question is made more complicated by frequent references to a *community power structure* when Americans discuss an action, or perhaps inaction, by their city government. Such references suggest a belief that an economic elite, possessing wealth and social status, shapes decisions within the city. These references tend to tarnish the public's image of local government's decision making, but are the references accurate? Is there in many (or most) U.S. cities a set of persons who control governmental decisions, or who at least bring to bear considerable influence on governmental decisions? If the answer is affirmative, how do we incorporate that into our understanding of the prospects for local-level democracy? How important is the question of who actually sits at the levers of control in our city governments? Clearly, the popular references to community power structures reflect the belief that if we know *who,* we also will know much about *what, why,* and *for whom.*

Although a huge amount of scholarly research into patterns of decision making and influence within cities was undertaken by social scientists, primarily sociologists and political scientists, in the past half century or so, the findings were far from conclusive. The research generated much disagreement among scholars in each field and even more disagreement between the fields. Intense debate flared during the late 1950s and much of the 1960s. More recently, the intensity of debate has diminished as numerous areas of agreement have emerged, and the findings of that research will be examined in the later pages of this chapter. But first, the terms used in the phrase *community power structure* should be clarified.

Power or Resources?

Because Chapter 1 discussed the meaning of community, attention now may be directed toward the second term in the phrase, *community power structure.* The word "power," for all of its popularity in ordinary conversation, seems to defy accurate definition that easily offers a basis for research by scholars. For example, most writers using the term *power* have chosen to speak of types or classifications of power in order to develop their analyses, but few authors seem to agree on which classification scheme to use. Thus categories such as positive power, veto power, and filter power were used by M. Kent Jennings, while Nobel Laureate Kenneth Boulding[2] used the categories of "threat power, economic, and integrative power—the stick, the carrot, and the hug."

As a consequence of the difficulty of obtaining agreement on analytic categories, some scholars have abandoned the term altogether and have thought and written about "resources" instead. While the authors of *Camelot* do not endorse all of the conclusions of this group of scholars, the authors believe that students probably can understand their own communities more easily and accurately by thinking in terms of resources rather than power.

Use of the term *resources* permits us to see that the components of power—in other words, the resources—are both numerous and varied. It also enables us to see that power has limits, for resources can be used up. Another benefit of using the concept of resources is that it becomes easier to see that some people use a particular resource with skill while others may use that same type of resource unskillfully or even wastefully. We employ the notion of resources in this discussion to take advantage of the greater accuracy and flexibility achievable with that concept.

What Is the Degree of Structuring in Community Decision Making?

Turning now to the word *structure* in the phrase *community power structure,* we will see that this term, too, must be used cautiously. Whether there really is a "structure" in a particular community, and if there is, how strong and durable it is, and what its pattern or configuration is, are empirical questions. They are questions to be investigated by the collection of information. The answers are not to be assumed or answered uncritically without evidence. Indeed, there are numerous communities (including perhaps your own?) where one must wonder whether any person or group of persons is capable of making effective decisions. But that answer may depend in part on the subject matter of the decisions. Different topics are likely to require different resources. Thus one sees that the possibility of difference or variation from one topic to the next adds another wrinkle of complexity to the challenge of understanding community decision making.

---

2. M. Kent Jennings, *Community Influentials: The Elites of Atlanta* (New York: The Free Press of Glencoe, 1964); Kenneth E. Boulding, *Three Faces of Power* (Newbury Park, CA: Sage Publications, 1990).

EVOLUTION OF COMMUNITY
POWER PATTERNS

It was stated earlier that, despite frequent and often intense disagreement among scholars with respect to many aspects of community power study, numerous areas of agreement have emerged. The first area of agreement concerns change over time. There is virtual unanimity among scholars today on the proposition that patterns of influence—that is, the structure of influence—differed in the United States in the nineteenth century from what we observe today. Though we must be ever mindful that there was then, as now, substantial variation from one community to another, when one traces the influence pattern (or structure) through a period of time in a single U.S. community, one usually finds that in the nineteenth century and the earlier decades of the twentieth century, the community displayed a higher degree of structuring than is seen at present. Prior to the turn of the twentieth century, in a given community there appears to have been a greater concentration of resources having political significance in the hands of a smaller number of persons. Thus it is accurate to say that more influence was concentrated in the hands of fewer persons than is true today.[3] In the past, resources tended to accumulate, rather like kernels of popcorn being stuck onto a popcorn ball. An owner-manager of a prosperous business also was likely to hold local offices such as mayor or member of council during the course of a lifetime. Moreover, the social structure of the community was likely to reinforce the patterns found in the workplace and in politics. Thus, individuals who were more successful in terms of wealth and social status also tended to be more influential in community decision making. Even in towns or cities where there was little evidence of corruption or bossism, voters tended to believe that wealth and social prestige were correlated with wisdom in political affairs. This "popcorn ball" effect was reinforced by the fact that people were less geographically mobile than they are today, which in turn meant that the social structure of a community was more stable, slower to change, than today.

Today's transfers of executives and managers from office to office and city to city as they climb the corporate ladder have been chronicled often and widely. And despite the development of efforts and practices to speed the assimilation of new arrivals, in most communities the level of commitment to the community and to civic affairs seems to be dwindling. Resources are more scattered than in the past. Education seems to loom larger as a resource, in part

---

3. For a thorough discussion of the concept of cumulative versus dispersed resources, see Robert A. Dahl, *Who Governs? Democracy and Power in an American City* (New Haven, CT: Yale University Press, 1961), 85–86.

because of the snowballing importance of expertise in technical fields and in part because of the divorce of ownership from professional management in the nation's large and medium-size business enterprises. Professional managers who report to superiors at a company's headquarters in a distant location are less likely to become involved in community controversy. They are more likely to limit their civic participation to matters for which a community consensus already exists, for many corporations are more concerned about their corporate image than about contributions to community life that their branch managers could make.

In today's world, it has become more difficult to find persons who are generally influential across a broad range of issues. The scattered distribution of resources, the great variety of resources, and limited commitment all combine to produce specialization of influence. There are few, if any, general power wielders. Different issues or topics are likely to be influenced by different persons with different resources available to them. As a consequence, the "richest man in town" no longer seems to carry the political weight of former years. Influence seems to be organized around more narrow specialties, and a winning coalition must be more broadly based. It must include more persons, along with their resources, than in the past. Looking at the matter from the other direction, in most American cities it is much more difficult to initiate, gain approval for, and implement a community decision today than in yesteryear. The reason is that the pattern of resource distribution is less concentrated today than in the earlier part of the twentieth century and in the nineteenth century. There seem to be more "popcorn balls" of influence today, but each popcorn ball appears to be somewhat smaller than in the past. In particular, "power generalists" believed to have influence across a broad range of issues are less numerous today.

Another point of agreement is that public officials have larger roles in decision making and are more influential than in the past. There are several reasons for this, but only two need detain us here. First, the growth of governmental bureaucracies has increased the number of officials with stakes in the implementation of governmental policies, and it has coincided with a trend toward greater professionalization of those officials, as can be seen in the rising educational standards and the lengthening job tenure within many municipal administrations. Second, greater emphasis on democratic accountability has increased the significance of tools of direct democracy such as the initiative and the referendum. This emphasis has given a larger role to those persons who have the resources (skill, position, knowledge, and time) to offer political leadership. Increasingly, these persons are public officials—persons with past experience in successful mobilization of voters. Votes can be an important resource for influencing some types of community decision.

Often one hears an argument that goes something like this: There must be a power structure in this community because the government officials so often take the actions requested by highly visible citizens such as land developers, factory owners, bankers, and publishers. The difficulty with this argument is that it fails to suggest evidence of a causal link. It begs the question; it *assumes* that developers, industrialists, bankers, and publishers are influential rather than *offering proof* that they are. That is to say, if A and B agree on a public issue, what basis is there for assuming that A is accepting orders from B? Why not the reverse? Should it always be assumed that the more wealthy person is giving orders to the less wealthy person? Might not A and B share a common perception of a common goal?

A thoughtful and challenging analysis has been suggested by Clarence Stone in an article describing "systemic power."[4] Stone agrees that the old debates about *who* has power seem profitless today. The more important question, as James Q. Wilson pointed out more than three decades ago, is what difference does it make?[5] Stone argues that there are certain tendencies and directions built into the operations of communities. Communities are, after all, work sites. Jobs are of vital importance, and in a society whose population is growing, it is essential that new jobs be formed to match the population increase. So it is, too, with communities. However, growth in jobs (economic development) almost always involves some changes in land use; new sites must be found for light manufacturing, for shopping facilities, for schools to accommodate workers' children, and so on. But neither the capitalist-entrepreneur nor the government official can achieve such economic development without assistance from the other. This means that the interests of the two—capitalist developer and government official—converge to a significant degree. Though they may quarrel over design details such as who shall pay for the costs of traffic engineering changes to accommodate the development, they have a common stake in its success. Thus casual observers may draw the mistaken inference of collusion between developer and official even though the better explanation is that their coinciding desires to see the development task completed produce the apparent convergence of goals. The developer reaps profit while the official reaps political credit for promoting jobs that have the incidental effect of augmenting the tax revenues of the city treasury. These augmented revenues, in turn, will give added flexibility to next year's budget—a point that is never lost on a public officer.

---

4. Clarence N. Stone, "Systemic Power in Community Decision Making: A Restatement of Stratification Theory," *American Political Science Review* 74 (December 1980), 978–990. Though Stone's more recent work develops a more complex scenario for such a situation, the greater complexity does not diminish the points made in this discussion. Interested readers may wish to pursue Clarence Stone, *Regime Politics: Governing Atlanta 1946–1988* (Lawrence, KS: University of Kansas Press, 1989).

5. Book Review, *American Political Science Review* 64 (March 1970), 198.

WHO GOVERNS IN CITIES TODAY?

The preceding section describes some changes that appear to have occurred over a span of many decades of American life. Resources that have political and governmental policy significance have become more varied, as can be seen by watching election returns on television. In addition, the emergence of a greater variety of resources that have policy-shaping potential seems to have been accompanied by wider distribution of control of those resources. However, this identification of changes and trends does not provide an answer to the question of whether democracy is to be found at the local government level.

The brief answer to the question, "Who governs?" is that it depends. The obvious follow-up then becomes, "On what does it depend?" The answer is offered here as a list of nine factors that have been found to affect patterns of decision making in American cities. Additional factors may occur to you, but this list will show the variety and complexity of the answer.

1. The size of a city's population is a factor. The larger the city's population, the more varied and complex will be the values and interests of the citizens. As the variety of values and interests increases, there will be more chances for conflicts spawned by clashes of values or interests. In addition, where there is more variety of values and interests, there are likely to be more-varied resources that have some potential for use in political conflict. Divergence rather than convergence of interests is the likely pattern as population size increases, and divergence of interests between holders of resources often leads to conflict, which in turn may reduce or constrain the influence of any of those holders of resources. The chances for conflict, then, increase when population size increases, for that usually produces greater social diversity.

2. The nature of a city's economic base is a factor. Here, too, diversity is a crucially important consideration. Greater concentrations of economic resources, as well as greater opportunities for wielding influence within a city, have been found most often where a single employer dominates an area's job market. Relatively few such examples survive today though the copper mines of Butte, Montana, or a steel plant in Gary, Indiana, might be cited. More frequently encountered is a concentration in a metropolitan area of several large firms belonging to a single industry. The dominance of packing houses in Kansas City, of automobiles in Detroit, of movie making in Hollywood, and of steel making in Pittsburgh provide examples of such concentration recent enough to be meaningful, even though the examples are less significant now than four decades ago.

   As the variety of manufacturing and commercial enterprises within a city increases, patterns of influence may be affected. Conflict between employees and managers is common and well understood, but it is less well understood that the diversity of enterprises within a city increases the chance that the interests of a company and its personnel will diverge from, and perhaps conflict with, the interests of another company and its personnel.

The familiar conflicts of capital, management, and labor within an organization may be overlaid by the varied needs and objectives of different types of
enterprises. Just as we discussed in the preceding paragraph, fragmented and
varied interests increase the chances of conflict and inhibit the concentration
of resources required for the appearance of a pattern in which influence is
concentrated in the hands of a few general power wielders.

3. The ethnic composition of a city's population is a significant factor. In the
   last half of the nineteenth century and early twentieth century a pattern of
   ethnic dominance existed in some cities. It developed when a large ethnic
   group discovered that votes could be used to influence others in ways advan-
   tageous to the group; the era of "machine politics" grew out of this discovery. Today, the competition between major ethnic groups may reduce the
   chance of offsetting with votes the economic resources available to merchants or managers.

4. The character of a city's labor forces is a significant factor as well. Especially
   important during the past fifty years has been the proportion of union membership within the labor force of the city. Though the proportion of workers
   who belong to a union is smaller today than three decades ago, unionization
   still has political significance.

5. History is a factor, too. Chance, or historical accident, may produce different
   patterns in communities that in many other ways are similar. And should
   anyone be surprised if an older city shows different behavior and character
   from that of a newer city? Cities that experienced rapid growth only after
   the development of automobiles may differ significantly from those based on
   earlier growth. Boston differs from San Diego, as does Minneapolis from Las
   Vegas, and the differences are in part historical, not simply geographic.

6. The degree of interparty competition in a city can be a factor of significance. For more than a hundred years, political parties have helped recruit
   and mobilize members of the American electorate, urging them to support
   the party's candidates on election day. In the process of doing this they have
   created an additional cleavage among competing social and economic groups
   holding conflicting views about which governmental policies to pursue. The
   growth of nonpartisan elections in cities has diminished considerably the
   influence of political parties. Even so, there are nonpartisan cities where parties function effectively behind the scene, especially in the role of candidate
   recruitment.

7. Many cities use types of ballots that tend to inhibit and discourage the operation of parties in local elections. Chapter 6 will examine the impact of nonpartisan ballots and the at-large method of selection in more detail.

8. Since the end of World War II, the metropolitan areas of the United States
   have experienced a movement of people outward, toward the suburban
   areas; this fact is widely recognized. Not so well understood is the fact that
   many jobs have either moved to the suburbs or been newly established in
   suburban areas. The result is that the proportion of workers who must cross

one or more municipal boundary lines in going from home to work has increased dramatically. Since persons having more years of formal education tend to have higher incomes than those with less schooling, this permits them to follow their preference for suburban living. And because educational attainment correlates significantly with various leadership skills and resources, the central cities of the United States have experienced a net decline in the number of persons residing within the central city who possess many of the resources useful for leadership. Those leadership resources include, but are not limited to, past leadership experience, flexible work schedules, secretarial support, a network of acquaintances to tap for information and counsel, and practice in the persuasive expression of their judgments and preferences.

9. The type of issue being addressed is the final item on this list of factors that help answer the question of who governs. The type of issue is important because resources that are quite useful in addressing today's issue may not be helpful in addressing tomorrow's.

   For example, if today's issue is more effective enforcement of traffic laws, the alignment of interested persons likely will differ from the alignment on tomorrow's issue, which might be storm-water flooding in some recently built residential areas. Complaints about traffic enforcement may come from any sector of the city. But in the discussion of flooding, irate homeowners from the affected neighborhoods may appear in the council chamber to confront officials. A developer who wishes to sell more houses (and who thinks the problem is due to the inadequacy of city trunk sewers rather than to the storm sewers he installed in his own subdivision) may urge officials to order an engineering survey as the first step toward correction of the problem.

   On yet another issue, a petition of voters throughout the city may be useful. Sometimes, immediately available funds may be the most important resource when legal talent must be hired by citizens to file a lawsuit challenging the city's authority to invest public funds in the development of an industrial park as a joint venture with certain private investors.

WHAT CAN WE CONCLUDE?

1. The first conclusion to be drawn from the preceding discussion is that decision patterns vary greatly: They vary by decade and they also vary by locale; city-to-city variation is common. In addition, decision patterns vary according to the type of issue, for the resources useful for one issue may be not at all appropriate for the next.

2. The second conclusion to be drawn is that the popular notion of a community power structure tends to be exaggerated. There are three reasons for this. First, the very term *power structure* suggests to the reader or listener that a group of persons, or a segment of society, is able to impose its preferences on the rest of the citizens. But the reality often is disagreement, even fragmentation. The notion of "power structure" overlooks possible conflicts and

disagreements among the persons who possess resources that can be put to political use in a dispute.

The second reason is that some, perhaps many, of the resources available for use by a power structure will be depleted by use. Issues arise in connection with many different topics, and since resources are quite varied in type, it is almost certain that some of the resources available for use by a power structure will be diminished by the very fact of their use. Time is a resource, for example, and as any student knows all too well, time spent studying for tomorrow's exam cannot also be used to study for the exam to be held the day after tomorrow. The same point can be made about money: Dollars are used up as they go to pay for advertising one's argument in the newspaper, on radio, and on television, or perhaps to pay for the campaign expenses of a candidate or to support the lobbying activities of an interest group. Sometimes a desired outcome may be obtained simply by display of a large amount of money, as Mark Twain showed in his story of "The Thousand Dollar Bank Note." In the story, the bill was never spent; in fact it was counterfeit. But displaying it was enough to persuade many people to extend credit, hospitality, and even friendship. Thus it can be seen that the problem of sorting out the effects of "anticipatory behavior" by persons who defer to wealth or other resources (whether those resources are real or illusory, as in the story of "The Emperor's New Clothes") is very difficult. Of course, more often than not the money must be spent if it is to achieve a desired purpose. The lesson to be drawn is that members of any power structure must calculate the possible gains and losses as they consider whether, and how, they wish to commit resources in the "game" of civic influence.

Third, commentators often fail to understand that skill in employing a resource is, itself, an additional resource. Unskillful use of one's resources will hasten their depletion and thereby make the pursuit of power (or influence) more costly.

3. The third conclusion that can be drawn about power structures today is that the distribution of resources is very uneven in U.S. cities. Moreover, the skill used in employing those resources, itself an additional resource, also is unevenly distributed. Clearly, these uneven distributions are important to our understanding of patterns of influence in cities.

Notice that each of these preceding statements is important for understanding agenda setting within cities. And observers of politics often argue that the persons who control the agenda control the outcome. Thus, although the head of a local labor union can gather signatures on a petition and thereby gain access to officials to discuss the petition's concern, the more pertinent question is whether he or she could get through to those same officials by phone as easily as could a local factory manager or owner.

Differences in ease of access (i.e., the costs of access) may mean that some persons or groups must spend a significant amount of their resources simply to obtain a hearing—to get on the discussion agenda—while others need only pick up the telephone. Thus, the owner of a local shoe store, concerned about inadequate parking in the vicinity of the store, may have to put those concerns in writing because a conversation with an official lies beyond reach of the owner's resources—in part because of the constraint imposed by the time the owner must commit to operating the store. And if neither the owner's name nor the name of the store will be recognized by an official to whom a complaint is addressed, how would we evaluate that owner's resources in comparison with the resources of a merchant whose past activities have created a first-name acquaintance with the official?

4. The final conclusion to be drawn about power structures in U.S. cities today is that democracy is not foreclosed; democracy is possible despite all that has been written and said about power structures. Skeptics may point to unequal distribution of resources as evidence of democracy's failure, but the more important point is that democracy is a matter of degree. Though democracy never is perfectly achieved, important questions must be asked about the degree to which a democratic ideal can be approached.

   Though resources are distributed unevenly, it often is possible to collect or accumulate a particular type of resource, as when owners of small businesses each contribute modest amounts to some political purpose or when the head of a labor union recommends contributions to a political action committee. Sometimes one type of resource can be used to oppose a different type of resource, such as when the votes of a labor union are used to counteract the dollars spent to advertise the political message of a local chamber of commerce.

In sum, the presence of elites—persons who have a disproportionate amount of some valued resource, whether that resource be money, status, control over jobs or credit, education, or any of the other resources that one might identify as having some potential for community decision making—does not tell us whether or how those resources are being employed. Nor does it tell us whether or how resources might be employed tomorrow. Perhaps certain resources will be used by their possessors in an effort to influence an outcome; perhaps not. And if resources are committed to such a use, perhaps they will suffice, perhaps not.

Voters also have resources to commit when they enter the polling places. So the question raised in preceding paragraphs is not simply whether elites have some potential for intervention and control. They very definitely do. The question also is whether the citizenry has some potential for intervention and control, too. Here, also, the answer is that they very definitely do.

The basic questions remain: Who governs? And to what ends? But there is no answer generally applicable to either of those questions. The answers are multiple and varied, for they depend on time and place, on the nature of issues being examined, and on the interests and skills of persons possessing resources. They must ponder needs and the costs of resources if they choose to become involved.

3

The Legal Authority
of Cities: Constraints
and Powers

The dividing and re-dividing of national decision-making authority was part of the grand design of the authors of the U.S. Constitution. This is referred to as "separation of powers," which we see in the U.S. national government, in every state government, and in many city governments. The federal system, which further divided power, this time between the states and the national levels of government, fit perfectly into the scheme. And that is just about where the dividing ended. One might think that the states would eagerly follow what seemed to be the established trend and divide power once again, giving cities specific powers of their own, keeping some powers for themselves, and then blending or sharing a few between states and cities. In fact, quite the opposite has occurred. States, for the most part, have jealously guarded state authority over cities, limiting the cities' decision making to certain specified subjects.

To many a harried mayor or perplexed council member the *limits* on city governments endeavoring to cope with community needs may appear greater than the legal *authority* to cope with those needs. This chapter describes the constraints cities experience and the consequences of those constraints. With the constraints in mind, the chapter then describes some of the powers the cities do have.

The first step toward understanding the legal authority of cities is to remember that the term *city* has two rather different meanings. As used here, the word *city* refers to a unit of government having a defined geographic juris-diction and a relatively high-density population. In the United States, a city in this sense of the word is called a *municipal corporation.* The second meaning of the word *city* is less precise, but an illustration or two may make it clearer. If you said that your family is going to move to Chicago, it would not be clear to a listener whether your family home will be located in the municipal corporation named Chicago, as contrasted to suburban municipal corporations such as Winnetka, Oak Park, Homewood, or Western Springs. If you announced that your family is going to move to Washington DC, not even the *state* of residence would be understood, for suburban Washington includes Arlington, Alexandria, and Fairfax in Virginia, and Rockville, Silver Spring, and Wheaton north of the Potomac in Maryland. Thus the word *city* may refer to a municipal corporation or, in a more general way, to a metropolitan area. In *Camelot* the word will refer to municipal corporations, or municipalities.

The second step in understanding the legal authority of cities is to exam-ine the significance of municipal incorporation. Any corporation, whether it be General Motors or the City of Los Angeles, is a legal entity authorized by the state in which it resides. (The legal capacity of Congress to create corpo-rations has been used only rarely and has been limited to public or semi-public purposes.) Whether municipal or private, an important purpose of a corpora-tion is to facilitate collective action. In the case of the private corporation, aggregation of capital is the collective purpose served, and, in the process, the legal liability of stockholders for the debts of the corporation is limited, usu-ally to the value of the stock shares owned by each stockholder. In the case of municipal corporations, the collective purposes are to make binding rules of behavior (called *ordinances*) and to collect taxes for activities such as fire pro-tection and street maintenance that are undertaken for the benefit of all citi-zens. Both categories of corporation, municipal and private, are limited to those activities authorized by the incorporating authority—the state. For rea-sons that extend many centuries into English history, such a grant of author-ity is called a charter, and it is the city charter that establishes the city's legal existence and identifies the scope of its authority.

The parallel between private and municipal corporations ends when the notions of ownership and citizenship are compared. The stockholder purchases an ownership share and may later choose to sell it. However, you become a cit-izen of a municipal corporation simply by residing within its boundaries, and if you choose to move you cannot sell to someone else your fractional share in a fire truck or a police car.

In the nineteenth century, state legislatures often intervened in the detailed affairs of the cities they had created, so much so that many states adopted con-stitutional amendments forbidding "special legislation"—legislation having application only to a special situation or to a single city—and requiring that all legislation have more general application. This, in turn, brought the courts prominently into the picture to settle disputes over whether statutes were special or general. Moreover, the courts had an additional role to play in interpreting the grants of power to the cities. Unlike the grants of power to the federal government, which are interpreted broadly under the principle of "implied powers" first announced in the landmark case of *McCulloch v. Maryland* (1819), the grants of power to cities are interpreted narrowly. The rule of interpretation was summarized many decades ago by Judge Dillon in his textbook on municipal law when he wrote that "any fair, reasonable substantial doubt concerning the existence of [the] power must be resolved by the courts against the corporation, and the power is denied."[1] The application of Dillon's Rule, as it has come to be called because of the succinctness of his summary, has given judges and lawyers a major outlet for their energies; litigation has abounded, and city officials cannot be certain of the legality of innovative actions unless they have obtained a court decision on the particular ordinance or expenditure in question. In short, municipal corporations are constrained quite severely by their legal position as creations of the state.

There is, however, a complicating matter to pursue. To understand it we must recall the history of urban reform in the first decade of the last century. Efforts toward urban reform included the notion of "home rule" for cities. Cities were to be given the capacity to determine their own scope of authority as long as municipal actions did not conflict with the state constitution or with general laws adopted by the state legislature. In some states—for example, Indiana—the idea of home rule never caught on. In other states, home rule was accorded to the cities by state statute. In still other states, such as Ohio, attempts were made to grant home rule to cities by directive language in an amendment to the state constitution. But irrespective of the method employed, the cities found themselves substantially constrained by the spirit of Dillon's Rule, which the courts continued to apply as they interpreted legislative grants of authority. To illustrate, Ohio's Home Rule Amendment, adopted in 1911, specifies that each municipal corporation may exercise all powers of local government. Despite the apparent sweep of such language, the amendment is significant chiefly for conferring upon municipalities the power to tailor the *form* of their government to the particular taste of that community and, within certain limits, to control land use within the community. Home rule did not repeal Dillon's Rule, and state judges continue to have an active role in determining the limits of municipal authority.

Although efforts of reformers fell short of their objectives, cities do in fact have some important powers as they seek to control their own destiny. By and

---

1. John F. Dillon, *Commentaries on the Law of Municipal Corporations,* 5th ed. (Boston: Little Brown, 1911), vol. 1, sec. 237.

large, most of these powers do not come from constitutional grants of authority, but rather from specific powers conferred by a legislature's or from state-
court approved activities. No attempt will be made to provide an inclusive list
of the powers of cities, but four important powers merit attention. Two of
these were mentioned above: (1) control over land use within the community,
subject to the requirements of *due process of law* under the U.S. Constitution
and (2) the power to determine the form (or structure) of the local government. In addition, a brief introduction is provided to the "housekeeping"
functions of cities, and the final topic will be the expanded use by cities of the
power of eminent domain.

LAND-USE CONTROL

Ever since 1926, when the U.S. Supreme Court decided *Village of Euclid, Ohio
vs. Ambler Realty Company* (272 U.S. 365), there has been little question that local
governments can, if they choose, decide how land shall be used within their corporate limits. The usual process is for the city or village to authorize the mayor
and council to appoint a planning commission having authority to develop a
master plan. The plan divides the city (or village, or township, or county) into
zones of permitted uses: single-family housing, multiple-family housing, commercial (often subdivided into various categories), and industrial. This is a simplified sketch; usually the zones are more numerous and more detailed, treating
such matters as height of buildings, required minimum setback from the street,
and minimum side yard. In addition to specific restrictions within each zone,
uses permitted within the zone are carefully described. Boston, Massachusetts,
for example, once created a special zone for X-rated movie houses and bookstores, and sex paraphernalia shops. It became known as "the combat zone"
because of the high incidence of crime and violence that developed despite
intensive policing, and the experiment has been regarded as a failure.

Zoning can, of course, be abused. The theory on which zoning regulations
originally were upheld by the courts is a theory of mutual protection. The
zoning code may prevent you from operating a motorcycle repair business in
the garage of your home, but it also prevents the house next door from being
turned into a disco bar specializing in half-price drinks every Thursday night.
By each of you giving up a little bit of freedom, your investment in your home
is protected against your neighbor's actions, and the value of your neighbor's
home is protected against your actions. But sometimes the mutuality of benefits, the two-way flow of benefits, can be lost.

In the example just given, and in zoning codes generally, much weight is
given to maintaining the lifestyles preferred by the property owners and fostered
by the physical characteristics of the structures and lots in the neighborhood.

Protection of the stability of values and behaviors is an important factor in the public's evaluation of a zoning code. But how far should that be carried? Would it be appropriate in a neighborhood of retirees to amend the zoning ordinance so as to prohibit residents under the age of 25? Could children be excluded for the convenience of owners if the majority of owners so wished and the city council concurred?

We all understand that the courts of the land consistently hold that a zoning code attempting to exclude persons of a particular complexion, or a particular religion, or who speak a particular language would be unconstitutional. But what about fraternity houses? To exclude them from all sectors of the city in which a college is located probably would violate some constitutional provisions, but restricting them to streets proximate to the college attended by their members apparently is reasonable and therefore permissible.

Sometimes the regulatory action can be ambiguous—apparently lawful but possibly stemming from questionable motives. One example is a rather common type of zoning provision—a provision that limits occupancy of any dwelling unit to no more than four (or perhaps five or six in some cities) "persons unrelated by blood, marriage or adoption." This means that if, in a university town, the legislated number is four, no apartment unit or single-family dwelling can lawfully house more than four students since it would be almost impossible to find five or more students who are related to each other by blood or marriage and who wish to share a housing unit. Two of the authors have experience with just such a zoning problem. (One was a former council member; the other was chairman of the planning commission.) When a zoning code amendment was adopted that reduced the maximum number of unrelated persons occupying a dwelling from five to four, the practical effect was that the rental income to landlords would be reduced unless they raised their rents. The renters were mostly students, but there were some owner-occupied homes as well, for the area was in transition. Though renters usually are critical of landlords, who often reciprocate in kind, in this instance both sides had a common interest. Nevertheless, the landlords lost because of widespread concerns about health and fire safety within the structures and about area problems that included excessive noise (especially late at night), litter, drunken behavior, vandalism, serious shortages of parking, and other concerns that accompany the conversion of land from single-family use to more intensive uses.

Were these actions aimed at students as a class? Or were they aimed at landlords whose exploitation of an inelastic market led some students to accept living conditions that most readers would consider unacceptable from the standpoint of both safety and health? To take an example known to the authors, how many of us would be willing to rent a newly constructed living unit that had only 78 inches (6.5 feet) between floor and ceiling? Perhaps each explanation is part of the truth.

Even more restrictive was the action of a small community near the State University of New York at Stony Brook: The maximum number of unrelated persons who could share a dwelling unit there was set at two (*Village of Belle Terre v. Boraas,* 416 U.S. 1, 1974). But a caution should be borne in mind: Because the law of zoning continues to develop in response to changing needs and circumstances, it would be unwise to form opinions about one's own case on the basis of the few remarks that can be offered here.

CHOOSING THE FORM
OF LOCAL GOVERNMENT

As stated earlier in this chapter, municipalities operating under Home Rule may choose their form of government. They can have a manager-council form of government, or the strong-mayor form, or something else. They may decide on the size of the council, the length of term of the mayor and of council members, and whether elections shall be partisan or non-partisan (except in states such as California, where all local elections are non-partisan), just to name some of the decisions they can make. Local governments can decide how power will be divided—that is, whether the mayor will have a veto power, whether the planning commission will have final approval authority (this is rare) or have its recommendations be advisory only (this is typical). If a manager-council form is chosen, more decisions have to be made at the local level. Shall the manager have sole power to appoint department heads, or is approval by the city council required? Can the manager fire these individuals without council approval? What is the relationship between the mayor and the manager? The decisions described in this paragraph are but a small sample of those that must be made when a local government is being established or reorganized.

HOUSEKEEPING FUNCTIONS

The traditional definition of the powers reserved to the states and cities by the U.S. Constitution is that they have authority to "protect the health, safety, welfare, and morals" of the citizens. These originally were called "police functions," but it is more useful today to think of them as housekeeping functions. Clearly, there is little question about the authority of local governments in the areas of safety: street construction and maintenance, traffic regulation and control, and police and fire protection. More recently, local governments have added the safety of users and occupants of homes and commercial buildings to their responsibilities by means of the licensing of building crafts such as carpenters, plumbers, and electricians, by occupancy codes, by building codes, and by inspection of electrical wiring, plumbing, occupancy patterns, and fire hazards.

Almost all cities now have health departments that concern themselves with the fluoridation and chlorination of local water. Some cities add chemicals to the water to eliminate iron particles and soften the water. Under the same umbrella of authority, cities maintain restaurant inspection, and many have developed an array of activities to reduce drug use. In addition, local governments must address solutions to the problems presented by crumbling sewer systems of inadequate size and by the disposal of solid waste and hazardous waste. Local governments today carry out a multiplicity of functions never dreamed of by those who first defined the "police functions" described here. Examples include life squads, recreation programs, paramedics, historic preservation, recycling, sports arenas, and parking garages.

What about noise control, or open containers of alcoholic beverages carried on the street, or topless bars? Do cities have the authority to outlaw such activities? Neither state legislatures, state courts, nor the U.S. courts have provided consistent guidance over time that would allow a confident answer. Yet local governments, even when they are unsure of their authority, try to respond to the demands of local citizenry by approving or disapproving various activities, behaviors, and businesses. Local legislators are expected to be experts on difficult and complex matters, and many of the decisions they must make on technical issues require far more knowledge than most of us have.

For example, townships are perhaps the most local of local governments. Though the powers of trustees are quite limited, if a trustee wishes to be reasonably effective, it is remarkable how wide is the range of specific knowledge he or she should have. A review of township meeting agendas in a typical year revealed that a trustee should have knowledge about road maintenance equipment, including backhoes, trucks, and snow removal blades; banking practices relating to borrowing for major purchases; construction costs and preferred materials; and the laws regulating a driveway common to two residential properties.

THE NEWER USES OF EMINENT DOMAIN

When the U.S. Constitution was written, the Founding Fathers had experienced firsthand the misuse of governmental authority, especially the taking of private property without any compensation. They were determined to protect citizens in the future from this kind of abuse. At the same time, they recognized that government, as the instrument of the citizenry, may sometimes need a particular parcel of land for a public purpose to serve the public good.

An example might be the need for some land on either side of a river in order to build a new bridge at that location. But even though the public good requires that a particular parcel of land be available for public use, there is no reason why the public that is to benefit should not pay for the benefit by reimbursing the owner from the public treasury for the fair market value of the land. The alternative, having the landowner bear the loss when the land is taken for a public purpose, would violate our sense of fairness. Thus developed the concept of eminent domain, whereby the government may compel the transfer of property even though the owner is unwilling to sell. But if the government and the private owner cannot agree on a fair value, the value can be set by a jury. Thus the owner is protected against dollar loss, and the government is protected against the risk that private preference could block a public project indefinitely.

In short, the federal government, the state, or the city may take your property, but it must be for a public use and you must be compensated for the loss. However, two key phrases are left undefined: What is *private property*? And, what is *public use*? Although it is not the purpose of this chapter to provide lengthy discussion of legal definitions, it is worth noting that the concept of eminent domain has been expanded in recent years in quite remarkable ways. One of the significant ways in which the concept was expanded occurred as a result of the urban renewal program of the late 1950s and 1960s when federal grants were combined with local government's power of eminent domain to achieve slum clearance and redevelopment.

More recently, and in a topic area further removed from our usual understanding of government, the owner of the Oakland Raiders decided to move the team to the Los Angeles area. The City of Oakland was upset by the move and voted to use the power of eminent domain to buy the team in order to keep it in Oakland. This raised the legal question as to whether a city could use its eminent domain powers to buy a football team. The case went to court, and the California Court of Appeals ruled in December of 1983 that the City of Oakland had the right to acquire the Oakland Raiders professional football franchise under its power of eminent domain. The court stated: "The acquisition and, indeed, the operation of a sports franchise may well be an appropriate municipal function. That being so, the statutes discussed herein afford the city the power to acquire by eminent domain any property necessary to carry out that function."[2] The California court had given the city of Oakland the authority to use the power of eminent domain to buy the Raiders football team. Unfortunately for Oakland, the owners of the Raiders simply moved the team to Los Angeles before Oakland could complete the purchase. Neither the

---

2. *New York Times,* December 30, 1984, I, p. 20: 5.

California court nor the U.S. Supreme Court would agree that Oakland had authority to force the Raiders back to Oakland.

Other examples abound:

- Although the next situation never reached the state of a formal action, an op-ed article in the June 4, 1984, issue of the *New York Times* argued that the City of New York should buy the New York Yankees, using eminent domain, because of the demoralization of the team under the ownership of George Steinbrenner.[3]

- The June 10, 1984, issue of the *New York Times* reported that the mayor of New Bedford, Massachusetts, had stated that the city was prepared to use eminent domain to buy the Morse Cutting Tool division of Gulf and Western Industries if that would keep the plant functioning and save the jobs of the plant's 450 employees. The mayor claimed to have legal support for his recommendation.[4]

- A federal judge ordered the City of Yonkers, New York, to buy private land through eminent domain in order to build public housing that would end discriminatory housing patterns.[5]

- In 1984, Missouri passed a law stating that, in certain cases, after local governments have approved a developer's plan for a site, the local government power of eminent domain may be passed to the developer. For example, the Kansas City Planning Commission approved a developer's proposal to use eminent domain to acquire and demolish four apartment buildings because the buildings were "functionally blighted and because they do not have enough parking spaces and are economically blighted because they bring in far less revenue than the [proposed] office buildings would."[6]

- *U.S. News & World Report* reported that a large mall in Hurst, Texas, a suburb of Fort Worth, wished to expand. The space required by the mall involved 129 relatively new private homes. Most of those affected willingly agreed to sell at prices "well over their houses' assessed values." But about a dozen refused. Because the mall was the biggest taxpayer in the town, the city council used its eminent domain powers to force the reluctant homeowners to give up their homes. They took their case to the Texas District Court, which approved the demolition.[7]

The action by the Hurst City Council had become possible because of a 1987 amendment to the Texas Constitution that allowed the use of public funds to assist private development. The amendment had been approved because of the dismal state of the Texas economy at the time. Later, the Texas

3. *New York Times,* June 4, 1984, I, p. 19: 3.

4. *New York Times,* June 10, 1984, IV, p. 2: 3.

5. *New York Times,* December 25, 1987, II, p. 4: 6.

6. *Washington Post* National Weekly Edition, November 12, 1984, p. 33.

7. *U.S. News & World Report,* September 15, 1997, pp. 42–43.

legislature gave eminent domain powers to local economic development corporations.

That same article also reported that eminent domain was used (1) by Atlantic City to give the Trump Plaza Hotel & Casino space for more lawn and for limousine parking, (2) by Arlington, Texas, for a new stadium for the Texas Rangers, and (3) for a race track in Fort Worth. However, when the Trump Plaza "taking" was challenged in court, the New Jersey Superior Court held that the New Jersey statute was flawed because it set no limits on how the land could be used once it was acquired through eminent domain. In short, because there was no guarantee that the taking would be for a public purpose or benefit, the statute was invalid.[8]

THE IMPACT OF FEDERAL AND STATE REGULATION ON CITIES

There is one other topic that must be included in this discussion: the increasingly rapid and dramatic changes in the relationships among the federal, state, and local levels of government. The familiar name for this is *intergovernmental relations*. But however familiar this term becomes to the student of politics or public administration, it cannot convey the rich complexity of recent changes and current trends in federal and state regulation of cities.

There was a time when it was possible to discuss the powers of the federal government and those of the states as if there were a fairly clear distinction between the two. It was said that the federal government had the authority to carry out certain functions; was denied the authority to do certain things; and that authority not granted to the federal government "belonged to the states or to the people." That was long ago. Over the past half-century, as will be discussed in Chapter 4, federal grants have become important sources of funds for state and local governments. More recently, the federal government has mandated various state and local government actions as a condition of receiving certain grants. For example, Title IX of the Education Act Amendments of 1972 has had a profound impact on women's athletics at the high school and the college level. More recently, in the 1990s, Congress adopted legislation stipulating that, in order to remain eligible to receive federal funds for highway construction and maintenance, each state must set the minimum age for drinking alcoholic beverages at not lower than twenty-one. A state that failed to conform would find funds cut off. Thus, while the states are legally free to maintain their individuality on this topic by refusing to comply with the federal mandate, no state can afford to give up federal highway funding.

---

8. *USA Today*, July 21, 1998, p. 6A.

An even broader extension of federal authority has developed over the past thirty years through adoption of laws to implement civil rights and promote equal opportunities by prohibiting discrimination based on race, religion, age, gender, ethnic origin, or physical disability in employment, housing, and education.

Some observers have concluded that the concept of federalism, which is of shared power between the states and federal government, either does not, or soon will not, apply. In their view, the states will simply become administrative units of the federal government. Others view the trend differently. State and local governments may have lost their exclusive control over certain areas of responsibility (civil rights and highways, for example), but they are not without *political* resources to resist at times, or to modify programs. State and city agencies and political leaders have created national organizations. There are national associations of governors, mayors, city managers, city planners, and other officials whose responsibilities are even more specific in focus. For example, an author of this text once conducted interviews in many states as part of a research project for The National Association of State and Local Food and Drug Officials.

In practice, the federal bureaucrats who allocate the funds and the state and local bureaucrats who expend the funds in support of their programs become natural allies when federal funds are involved. The federal agencies benefit from being able to establish fiscal priorities, the state and local agencies benefit from use of the funds, the political leaders benefit politically from having the funds spent within their states and districts, and labor and businesses benefit from the application of the funds to the economy. Everyone involved has a stake; everyone benefits; everyone is dependent on everyone else. The federal agencies need to keep the state and local people on their side simply because the political organizations are at the local level. And the national organizations of state officials, city officials, and agencies are increasingly active.

Professor Deil Wright of the University of North Carolina has noted in a widely read book that the term "intergovernmental relations" (IGR) describes processes and activities rather than circumstances that involve spheres of power that embrace federal, state, and local governments. His concluding remarks are pertinent for our understanding here.

> Whatever directions IGR follows in the coming decades, one theme . . .
> seems likely to be applicable to any and all future circumstances. That lesson
> involves bargaining, negotiation, and exchange relationships. The effective
> public administrator . . . will be like a skillful architect-builder who realizes
> that IGR in the United States is like a huge, complex building under continual
> construction and reconstruction. The edifice has no single deliberate overall
> design or consistent architectural motif. There is nonstop remodeling and
> renovation, plus minor and major interior repairs; there is even selective razing

and often whole new floors and wings are added. But the old foundations of the original structure remain intact. They have been extended with reasonable ease to support many more occupants and many new, varied uses to which the building has been put. Barring catastrophes or calamities, it appears that the structure will survive and remain useful in the foreseeable future.[9]

---

9. Deil S. Wright, *Understanding Intergovernmental Relations* (Belmont, CA: Brooks/Cole, a division of Wadsworth Publishing Co., 1988), 466–467.

4

Sources of Local Government Revenues and Their Constraints

Chapter 3 pointed out that each city (municipal corporation) is a creature of the state in which it is located. In no respect is this more true than in the matter of local government revenues. Without the authorization of the state legislature, cities can do nothing to provide financing for their own activities. The state legislature decides which revenue sources can be used by cities; it decides the amount or share of each source the cities can tap; and it can impose restrictions on the purposes for which particular revenues are expended. The state may designate (or *earmark*) a percentage of the proceeds from a particular state tax to be used by local government. In Ohio, for example, the tax on estates of decedents is shared with local governments and with library districts in particular. Most states specify the number of cents on each gallon of gasoline sold that shall be paid to local governments for building and maintaining streets and highways within the city limits. But whatever the specifics, the more general point is that an American city is not master of its own fiscal destiny. And the city of Camelot is no different from any other city in the United States.

The next section reviews the several sources of local government revenues—taxes, user fees, intergovernmental transfers, and profits from gambling or a lottery. Borrowing, usually allowed only for capital improvements rather than for current operating expenses, is not considered revenue because it must be repaid, but it is discussed in this section because of its effects on the revenue stream.

The final section of the chapter is devoted to the problems encountered in using these types of revenues, and it examines the constraints created for local governments.

REVENUE SOURCES

Property Tax

Property is classified for tax purposes into two types, real and personal. Real property consists of land and all the structures and improvements thereon. Personal property consists of all other property. (A subclassification of personal property into tangible and intangible need not concern us here.) Real property has been a staple of local government treasuries throughout the history of the United States even though its dominance has declined significantly in the past five decades. The real property tax actually consists of a number of different taxes earmarked for various purposes and packaged together into one total tax bill. Thus, a bill of $1,000 for six months of taxes on a home or place of business might include monies earmarked for the municipality's general operations, for the local school district, for a community college, for mosquito abatement, for public libraries, for operating the county government offices, for funding mental health and children's services within the county, and for interest and repayment of some of the principal on bonded indebtedness incurred when the local sports arena was built.

In many states, businesses are also subject to personal property taxes on the value of their inventories, and the revenue received by local governments from such a tax is prized by local governments. Some states exempt inventories of items held for resale, taxing only items such as the firm's office furniture and computers.

A third type of property tax is that imposed on all the assets of a person who recently died—an estate tax. Clearly, this is not a source of revenue for which local governments can plan with precision, and it will not be used in the simulation even though the arrival of such distributions from the county treasurer is a welcome supplement.

Of the three types of property taxes mentioned, only real property taxes can be locally determined, and that is why the Camelot city council may have this as an issue.

"Income" Tax

The word "income" in the title of this subsection has been placed within quotes to remind you that, at the local level, the tax seldom is levied on all income. Rather, for reasons of administrative feasibility, it more often is a wage tax that makes no attempt to catch dividends from investments or interest on bank deposits in the net of taxation. Although fewer than one-fourth of the states permit local government to impose a tax on wages or on income, we have chosen to give that city the authority to impose an income tax in the interest of fiscal flexibility. Where it is available, this tax quickly becomes an important element in the tax mix. Unless the legislature has forbidden it, the tax can be levied on both residents and persons who reside elsewhere but are employed within the city. Or, if the legislature chooses, it may direct that the tax be split between the city of residence and the city of employment. Thus its popularity with councils straining to cope with the costs of commuter traffic is quite understandable.

Sales Tax

A tax based on the price of commodities when they are sold is widely used among the states, but use of such a sales tax for municipal revenue is quite uneven across the United States. Nearly half of the states have not authorized municipalities to levy a sales tax, and the cities that do levy a sales tax vary greatly in the extent of their reliance on it. In Ohio, though municipalities are not authorized to impose a sales tax, counties may do so. In one metropolitan area in Ohio the county imposed a tax of 0.5 percent and later added another 0.5 percent tax in order to pay off bonds for a new stadium to be leased to a professional football team. But a large city in that same metropolitan area, wishing to enlarge its convention center, could not adopt a sales tax to help finance the project. A recent trend among the states to extend their sales tax to services as well as to commodities is likely to be reflected among the cities that impose a sales tax, as is explained in the next paragraph.

Sales tax revenues are of two types. The state-imposed sales tax is usually a shared tax. The usual pattern is for the state to keep for itself a percentage of the revenues generated and share portions of the revenue among the local governments—counties, townships, cities, villages, etc. In addition, some states have authorized cities (as well as townships and/or school districts) to "piggyback" on the state sales tax a relatively small sales tax for local use.

It should be mentioned that the states often impose a tax on the sale of a particular commodity. This is usually called an excise tax, though as a practical matter it is simply a sales tax limited to a particular commodity or service rather than placed on a broad range of commodities or services. Examples of commodities so taxed are cigarettes, alcoholic beverages, and gasoline. Recently, hotel occupancy taxes have been imposed in many cities, often going as high as 10 percent or 12 percent, or even more, and imposed in addition to a state sales tax. These have been especially popular since they fall upon visitors, who do not vote in the elections of that city, rather than upon local citizens. In a city that hosts many conventions, such as Chicago, the revenues may be quite significant.

User Fees

Fees paid by those who choose to use a municipal service are being levied more frequently for several reasons. For services such as water and sewerage, for example, the price may function as a rationing mechanism. Those who use more pay more, and presumably the cost of the service becomes a factor in the user's decisions about quantity and frequency of use. The costs of amenities such as municipal golf courses and swimming pools can be borne in whole or in part, depending on the preference of the community, by the clientele using the facilities.

Some activities of local government do not lend themselves to user fees because the distribution of the benefit is a "public good." In other words, there is no reasonable way to exclude from the benefits of the service those members of the community who might choose not to purchase the good. Police and fire protection are examples of public goods seldom amenable to user fees. There are a few exceptions, as shown by the increasing popularity of gated communities (or subdivisions) that shift some of the tasks of policing to employees who are not sworn officers of the law. Also, in some suburban areas having low population densities and buildings spaced far apart, it may be feasible to allow home owners to decide whether they wish to contract for local fire protection services, as was done in many U.S. cities in the mid-nineteenth century. Parking meters offer an example of a former public good—street parking space—that is rationed by the installation of meters and the threat of fines.

Miscellaneous Fees

Local governments often receive a share of other state-assessed fees, such as motor vehicle license fees and liquor permit fees.

Intergovernmental Transfers

An excellent argument can be made for the assertion that the most important change affecting cities in the past four decades has been the growth in the number and variety of intergovernmental grants. But along with the grants have come terms and conditions tied to the acceptance of the grants. To put it briefly, the grants come with strings attached. And the strings are becoming more numerous and more varied in their purposes. Grants to the cities may come through a variety of channels. Some come from the states, from the state treasuries; some come from the federal government, from the federal treasury; and some come from the federal treasury via the states, which administer the details and parcel out the money to qualifying recipients. The grants may aim toward familiar goals such as highway construction and maintenance, law enforcement, and upgrading of sewage treatment, but other grants may aim toward innovations, new programs, or new approaches to old program objectives. The grants can be just as imaginative as the administrators who proposed and the legislators who approved them.

Borrowing

Most cities are forbidden by state law to go into debt in their current operating budget. Although they may be able to borrow for large construction projects requiring capital that will be paid off over a span of years (somewhat like a mortgage on your home), they cannot borrow today to meet next week's payroll with a promise to pay it back next year. Typically, numerous strings limit both the manner of incurring debt and the purposes for which indebtedness may be incurred. The indebtedness usually must be for some capital investment such as construction or land acquisition rather than current operating costs, and often the voters must approve the indebtedness by voting on the matter at an election. In addition, the referendum proposal often is tied to an earmarked tax whose proceeds will be used to pay off the indebtedness. Alternatively, the indebtedness may be for a revenue-generating facility such as a stadium, in which case the rentals will be earmarked for the indebtedness (i.e., the revenue from rentals will be the security for interest-bearing bonds that are sold to raise the construction money).

Gambling and Lotteries

As states and cities have searched for new sources of revenue in the past three decades, they have turned increasingly to taxation of gambling. Today one can engage in some form of lawful gambling in every state except Utah, Tennessee, and Hawaii. Lotteries are allowed in thirty-seven states and the District of Columbia; there are casinos is twenty-eight states, including "destination" casinos in Nevada and Atlantic City, one hundred riverboat and dockside casinos in six states, plus 260 casinos on Indian reservations. In addition, pari-mutuel betting on horse racing is allowed in forty-three states.[1]

One of the most important arguments put forth by gambling's supporters was that it would provide a new source of revenue for cities and states that would not be a tax on property or income. According to testimony given the National Gambling Impact Study Commission (NGISC), in 1995 the legalized gambling industry had revenues of between $22 billion and $25 billion, and paid a total of $2.9 billion in taxes. However, no breakdown by state or city or by type of gambling was provided by the report, nor was the source of those figures identified.

---

1. This section draws heavily on the final report of The National Gambling Impact Study Commission, June 1, 1999.

The amount of tax revenues received by the states and cities is but one side of the coin. Equally important is the question of costs incurred by permitting gambling. On this point, the following quotation is revealing:

> The key question is this: How do gambling's benefits measure against its costs? Even after the NGISC's 2 years of extensive research, the question cannot be definitely answered. The overall amount of high-quality and relevant research in this area is still extremely limited. Indeed, much of the previously existing research is flawed by insufficient data, poor or underdeveloped methodology, or researchers' biases.[2]

For the states and cities, therefore, the decision of whether or not to permit some form of gambling as a means of increasing revenue must be made without reliable data on costs. And the following quote is equally sobering:

> Research indicates that lotteries fall far short of their promise of extra spending for desirable programs. Close studies of spending in such areas as education and senior citizens' programs suggest no increase due to the existence of lotteries.[3]

Moreover, there is an additional problem for states and cities emerging today in the form of Internet gambling. One report given to the commission stated that between 1997 and 1998, the number of potential Internet gamblers rose from 6.9 million to 14.5 million, and the revenue estimates during the same period went from $300 million to $651 million. Of course, the earlier caveat about the reliability of the data must be taken into account, but it is important to note that Internet gambling is a growing competitor for gambling dollars, and it is not now a source of revenue for either states or cities.

Overall, the record does not support conclusions that prosperity comes to town along with the casinos. Casino operators attempt to capture as much of the revenue for themselves as possible by offering a complete package of services, and unless the city has driven a hard bargain in licensing negotiations with the casino operators, the net financial benefit may be little more than the employment of some local citizens after they have been trained to be dealers, croupiers, bartenders, and servers. The profits will flow elsewhere.

TAXATION PROBLEMS FOR MUNICIPAL DECISION MAKERS

Financial constraints that restrict our freedom of choice in various ways are a fact of life for most of us in the United States, and much the same can be said of our cities. The fiscal capacities of municipal governments to undertake and

2. Ibid., p. 23.

3. Ibid., p. 14.

maintain activities are limited significantly by several different types of constraints. In addition, there are certain practical problems related to raising revenues that cities must face. This section of *Camelot* explores the nature of those constraints and problems, and it also looks at some of their consequences.

The Fairness Problem

Probably most citizens would endorse the proposition that for a tax to be fair, it must treat in the same manner persons who are in similar circumstances. The difficulty comes in determining what is meant by "similar circumstances." A cluster of similarly circumstanced persons who will pay taxes imposed on land ownership will not correspond closely to a cluster of similarly circumstanced persons when income is taxed. Sales taxes on consumer spending for such things as clothing, food, and automobiles will yield a third pattern of clustering, while taxing a single commodity, such as gasoline or cigarettes, will produce still another pattern. Since personal income is so important in our society, a tax imposed on personal income is likely to seem fairer to more people than a tax on real property, for some persons of substantial income own no real property. The income tax, in other words, casts a wider net.

The matter does not end there, however, for many (though certainly not all) citizens believe that a tax rate of, say, 1 percent applied to all personal incomes will hurt the worker earning thirty to forty thousand dollars per year more than it will hurt an executive earning four hundred thousand dollars per year or a professional athlete earning four million dollars per year. The reasoning is that the basics, such as food, shelter, clothing, transportation, and medical care, are unlikely to be ten times as costly for the executive as for the worker, nor three times as costly for the athlete as for the executive. Looking at it from the other side, the worker's wage goes chiefly for basics, such as food, shelter, clothing and health, while the executive and the athlete will have substantial amounts of money left over after the basics are supplied. For that reason, a tax of 1 percent on the worker will cut more severely into basics than will the same tax rate applied to the high income of the executive and the athlete. The economists would say that the executive and the athlete have more discretionary spending power. The remedy, if one concurs in this analysis, is to apply a higher percentage rate to the higher income. This will target the discretionary spending power of each taxpayer more accurately. In other words, the tax rate will be "progressive": it will impose a higher percentage rate on persons with higher incomes.

Now we have the information to see two problems of fairness in connection with municipal income taxes. First, because municipal income taxes are almost always flat rate taxes, they lack the progressivity that many persons believe to be necessary in a fair tax program. Second, because most of the municipal income taxes are really single-rate taxes on every dollar of wages (there are no deductions), but do not tax capital gains, royalties, interest income, and stock dividends, they clearly are regressive rather than progressive. Thus they tend to discriminate against wage earners and favor persons who enjoy substantial income from invested wealth.

There is another fairness problem in the estimate of many persons. The real estate tax once was thought to be a tax that was passed on to the consumer, but recent writings have challenged portions of that view. Farmers rather clearly cannot pass a real property tax increase on to the consumer when the market for farm products is a highly competitive international market. Tax increases on farm land in the United States in recent years seem to have become in part taxes on capital rather than entirely on income. If that is the case, virtually everyone would agree that this alters the intended effect of the tax, and many would argue that the alteration is unfair, that taxation should aim chiefly at income, not at capital. Our purpose here is not to argue that the real estate tax is unfair, for that involves questions of personal values, but we do argue that whenever there is a widespread perception of unfairness in the operation of a tax, that tax policy is in difficulty. An excellent example of this point occurred in California in 1978 when the voters approved by a two to one margin Proposition 13, a citizen-initiated referendum that rolled back real property taxes in that state.

User fees also create problems of fairness. The question of fees for emergency ambulance service is a bone of contention in many communities today. In small and medium-sized communities the prospect of profit may be too slight to attract private ambulance contractors, and if the municipality chooses to provide the service, a subsidy is almost certain. But should the subsidy be total? Should the users get a free ride in the fullest sense of the term? Or is it appropriate to impose a user fee to defray part of the expense? Because a user fee will serve to some degree as a rationing mechanism, is it wise social policy to impose such a calculation on persons of limited means who face a medical emergency? The question is even more complicated because some citizens have medical insurance that could pay part, or all, of the ambulance fee. Are taxpayers who pay for ambulances in effect giving the medical insurance company more profit? Is such cost shifting desirable? Or should emergency ambulance service be a public good? These are some of the practical questions facing council members today.

The Competition Problem

All governments have boundaries that, among other things, limit the geographic scope of any tax that may be imposed by a particular government. This becomes especially important to the policy makers of states and municipalities, for the competition to attract new industry, new commercial development, and affluent retirees can be fierce. For example, a high tax on real estate may discourage retirees, but the absence of a state tax on decedent's estates may encourage them. A high tax on real estate will be a factor, though seldom the sole factor, in location decisions of industry. Indeed, many cities and states have policies that allow certain new businesses a real property tax abatement (reduction) for some stipulated period in order to attract new investment. Probably you have noticed middle-class housing located outside municipalities in order to take advantage of the lower tax rates available because counties and townships usually provide fewer services than do municipalities of comparable population size.

The consequence of this potential for competition is that municipalities are limited in their capacity to tax. Although there are a few exceptional cases of cities that wish to avoid or sharply limit population growth, most cities are constrained by the risk that a tax rate too far out of line with taxes of other municipalities could limit the opportunity to attract and retain businesses and citizens having substantial tax-paying capacity.

The Enforcement Feasibility Problem

Policy makers must give thought to the enforcement feasibility of any tax they consider. To illustrate, a tax could be widely hailed as extremely fair, but if the collection costs would amount to 75 percent of the total revenue produced, that tax would be a very poor bargain indeed. A tax that is easily evaded can be corrosive of citizen morale, for it rewards dishonesty and penalizes lawful conduct. Taxes on personal property items that are undocumented fall into this category, which in turn explains why legislators prefer to tax securities, bank deposits, and automobiles—all of which carry title documentation—rather than furniture, watches, and jewelry, as was done in the past. By contrast, real property cannot be concealed or moved out of the taxing jurisdiction, which helps account for its importance as a revenue source through several centuries of our history. Nevertheless, there is an administrative problem in assuring that evaluations are accurate and the tax fair: There must be an appeals process for persons who think the tax assessor is in error. While relatively few appeals are carried forward by the citizenry, the potential for doing so tends to hold down all of the valuations. (If you think you received the benefit of the doubt, whether from a tax assessor or from a professor grading an exam, aren't you less likely to appeal?) Some states, such as Ohio, have a formal policy of undervaluing, probably to encourage each property owner to accept the tax assessor's evaluation rather than challenge it.

Enforcement of income taxes is relatively easy because the administrative costs of withholding and collection can be placed upon each employer in the same way the federal government requires federal withholding. Because a county or city tax almost always is flat rate, with no deductions and no exemptions, the administrative costs are only a small percentage of the revenues generated.

User fees and licenses usually are easily enforced, provided that one is not dealing with a public good. Delinquent accounts may have the water shut off, people unwilling to pay admission fees are excluded at the door, and licenses must be displayed for easy inspection.

Sales taxes are costly and troublesome to enforce at the local government level unless they can be "piggybacked" onto an existing state sales tax. If they can, administration is easy, but the risks of competition discussed earlier may inhibit the magnitude of the tax rate.

The Problem of Earmarking

Earmarking a tax for a particular activity or cluster of related activities is a time-honored method of increasing the chance of enactment, whether the enactment is by a legislative assembly or by the citizenry in a referendum, but it creates several problems. First, it is feasible for the more popular and appealing types of government activities, such as emergency ambulance service or parks and recreation, but other activities, perhaps unglamorous though important, are unlikely to benefit from it. Garbage collection, street sweeping, and snow removal spring to mind as examples of this point.

The second difficulty with earmarking is that it tends to be inefficient and inflexible. It sets aside funds according to a certain formula but not in accordance with any current estimate of need. Usually the funds cannot be transferred elsewhere, even in an emergency. Moreover, if it should happen that the earmarked funds become inadequate with the passage of time, there may be some hesitation about increasing them, because, after all, the funded activity already has a special tax dedicated to it.

The Problem of Preemption and Mandates

In Chapter 3, we examined the legal position of municipalities and noted their subordination to the state in which each is located. A further illustration of this subordination is found in the doctrine of preemption, the doctrine that a state's entry into a particular field of taxation excludes municipalities from collecting a tax on the same subject unless the state legislature specifically authorizes the municipal tax.

Compounding the fiscal difficulties of cities is the fact that the states can, and very often do, mandate (impose) a certain activity or responsibility to the cities without bothering to furnish funds to implement the mandate. These *unfunded mandates* are disliked intensely by the cities, just as unfunded mandates imposed by the federal government on the states are disliked intensely by the states. But for the states, as for individuals, there often is a lack of symmetry between their hostility toward what is done *to* them and their justification of what is done *by* them. Which, in turn, explains why unfunded mandates are likely to pose problems for the cities for the foreseeable future. And the doctrine of preemption limits a city's search for additional revenue.

The Problem of Terms and Conditions of Grants

Some of the conditions tied to grants may seem unlikely to chafe. Accounting requirements, for example, seem innocuous enough, but many municipal officers, especially in moderately sized cities, will contend that the cumulative cost of compliance with federal reporting standards, no matter how reasonable each may appear by itself, is significantly burdensome for the reporting city. Other conditions may be welcomed by most because of their worthy purpose when legislated but disliked by some when the administrative regulations that implement the law are announced a year or two later. To take an example that is not municipal but that is likely to be especially significant to many of the people who read these words, Title IX of the Education Act Amendments of 1972 was instrumental in opening up more opportunities for women to participate in intercollegiate athletics. That particular condition was fastened onto the broad array of federal grants, contracts, and scholarships that connect colleges and universities, both public and private, to various federal agencies.

A consequence of the increase in grants is that, paradoxically, the cities are losing some of their spending discretion. One must be careful not to exaggerate this point, but when a grant requires, as many do, a matching or partially matching fiscal contribution by the city toward the total cost of the endeavor for which the grant is awarded, then the pressure to give fiscal priority to the grant match is felt keenly by all officials. The consequence, in other words, tends to boost the priority ranking of the grant's objectives, and some competing claims on the city treasury may have to be subordinated or postponed.

Other Administrative Costs

To the casual observer, real estate property taxes would seem to be simple to administer: A value is placed on the property and, based on that assessed value multiplied by the tax rate, the property tax is computed (e.g., twenty mills, or $20 per thousand of assessed valuation). Unfortunately, in addition to the fairness problem discussed earlier, this tax is anything but simple to administer. The first problem is to get an accurate valuation of real estate. Property values are related to location. As every real estate dealer will remind both buyers and sellers, the three most important factors determining the value of a particular piece of real estate are location, location, and location. Also, there is frequently a time lag in keeping assessments up-to-date. Assessed values are expensive to determine, and thus appraisals are infrequent. In addition, the accuracy of such appraisals may drift a bit unless a recent sale has indicated the market value of a given property. These two factors—the cost of reappraisals at regular intervals plus the inevitable risk of moderate errors of judgment in appraising the land and buildings—constrain the amount of revenue that is feasible to raise through real estate taxation.

Problems of administration would multiply if the real estate tax were to be used by state government, for achieving reasonable accuracy in evaluations throughout the entire state would be much more difficult than achieving accuracy within a single county, as is now the case. The result is that the real estate tax in the United States is overwhelmingly a local tax, and a large portion of the revenues derived from it is earmarked for local education (K–12).

In summary, for American cities each of the several tax sources has its own type of constraint. Some taxes create problems of fairness and equity; some have problems of enforcement feasibility; others could have adverse consequences for local employers or merchants in a competitive market; and, lastly, the unavoidable risk of unforeseen consequences may dampen any impulse toward experimentation with a new tax.

The fiscal problem for cities is complicated further by the possibility that the state may preempt one or more of the cities' sources of income, while at the same time requiring cities to carry out state-specified activities paid from city funds. Finally, although cities may find it helpful to receive income in the form of grants from the state or federal government, the grant money typically has numerous conditions attached, conditions that direct how the money shall be spent and specifying conditions that must be met before the funds will be allocated or continued.

5

Organized Interests in the Decision-Making Process

WHAT ARE ORGANIZED INTERESTS?

An *organized interest* is any cluster or set of persons that, at times, tries to influence the decision-making process. And the reason many scholars today prefer the term *organized interest* is because it is a broader and more accurate descriptive term than *interest group*. In this first section we examine various types of groups with respect to leadership, revenue sources, and opportunity for member interactions.

Until recently, studies of organized interests concentrated on groups that had identifiable membership. In such groups, membership lists were maintained, members often paid dues, and the members interacted. The group provided a sense of continuity to its members and to those it attempted to influence. Some of these groups still can be found, but other types of groups have emerged and flourished in recent years.

Today, for example, scholars find organizations, such as corporations, public interest law firms, and governmental actors (domestic, foreign, intergovernmental), operating in the political world. Some have dues-paying members; others do not. Some do not even have membership lists.

There are organizations composed primarily of "check-book members," i.e., individuals whose participation is limited to making contributions. There is often a fluidity of both leadership and membership. And the techniques used to influence political decision making vary by topic, by region, and by year.

Another type of organized interest is referred to as *ad hoc*. It may appear suddenly, perhaps in response to an issue such as a zoning question, and then may disappear almost as quickly. It may or may not have identifiable leadership, membership rosters, and dues-paying members. Members are likely to feel they have an important stake in the issue.

In *Culture Wars and Local Politics,* Elaine B. Sharp has pointed out that certain groups focus with intensity and persistence on particular moral issues.[1] Such issues can derail political processes designed to find a common ground for agreement or intended to foster consensus.

Because the primary focus of *Camelot* is on local politics, the pages following examine the types of organized interests one might expect to find in a city such as Camelot. Where and when do they appear in the decision-making process; who are their members; and how effective can they be in influencing decision outcomes?

ORGANIZED INTERESTS OPERATIONS

It is not helpful to answer the question "who joins?" by saying "everyone." Some people never join such groups; never try to influence the political process in any way. Other people are deeply involved. As was suggested in Chapter 2, the more political resources you possess (education, intelligence, social status, occupational status, income, vitality, and energy), the more likely it is you will be active in various ways. However, a scale that predicts activity in general does not necessarily predict activity in particular. The fact that you have the time and skills to be active politically doesn't mean you will commit those resources to politics, nor does the fact that someone now is politically inactive mean he or she will always be inactive. Obviously, it depends on how important the issue is to a person; that is, it depends on the *saliency* of the issue.

Issues vary in terms of the number of people affected, as well as how intensely each individual feels about the issues. For instance, if someone proposes that property taxes be doubled, many normally quiescent, even submissive, citizens can become militant activists. There is a positive correlation between having a stake, real or intangible, in an issue and having a willingness to try to influence the political decision-making process. Moreover, the greater one's political resources, the more likely one is to join an organized interest and be

---

1. Elaine B. Sharp, ed., *Culture Wars and Local Politics* (Lawrence, KS: University Press of Kansas, 1999).

active in its efforts. The irony is that those who have the most to gain from organization, the poor, are least likely to organize, to join organizations, or to try to influence political decisions.

Institutional Groups

An *institutional group* is an organized interest that is intimately tied to the political system; it is a functioning part of the system. Let us suppose that the police department has requested additional funds for more-powerful weapons, for special equipment for a SWAT team, or for additional personnel. If the mayor or city manager has included the request in the proposed budget for next year, it then is an item on city council's agenda and thus will receive at least a careful, perhaps even a sympathetic, response. You see an example of this in *Camelot* when the Officer Protection issue is considered. However, organized interests outside the system do not have that advantage. They must first of all try to convince someone in the system (mayor, city manager, members of council) that their request deserves to be heard. Formal action—a motion to approve or to appropriate dollars for the requested purpose—must await a place on the agenda.

Some groups have more bargaining chips than others. This became clear to the citizens of Dayton, Ohio, several decades ago, when there was a dispute over salaries of firefighters. Firefighters refused to put out any fire in which human life was not endangered. Many buildings burned, and the Dayton City Commission received a crash course on the topic of the power of an institutional group.

Economic Interest Groups

Those who own land often seek to maximize the use of their property in order to increase the value of their land. In addition, reference was made in Chapter 2 to Clarence Stone's discussion of the shared interest that developers and government officials have in economic development, the developer seeking profit and the government official seeking increased revenues in order to provide improved services. It is not unusual, therefore, for city planning commissions and city councils to look favorably on proposals that seem to promise more intensive use of land, whether that be sport stadiums and convention centers that attract dollars from outside the city or new construction that will restore a dying downtown area. The Downtown Hotel Plaza Issue is an example of this.

Such issues can become contentious when that development evokes opposition from individuals who expect no economic benefit from the development but who fear social costs. This is one of the underlying questions raised by the Downtown Hotel Plaza Issue and the Eminent Domain Issue. Political decision makers then may seek solutions that will placate those harmed by the economic development, without discouraging the developers so much that the project is abandoned.

Ad Hoc Groups

The words *ad hoc* mean something that is created for a single purpose, as an *ad hoc* committee. Frequently it is an improvised action, or group, designed to meet a particular need, often at a particular time. Ad hoc groups tend to spring up, flower briefly, and then disappear, usually never to be heard of again. For instance, a group of neighbors may organize to protest a zoning change or to ask for one; or a group may form to save a building or to stop a restaurant from being built; a different group may try to revise the city charter or call for a referendum on a recent city ordinance. It is not unusual for such issues to be emotionally charged and to involve individuals who would otherwise never take part in political decision making. On this issue they have a stake in the outcome, whether for or against. You will discover examples of this in several issues in *Camelot:* The Massage Therapy Facility Issue, The Noise Ordinance Issue, and The Rights of a Home Owner Issue are examples.

In the small town where several of the authors live, a recent issue was whether or not an unused, historic water tower should be torn down. The "Preserve the Tower Group" and the "Tear It Down Group" were each determined to win the day. Members of city council who voted to tear down the water tower received threatening letters, and eggs were thrown at some homes. This was despite a nonbinding public referendum that, by a 60–40 vote, said "tear it down." City council remained firm in its support of the voting majority, and the tower was torn down. The life span of the two opposing ad hoc groups was perhaps three weeks. Similar examples can be found in your local paper almost every day.

The reasons why local ad hoc groups may be influential are easy to understand. First, it is easier at the local level to gain access to the political decision makers. Ad hoc groups, therefore, have a sense that they can have an immediate impact. Second, a local-level ad hoc group may be composed in part of friends, neighbors, or acquaintances of the members of city council, which means that the council members may have fairly frequent contact with individuals who possess similar values and status. In some communities, all may be part of the same social circle. The ad hoc group members, therefore, are not persons who can be dismissed easily.

A third reason for the influence of ad hoc groups has to do with the scale of decision making. Policy making is not a complex process in most cities. Especially in small and medium-size cities, the bureaucracy is not large, and one can more easily identify who is in charge.

A fourth reason is the widespread use of nonpartisan local elections. Without political party organizations, the individual representative stands alone.

There is no political party that recruits and supports candidates for election and reelection, that identifies salient issues and offers public discussion of them, that sets the priorities for issues, or that protects the party members with an effective organization. Without a party organization, a nonpartisan candidate or office holder has no effective means to blunt opposition attacks, and there exists no organized group of supporters to rush to his or her defense. Thus nonpartisan elections increase the vulnerability of elected officials to ad hoc groups.

Culture War Issues[2]

As was suggested earlier, culture war issues are not amenable to "normal politics," in which the contending groups attempt to find areas of agreement and compromise. Culture war disagreements do not allow compromise. One can find little common ground between the positions of pro-life and pro-choice groups, or pro-gun and anti-gun supporters, or environmentalists and loggers. Clashing definitions of right and wrong, of good and bad differentiate the contending groups. The position of the moderate, seeking to find a resolution, often becomes untenable.

Such conflict is not new to American politics. The slavery issue in the nineteenth century evoked the same kind of intensity, and it took the deadliest war in American history to end the conflict. But even then it did not resolve problems of access to jobs, education, and ballots.

The prohibition movement in the late nineteenth and early twentieth centuries is another example of a culture war issue. It resulted in what has been called "The Noble Experiment," the Eighteenth Amendment to the U.S. Constitution, an attempt to end the production, sale, distribution, and consumption of alcohol. The experiment was a failure, and its negative impact on American attitudes toward the law was severe.

To use the language of armed conflicts, culture wars "take no prisoners." The purpose of *Camelot* is to give its participants an experience in conflict resolution. Unfortunately, a culture war conflict seldom can be resolved, for conflict resolution requires compromise. And few will consider compromise when the conflict involves intensely held beliefs like those on abortion, capital punishment, or animal experiments that cause great pain or discomfort. In culture wars, one side or the other may give up, but they never give in.

But when all is said and done, the organized interest that provides *the best information* has a head start toward achieving its goal, for most of us prefer to have evidence that supports our opinions and decisions. Moreover, because we believe that our nation is a democracy, we tend to be more deferential toward opinions that have majority support. Even when we believe that a majority opinion is erroneous, if we hold public office we must at times balance the

2. Sharp, Introduction.

weight of our own informed judgment on the one hand against our *commitment to democracy,* which includes the right of a majority to prevail in most matters. As a consequence, the organized interest that has both strong supporting information and significant numerical support among the citizenry is likely to prevail.

In summary, the organized interest is one of the key forces in political decision making, much more so than the individual voter. At the local level, institutional groups (e.g., police and fire departments) are particularly influential because they are part of the governmental system. Economic interest groups (e.g., land developers) are influential because new development brings the promise of jobs to citizens and of additional revenues to the city. Ad hoc groups (which frequently focus on land use questions) arise around issues that appear suddenly and fade when the issue is resolved. Finally, there are some moral issues so divisive that resolution of the conflict is not possible.

6

Implementing Democracy

POLICY INITIATION

The word *policy* in this section's title has a larger meaning than just a law. Technically, it includes anything from constitutional amendments, executive orders of the president of the United States, administrative rules of a government agency, and acts of Congress, at the federal level, to city ordinances and a mayor's orders to a police chief to put down a riot at the local level. However, this brief review of comparisons and contrasts between federal and local processes is limited to the *initiation* of legislation, that is, to enactments of the legislative bodies of the different governments.

Policy initiation is a somewhat forbidding phrase that actually refers to nothing more than discerning the need for a remedy or response to some problem or circumstance within the society and then urging a particular course of governmental action to meet or alleviate that need or circumstance. The most common descriptions of democracy usually address only one type of policy initiation, that which comes from citizen concerns and desires and is then transmitted by the citizens to legislators for effective action. But there is a second type of policy initiation, a type that springs from sources inside the apparatus of government. Both types of policy initiation will be examined here.

Citizen-Initiated Policy Proposals

At the local level, a citizen-initiated policy proposal might seek a change of zoning on certain tracts of land. Such an initiative could come from local interest groups, perhaps developers who want to build a housing development, mall, or gas station. Or perhaps an individual entrepreneur sees an economic opportunity through rezoning—seeking permission to open a restaurant, massage facility, or fitness center in an area that does not now permit such activities. Possibly homeowners wish to preserve the residential character of the neighborhood by making the area more restrictive than it is now. The thread that runs through these examples is that the decision does not require either the city administration or city council to address the ugly question of "How do we pay for this?" The proposed policy may indeed force the city council to choose between or among contending groups of local constituents. That will be painful enough. But at least the issue will not involve the additional problem of having to find new money through higher taxes or through the reduction of an existing program.

Citizen-initiated policy proposals that do not involve money, and that therefore have minimal budgetary implications, are less common at the national level of government than at the local level, for the national government has no provision for initiative and/or referendum procedures that could force citizen-initiated proposals onto a ballot for decision. By contrast, most states and many cities have such procedures. Examples may appear in the form of protest, such as "save the spotted owl," or as a petition to place a local structure on the National Register of Historic Places. Often an important purpose of these activities is to win media attention for their cause. Even at the state or local level, such activities seldom have significant budgetary implications, nor are they likely to loom large in the overall picture of government activities.

Administration-Initiated Policy Proposals

Many of the proposals at the national or local level will not come from individual citizens or from interest groups, and many of the proposals do in fact involve money. If an equal rights policy is adopted to eliminate discrimination based on race, gender, religion, or national origin, then an agency must be established to determine whether the law is being followed. If we want to have unadulterated foods, safe and effective drugs, clean water and clean air, then we must establish testing laboratories and hire agents to enforce the standards. The same impact occurs in areas of occupational safety and automobile safety. Examples are in the hundreds—and so are the agencies.

The point is that every need, every problem to be addressed by government, requires a specific proposal that can be considered, perhaps amended, and then approved or rejected. But where will the specific proposal come from?

Most of us are better able to articulate our needs and our fears than to articulate details of a workable remedy for those needs and fears. Where will detailed remedies come from? Who will develop and propose them? Increasingly the answer is the staff members of the executive offices of all levels of government. And it is these staff members of the executive offices who are responsible for most of the second type of policy initiation, the type that springs from sources lying within the apparatus of government. How does this policy initiation occur?

The popular image of governmental bureaucracies is that their chief activity is regulatory, but administrative offices actually perform very significant information-gathering functions. This information gathering tends to become intertwined with the budget-making process in a way that merits close examination. Preparation of the annual request for funds (the annual budget) begins at the lowest echelons. Each operating office prepares estimates of its needs for the coming year: personnel costs (including the cost of additional staff and pay raises for current staff); supplies such as postage and stationery; computer equipment, desks, chairs, and filing cabinets; funds for telephone; funds for transportation to meetings or conferences; and other items perhaps distinctive to the office and its mission. This request for funds is transmitted upward to the next level of the administrative pyramid, where it is reviewed alongside similar requests from other offices. Priorities are established by the supervisor, who then transmits the revised and consolidated recommendations for the several offices upward to the next higher echelon where these consolidated recommendations must compete with other consolidated recommendations from other supervisors in other parts of the administrative pyramid. And so it goes, ever upward, until the increasingly consolidated requests reach the apex of the pyramid—the central clearance point—the point to which all budget requests flow, be it the desk of the mayor, the city manager, the governor, or the president.

But there is more to it, for if the request were to travel upward without supporting documentation, chances of the request being fulfilled would be slender. To increase the persuasiveness of the request, the administrative office will send along a description of its recent activities, its successes, its hopes for the future, and an explanation of how the larger budget request will help to realize those hopes. In short, the budget request will be reinforced by an annual report pointing with pride to the agency's accomplishments, pointing with alarm to unmet needs, and suggesting useful ways in which money should be spent to meet those needs. The budget preparation process, therefore, pushing upward information about needs along with suggestions for meeting those needs, is a tremendously important source of policy initiatives. Information and suggestions for program innovation or modification are thrust upward along with the requests for funding until all reach the desk of the chief executive, the central clearance point.

The consequence is that the chief executive, the head of this administrative apparatus, has important resources of information, ideas, suggestions, and expertise. These resources have led increasingly to domination of policy initiatives by the executive. At the same time, the legislature's role has become reactive rather than proactive, responding rather than innovating. The chief executive has the resources that produce the new ideas, plus documentation of the need to take action. And this dominance—this near monopoly of policy initiatives—by the chief executive became perhaps the most important fact of political life in twentieth-century America. And it continues into the twenty-first century. Thus it is that legislative agendas, at both national and local levels, have come to be responsive more to the priorities and policy preferences of chief executives than to citizen groups outside the government.

AGENDA SETTING AND THE POLICY PROCESS

Although the preceding sections identified several sources of initiation of specific policy proposals, it should be noted that in the past several decades a somewhat broader set of concerns has claimed the attention of political scientists as they have pondered the question of how public agendas are constructed. How do issues become recognized as issues? How do they make their way toward achievement of the recognition essential to getting a place on the public agenda for discussion and possible action? How do they then move through successive stages of the policy processes of government? Here the focus is on how certain problems become political issues that claim the attention of government while other problems never become issues and never obtain that attention. Or, to change the perspective slightly, it is important to ask who has a right to participate in the process of determining what issues will be addressed by government? Who will define the terms employed in discussion of those issues?

Perhaps the most commonly offered answer to those questions is that agendas are created by the interactions of groups of citizens, or *organized interests,* in the more common terminology. The term *pluralism* often is used to describe that interpretation. In a series of works culminating in his study of New Haven, Connecticut, Robert Dahl argued that resources are neither evenly distributed nor heavily concentrated. He advanced the notion of "dispersed inequalities" to moderate somewhat the impression of an interest group free-for-all that readers could derive from writings of some of the most thorough-going pluralists. But the difficulty for many observers was captured by E. E. Schattschneider in his remark that "the flaw in the pluralist heaven is that the heavenly chorus sings with a strong upper class accent."[1] He went on to argue that the majority of citizens don't, or perhaps can't, get into the system of interest groups.

In highly influential books about agenda setting, Roger Cobb and Charles Elder[2] and Charles Jones[3] offered an even broader view as they suggested that an issue first must gain recognition within the society as a problem—a recognition that may come in response to changes in demographics or technology—then it must get onto the discussion docket of governmental institutions, perhaps in response to the activities of interest groups. Last, it must receive enough attention within government to reach the stage of policy action or decision.

Once a problem has moved onto the agenda, there are additional stages to be passed through as the policy process unfolds. The most widely used formulation of those stages describes a six-fold sequence subsequent to agenda setting. (See Figure 6-1.) The six stages are as follows:

1. *policy formulation*—articulating goals and drafting strategies to attain them;
2. *policy legitimation*—gathering political support and achieving formal adoption through legislation, an administrative rule, an executive order, or some other means;
3. *appropriation of funds for the policy*—to have available the necessary financial resources;
4. *policy implementation*—day-to-day administration through use of the institutional resources of government;
5. *policy evaluation*—determining whether the goals are being attained and analyzing costs and benefits;
6. *policy termination or revision*—revision that could occur through modification of goals or of methods for pursuing those goals.

Perhaps the most important point to be derived from an understanding of the process is that policy making is an endless process that reminds us of the treads on military tanks and Caterpillar bulldozers. Or, to use the language of system analysis, the process derives continuity and self-adjustment from the feedback loop.

---

1. E. E. Schattschneider, *The Semi-Sovereign People* (New York: Holt, Rinehart & Winston, 1960), p. 35.

2. Roger W. Cobb and Charles Elder, *Participation in American Politics: The Dynamics of Agenda Building*, 2nd ed. (Baltimore, MD: The Johns Hopkins University Press, 1983).

3. Charles O. Jones, *An Introduction to the Study of Public Policy*, 2nd ed. (North Scituate, MA: Duxbury, 1977).

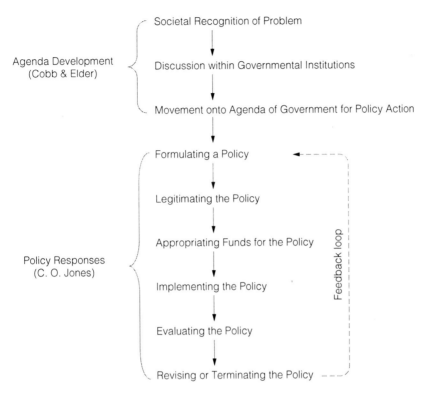

FIGURE 6-1 Forming Public Policy

POLITICAL RECRUITMENT

Who Runs?

Political scientists speak of "political recruitment" to describe the processes by which a citizen is identified and persuaded to run for elective office. Sometimes it is a matter of self-selection and self-persuasion. Sometimes others urge the citizen to run in the name of civic duty or of concern for the party or for the cause. Of course, not all U.S. senators and representatives are recruited in the same way, but the federal government's legislators display less diversity in that regard than do the council members of this nation's municipal corporations. Space limitations preclude an extended discussion, but the more pronounced contrasts are discussed here.

The most striking contrast between federal legislators and city council members is that, in all but the largest cities, service on the municipal council is likely to be by volunteers, not by careerists. Most members of the U.S. House of Representatives hope to remain as members unless they have an opportunity to run for the Senate, but most council members see themselves as citizen volunteers serving for a limited time. The council post typically is not a stepping-stone to bigger things; it is not the first rung on a political career ladder.

The members of Congress can live reasonably well, even in Washington, on the salary and expense account that go with the office, but many council members receive modest salaries, in some instances only token salaries. Should they receive more? The majority of cities in the United States are small to medium in size, and their council members are likely to be part-time council members and full-time something else. Thus, the number of hours spent each week on official responsibilities is necessarily moderate rather than large. But even a moderate number of hours can be burdensome when added to the demands of full-time employment elsewhere. As a rule of thumb one can say that the larger the city, the larger the amount of time that will be spent by council members on municipal affairs, but the relationship between those time demands on the one hand and salary on the other is very crude and includes some widely deviating instances.

The time of day used for council meetings and the frequency of those meetings furnish useful clues to just how strongly the spirit of volunteerism imbues the council. Fortnightly meetings in the evening permit many persons in the community to consider running for council, but afternoon meetings one or two times each week will discourage volunteerism and promote professionalism. (The word *professionalism* is used here to refer to the commitment of relatively large amounts of time, skill, and energy to council activities. *Professionalism* may be of limited duration, in contrast to *careerism,* which suggests a longer-range pattern of activity.)

How are these candidates recruited? That is, what happens to them, or what do they do, that results in their names being on the ballot on election day? There is no single answer, but perhaps several answers can be arranged in such a way that a pattern emerges.

Individuals do not often decide to run for office in solitary contemplation. Even the most ambitious and brash are likely to discuss the possibility with friends, with persons of political experience and judgment, and with persons who might be called upon to help in the campaign. But often candidates are sought out and encouraged to run by persons who wish to strengthen the quality of competition at the next election.

Who may wish to strengthen the quality of competition? A part of the answer is that persons active within a political party may wish to strengthen the party by filling the party's slate with quality candidates. Many council candidates in this nation run on partisan ballots, just as do candidates for the state legislature and for the U.S. House of Representatives and the Senate. But today more than two-thirds of the council members in the United States run on a nonpartisan ballot. *Nonpartisan* simply means that the party preference or affil-iation of the candidate cannot be determined by inspecting the ballot. From this fact, may we conclude that in more than two-thirds of U.S. cities (i.e., in the nonpartisan cities) prospective candidates travel alone across the electoral landscape? Not necessarily.

In some cities, to be sure, a candidate's decision to run is unsolicited and made in solitude. But in many cities there are solicitations and persuasion by a slate-making group that tries to identify able citizens and encourage them to run. That slate-making group may be a political party operating behind the scenes even though the form of the printed ballot omits the party label. Or it can be a group of citizens organized for some other purpose but possessing a civic interest. Examples might include a chamber of commerce, a community improvement association, or a labor union. Still another possibility is that a group may be organized especially for the purpose of creating a local slate of candidates. For example, two of the authors were instrumental in establishing a local slate-making group, limited to former members of the council, that func-tioned for more than a decade.

Whatever the basis of organization and action may be, the result can help to structure the process and make selection of candidates for office less haphazard.

How Are They Selected?

The two-stage elections of members of Congress and U.S. senators—nomination in primary elections and then final election in November—are too familiar to require description. City elections are in many respects similar, but there are three significant differences.

The first difference is that many of the smaller communities use nomina-tion by petition instead of primary-election nomination. Most of the time in a city of, say, twenty thousand, there will not be so many candidates that the screening (or winnowing) effect of a primary election is needed. A petition requiring fifty, one hundred, or even two hundred signatures will suffice to weed out the most frivolous or eccentric persons, and as for the rest, they can be screened by the electorate in the November election. Savings of time, effort, and money result from using this simple procedure.

The second difference is that nonpartisan elections give significant advantage to incumbents. Incumbency carries an advantage even with partisan elections, but without a party label on the ballot to offer at least a shred of information to assist voters' decisions, the name-recognition advantage of incumbents is even greater. Another way of understanding the effect of nonpartisan elections is to say that such elections reduce the ability of a political system to organize conflict around socioeconomic class differences or interests, and as a consequence the value of name recognition (and incumbency) rises.

The third difference is that many cities elect council members *at large* rather than from districts or wards. This has two significant consequences; the first consequence being that "protest" voting is difficult or impossible. Councilors elected at large represent the entire city rather than a district (or ward) within the city. At-large elections usually give each citizen as many votes as there are seats to be filled, with a proviso that no candidate may receive more than one vote from any one person. Thus, if city council has seven members and all seats are up for election now, each citizen will be allowed seven choices. And the seven highest vote getters will win. Although this system permits voters to organize to *elect* one or more candidates they prefer, voters would find it very difficult to organize to *defeat* a particular candidate inasmuch as the only way to defeat Jones would be to ensure that there are seven candidates who receive more votes than Jones.

The second consequence of at-large elections is that citizens who consider themselves part of a minority group (perhaps identified by a trait such as national origin, ethnicity, religion, or race) may feel that the system tilts to their disadvantage. They may prefer representation from districts (or wards) instead of at-large representation, for a group that is only 20 percent of the population within a city may comprise the majority of voters within a ward or district. This, in turn, could permit those voters to elect "one of their own" to a council seat if they chose to unite.

The preceding paragraphs help us understand two recent developments concerning at-large elections. First, when cities have occasion to review their method of selecting council members, there is a clear tendency for any changes in the method of representation to move in the direction of a hybrid plan. That is, the cities tend to choose a mixture of a few council members elected at large and other members each elected from one of the council districts into which the city has been divided. The second recent development is that some lawsuits have challenged at-large elections in certain cities on the ground that they disadvantage minorities (particularly racial minorities). In those cases where evidence showed there was a deliberate choice of at-large elections for the purpose of reducing the political influence of one or more minorities, courts have found such behavior to conflict with the Fourteenth Amendment's Equal Protection Clause, and a change either to some wards (hybrid) or entirely to wards has been ordered. But there has not been any court ruling that at-large elections are *inherently* racially discriminatory. At-large elections appear to be lawful unless adopted for reasons of racial disadvantage or (perhaps) ethnic disadvantage as well. Whether we have yet heard the last word on all the variations and permutations of this question is unclear.

LOCAL GOVERNMENT ISSUES

Two Types of Issues

A novice student of government quickly discovers that decision-making processes will vary according to the type of issue or the problem to be addressed. That suggests the wisdom of examining issues and problems typical of city governments. Despite some risk of overgeneralizing, it can be argued that the activities of government at the local level cluster to a significant degree around two major concerns: The first concern is to maintain the personal health and safety of the citizens; the second concern is to assure the security of property belonging to the citizens and to their organizations and institutions.

The example of a municipal water supply touches both concerns. The *quality* of the water is of critical importance to *health*. Through proper treatment of the water, typhus and cholera are controlled, and in many cities the dental health of children has been improved through fluoridation. Water also is important to the *safety* of the citizens and of their property because the *adequacy* of the supply and of the delivery system affects fire-fighting capabilities in the city. And it is worth noting that inadequate supplies of water can limit a city's capacity to promote economic development, for both new industry and residential construction add to the demand for water.

In addition to water quality, other municipal undertakings that have important consequences for the health of the citizens include: sewage collection and treatment, garbage and trash collection, and some hospitals and urgent care centers and clinics, particularly in target areas of widespread poverty. Ambulance service, especially in emergencies, now falls most often within the domain of local government.

Personal safety is promoted through police enforcement of laws, traffic engineering and enforcement, inspection of new construction (often performed by local inspectors even when they are enforcing state building codes), and inspection of rental property for compliance with fire and safety regulations. Property security is promoted through police enforcement of laws, fire protection and prevention, and regulation of land use so that one's own property will not be jeopardized by a neighbor who wishes to use land in a way that would depreciate the value of one's own.

In contrast, a large number of issues at the national and state levels cluster around income security—inflation, unemployment rates, unemployment insurance benefits, Social Security, and labor regulations quickly spring to mind as examples. In addition, national issues are more remote, often more durable through the years, and of broader range. Issues of war or peace, regulation and promotion of the economy, protection of the environment, protection and development of the nation's scenic resources, require the broad resources of the national government. At the individual level, Social Security and Medicare are so large, complex, and consequential that only the national government has the resources to manage them.

The Scale of Issues

Local government issues are smaller-scale issues than are the issues at other levels—that is to say, the territorial scope of an issue is necessarily quite limited. Citizens are quick to express their concern about the appearance of a neighborhood or about a perceived threat to the lifestyles of the neighborhood when the use of a parcel of land is to be changed by the owner. However, many local issues, though geographically of smaller scale than the issues at other levels, are too large for a single municipality. Many issues extend throughout the entire metropolitan area. We recall, for example, an instance in which a city built a major new street that ended at an intersection with a street that formed the boundary line between the city and a suburb, but the suburb refused to improve the intersecting street because the suburb opposed greater traffic flow through the suburb. Who can and will coordinate in such circumstances? Sometimes the answer is "no one." Sometimes the answer is that the central city, possessing the major share of a problem, will take some remedial steps even though you might think it better if a metropolitan area-wide effort could be launched. Occasionally, in some metropolitan areas, government reorganization has been undertaken in order to address such problems: Nashville, Jacksonville, Indianapolis, and Lexington, Kentucky, are examples. But there are many problems having a geographic scale well beyond the capacity of states and cities to address effectively, and in those circumstances calls for federal action often will be heard.

The Stakes of Issues

The topic "urban issues" tends to evoke images of conflict and debate, but it may be more useful to think about political struggles by comparing the stakes involved in municipal political issues to those involved in national or state issues. To illustrate, many of the stakes are more immediate in time at the local level than at the national or state level. The time span between decision and implementation at the local level tends to be short. A second characteristic of local-level stakes is that they are thought to be relatively low most of the time by most people. By contrast, stakes often seem higher at the national and state levels. (Students of public opinion would say that the "salience" of local issues is less than that of national or state issues.) For example, many of the stakes involve delivery of some municipal service to the citizens, but perhaps only one sector of the city will believe itself ill served or underserved.

Some issues that local government must confront seem to cut across the responsibilities and activities just mentioned. Race relations offer one example, and concerns for civil rights and liberties comprise another example. In these cases the question may not be whether a particular service is to be provided, but whether its distribution is fair and even-handed. Though such problems are common, they can be quite difficult to solve. They spread across the broad range of government activities. For example, should this parcel of land be used for middle-class housing or for housing that offers a subsidy to the poor? Do the police and fire departments try to recruit from minority groups as well as from the majority? Are decisions concerning promotions for city employees made on a "color-blind" basis? Are the streets in poverty-ridden neighborhoods swept as frequently as the streets in middle-class sections? Are the police courteous to all citizens? These questions and issues arise one by one, in piecemeal fashion, in the real world. It is only when we step back and try to understand them that we see the more general pattern that we label *race relations,* or *socioeconomic class rivalries.* Because the *Camelot* issues appear one by one, we have chosen a "direction of cut" for our analysis that parallels those issues. The question is rather like the question of how one chooses to slice a block of cheese: one may slice across the cheese with the knife pointed north, or one may slice along the length of the cheese with the knife pointed west. Thus, you will find in *Camelot* race relations considerations in some issues and not in others, but there is no package composed solely of race-relations issues.

When the stakes of national politics are examined, it can be seen that often those stakes are quite high; however, they often are more remote in time and are likely to be more enduring than the stakes of local-level decision. For example, such goals as equality of opportunity or equal protection of the law can be implemented more effectively at the national level than at the local level. Indeed, any pressure toward equality will have a tendency to move toward the national government's decision-making apparatus. As a consequence, ideological stakes are more prominent at the national than at the local level.

Citizen Access to Decision Makers

Another way of thinking usefully about the contrast between municipal issues and issues at other government levels is to examine the citizen's opportunity for access to decision makers and the decision-making process. Access at the local level is much easier and more open than at the state or national level *if* you are reasonably well educated and moderately skillful in interpersonal relations. Paths to access include running for office, speaking from the audience at city council meetings, voting and urging others to vote, circulating petitions on policy questions, and membership in civic groups that take positions from time to time. But this suggests a possible class bias in the responsiveness of local government, for if a person is not so well educated or not so skilled in dealing with others, then access is, for practical purposes, closed unless that person can find an interest group in which to participate.

At the national level, activity that goes beyond voting and supporting the party of one's choice is available to few. Access to decision makers is limited to a small fraction of the populace. It is fair to say that direct access is virtually nonexistent for citizen-voters. Most people must make their wishes felt through interest group activity, through support of their political party, and perhaps through letters or phone calls to their representatives in Congress.

Responsiveness of Decision Makers

When we examine the responsiveness of government to citizen desires, concerns, and complaints, the findings are uneven. As might be expected, responsiveness is significantly affected by city size: Large cities seem to have almost as much difficulty responding to citizen complaints and requests as have the state and national governments, but medium-sized and smaller cities often are more adaptable and responsive.

Responsiveness of the national government to individuals is negligible. There is no provision in the U.S. Constitution to permit a referendum on any issue, nor is there any opportunity for direct democracy to place a federal-level initiative on a ballot. There is no way in which the entire citizenry of the United States can express at the ballot box its opinion on *any* topic other than its choice for president. Indeed, when responsiveness does occur, it is likely to be cited on television or in the newspapers as an example of "the unusual instance that shows that democracy really does work."

Redistributive Policies

Another contrast between local governments and national governments is that some national policies have a redistributive effect. A "progressive" tax (imposing higher percentage rates on persons having higher incomes) is used to support a program that benefits all persons, or that perhaps targets the disadvantaged. The result is a redistribution of monetary resources via those taxing and spending policies. Medicare and Medicaid are examples, and various assistance programs for persons in need add to the list. But few local-level policies have a redistributive effect as described here, and the magnitude of any such redistribution will be slight.

A second reason preventing the use of redistributive policies at the local level is that city and county governments wish to encourage economic development. From the perspective of economics, the boundaries of cities are very porous, or permeable, in comparison to the nation's boundaries. Moving from one municipality to another is neither difficult nor costly. (Boundaries of the states fall somewhere in between—less permeable than cities but much more permeable than national boundaries.) Thus, desire to compete for new industries and jobs, combined with a desire to retain the taxpayers and revenues already in place, breeds caution among mayors and councilors searching for additional revenue sources.

Most local officials, most of the time, will regard the economic risks and the political risks of redistributive taxes and/or spending as too high. To modify an old saying, "Why drive away the geese that lay the golden eggs?" And there is widespread concern at the local level that proposals that could have a redistributive effect might prevent the flock from growing in number.

That concern, in turn, explains one of the most significant contrasts between national- and municipal-level issues. Political alignments based on socioeconomic class are quite important in state and national politics but are much less so in local politics. Indeed, many cities have adopted ballots with no political party designation next to the name of the candidates (the nonpartisan ballot) precisely so that they can insulate city affairs from political parties, which are the primary instruments for engaging in conflicts based on socioeconomic class differences and preferences.

CONCLUSION

When all is said and done, at every level of government in the United States most policy decisions originate within administrative departments or agencies. The process moves from a department's identification of needs to the development of priorities, thence to integration of those priorities into the department's annual budget proposal (a set of requests directed toward the legislative appropriation). To the department's annual budget proposal is added the department's annual report that points with pride to recent achievements and views that concern both continuing and newly emerging problems. The annual report also includes specific policy recommendations for coping with, or combating, these problems. The report is a set of policy recommendations integrated into a coherent set of spending proposals. When the chief executive, whether elected or appointed, reviews these reports and establishes priorities by adjusting the competing requests of the various departments before submitting the whole for legislative action, the "central clearance" process is complete.

7

Forms of Local Government

Nothing is very tidy in municipal politics. Thus it is that the forms (or plans) of municipal government include substantial variation. However, patterns do exist. It is important to understand that the descriptions that follow are only patterns. These arrangements are not carved in stone. You also should bear in mind that the phrase "form of municipal government" means the same as "plan of municipal government."

The four forms (or plans) of municipal government to be discussed are: (1) weak-mayor and council form, (2) strong-mayor and council form, (3) commission form, and (4) council-manager form. The description provided for each of these forms shows the typical arrangements. (See Figure 7-1.) In addition, the following pages will mention some examples of variations to be found within the four categories.

The council-manager form was chosen for Camelot. It is a popular choice for small and medium-size cities, and it is found in some of the larger cities. But for reasons that will be examined next, relatively few cities having populations larger than one million employ it despite the fact that each year witnesses additional cities selecting the council-manager form or a variant thereof. It would be quite understandable that a community having an educated electorate and a stable economic base (such as a major state university) would prefer the form of municipal government that stresses professionalism,

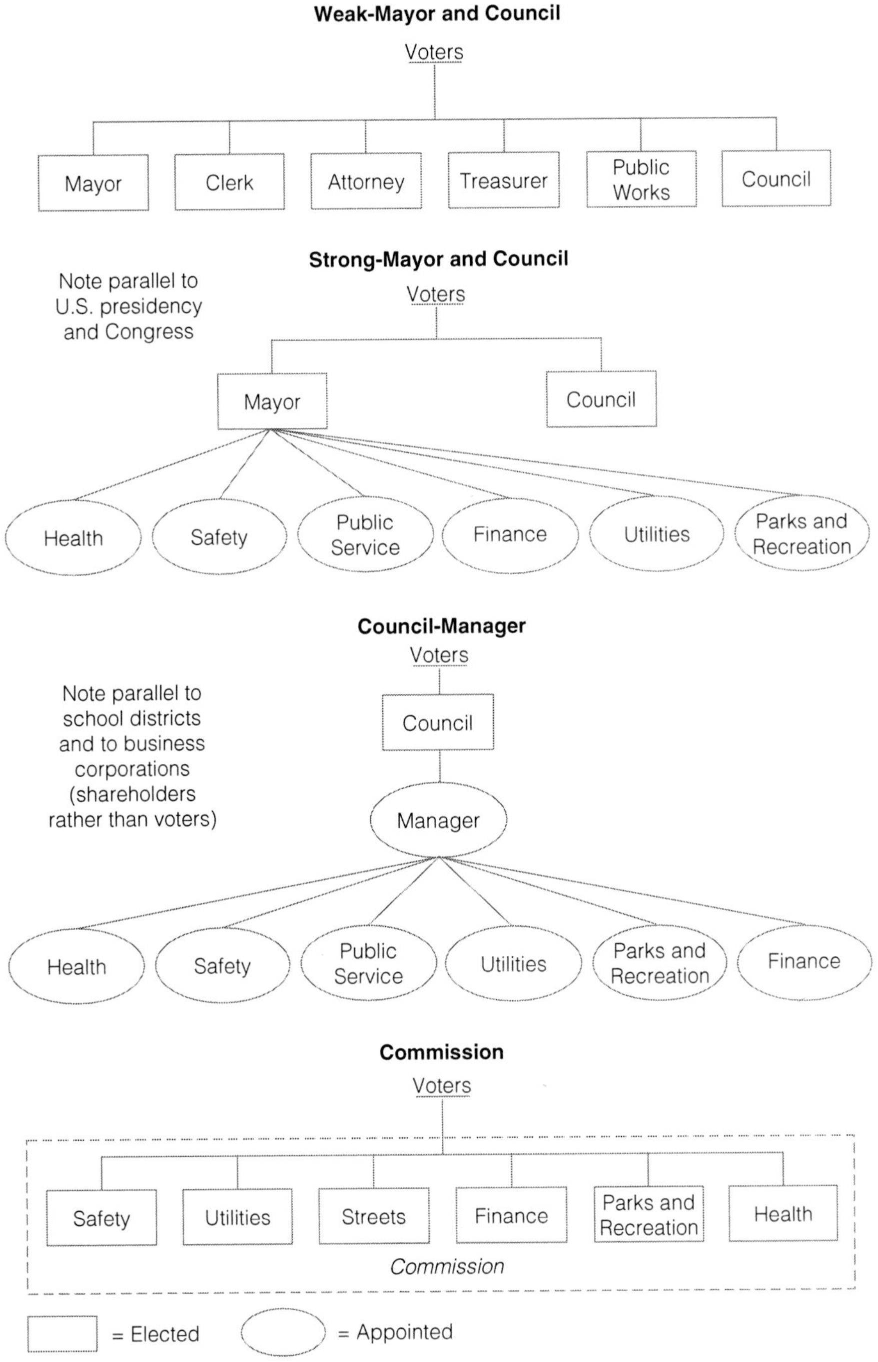

Weak-Mayor and Council

Voters

| Mayor | Clerk | Attorney | Treasurer | Public Works | Council |

Strong-Mayor and Council

Note parallel to
U.S. presidency
and Congress

Voters

Mayor   Council

Health   Safety   Public Service   Finance   Utilities   Parks and Recreation

Council-Manager

Voters

Note parallel to
school districts
and to business
corporations
(shareholders
rather than voters)

Council

Manager

Health   Safety   Public Service   Utilities   Parks and Recreation   Finance

Commission

Voters

| Safety | Utilities | Streets | Finance | Parks and Recreation | Health |

Commission

☐ = Elected   ◯ = Appointed

FIGURE 7-1 Forms of Government

good management practices, and the efficient providing of city services. These qualities tend to describe the council-manager form. But before undertaking a detailed examination of the council-manager form, it will be useful to discuss the principal features of each of the forms identified in Figure 7-1.

WEAK-MAYOR AND COUNCIL FORM

The majority of American towns and cities were established in the nineteenth century, a time when governmental organization and procedures were heavily influenced by "Jacksonian Democracy," a set of ideas for political reforms (or changes) that emerged in the 1820s and 1830s at about the time of the presidential campaigns of Andrew Jackson. Traits included short terms of office; many elected offices in the executive branch of both state and local governments; strong partisanship—including the spoils system of patronage; and a belief that while ordinary citizens can perform the duties of office, they ought not be kept in office very long lest they succumb to the various temptations and conceits inherent in office holding. Jacksonian Democracy dominated the structures and processes of state and local governments in the United States until the reformist efforts of the 1890–1910 era began to be heard.

As part of the lingering legacy of Jacksonian Democracy, the weak-mayor and council form remains a significant form of local government structure and distribution of authority, but its popularity and use are much diminished today. It is most often found in small communities that have not recently experienced the stresses associated with rapid growth. Its most apparent features are dispersal of authority and frequent elections. In practice this means that everyone (i.e., every member of council and the mayor) has to decide *everything*. When carried to its logical extreme in a small town, this has required council approval of (and these are actual examples) the purchase of a dozen pencils, two flashlight batteries, a new fire engine, and a broom. The mayor has *no* independent powers. He or she may preside over council but has no veto power and no authority to develop a budget; he or she cannot hire or fire anyone. The mayor may not even be authorized to prepare the agenda for the next council meeting! *Everything* is done by the mayor *and* council, which in practice means that a committee of council (probably, but not necessarily, including the mayor) makes a recommendation to the full council for final approval. Who shall be hired to fill a clerical vacancy? A committee of council reviews the credentials of the applicants, handles the interviews, and makes recommendations to council that a majority must approve. The same is true for the hiring of a police officer or a firefighter, the purchase of a water meter, or the resurfacing of a street. Members of the council thus have to make decisions requiring a level of expertise far exceeding that of the typical citizen.

The result is what one might expect: Amateurs are constantly making decisions on very technical problems, and supervision of the day-to-day operations of government is at best inconsistent and at worst nonexistent. The entire community pays the price. It is not simply inefficiency that results. That at least would be tolerable. It is often chaos. As an example, in one community the head of the water department knew where every water line and control valve was located. The diagram was in his head. He had never put anything down on paper, even though council repeatedly urged him to do it. One day he dropped dead of a heart attack. To this day, the city water department is still trying to find out where all the shut-off valves are located. And it still is being surprised, especially when there is a water-main break. There you have the principal weakness of the weak-mayor and council form: the inability to fix, or even find, responsibility. When everyone is in charge, no one is fully in charge. Decision making runs the gamut from infrequent to capricious and is often prone to cronyism.

Where the city or village is small, the inefficiencies are tolerable. In fact, the tax base may be so small that the citizens cannot afford to do anything but try to run everything themselves. There is nothing wrong with that. Government does not have to be efficient. It does, however, have to be effective—it must work. And when it no longer works, the citizenry begins to look for ways to correct things. Under this form of local government, the mayor and the members of council are, almost by definition, amateurs at running a city.

Typically they are full-time something else: merchants; realtors; insurance agents; professionals such as lawyers, accountants, and teachers; homemakers; or craftsmen and skilled workers. If the city or village is too small to afford hiring professional administrators, it obviously cannot hire a full-time mayor and pay members of council significant compensation for their time spent on public affairs. So amateurs run things, perhaps in their spare time, perhaps in time they ill can spare.

As a city grows, the problems of running it become more difficult. As the problems become more complex, specialists are needed to deal with them. In some cases, the citizens may decide not to alter the form of government in any basic way. All that is revised is the actual practice of running things. A city administrator will be hired to handle the day-to-day administration of the city, but the mayor remains little more than a figurehead. Council and council committees remain as the real power—or absence of it. Thus, when the citizenry becomes impatient with divided and limited authority, calls for a restructuring of the city government may be heard. One of the revision options then could be the strong-mayor and council form.

STRONG-MAYOR AND COUNCIL FORM

One way of focusing responsibility in city government is to give the mayor more powers, and this is exactly what the strong-mayor and council form does. Once again it must be stressed that there is not a checklist of items that must be met in order for the strong-mayor plan to be achieved. One looks instead for a pattern. Typically, in order to strengthen the authority of the mayor, and thus better to hold him or her responsible for what does or does not happen, one or more of the following powers will be granted:

1. authority to develop and propose a budget (council continues to have authority to approve, disapprove, or modify)
2. power to appoint and remove department heads and immediately subordinate staff personnel (within the limits of the city's civil service laws)
3. veto power over actions of council; but council can override the veto by a two-thirds, or perhaps a three-fourths, majority
4. authority to prepare agendas for council meetings

There are, of course, other powers, such as authority to reorganize the administrative departments of the city, authority to appoint investigative task forces, and to create a separate budget for the office of mayor. As can be seen, the total impact of these items is quite significant. Possession of even several of them will strengthen the leadership ability of the mayor and enable him or her to identify and pursue goals. The mayor is far from a dictator, however. Council still controls the purse strings and legislative authority, and council must be persuaded of the wisdom of any proposals. But at least the mayor should not have the feeling that she or he is hamstrung at every step of the way. Leadership is possible, and, depending on the amount of authority granted, the programs of the city can be administered in a coherent and responsible manner.

What are the limitations and weaknesses of the strong-mayor and council form? The people, of course, are the final authority in this as in the other forms of municipal government. They elect the mayor and the members of council independently of each other. And in their wisdom, the people often elect a council whose goals or personalities are in conflict with those of the mayor. Who, then, leads? The answer may be everyone and no one. Or perhaps more correctly, many try to lead. If a mayor is fortunate in belonging to a strong party organization that is capable of winning a majority of council seats, and if that mayor is skillful in promoting cohesive behaviors among the holders of those seats, opportunities for leadership by that mayor almost certainly will come. But in recent decades the strength of parties has diminished greatly in many cities, and in numerous other cities the ballot is nonpartisan. The consequence can be a real likelihood that the diversity of the groups and interests within the city, combined with the independence of the separately elected council members, may produce conflict rather than consensus, stalemate rather than objectives attained. In such a circumstance mayoral leadership may be effective if the mayor has skills as a coalition builder and "political entrepreneur."

But there is more to the story than matters of authority, powers, and leadership skills. In the first part of the chapter on "Implementing Democracy" (Chapter 6), there is a section on "Administration-Initiated Policy Proposals" in which the concept of *central clearance* is described and applied to local government. Central clearance processes, especially at budget-making time, will propel information upward within an administrative pyramid—and here, as in most areas of life, knowledge is power. Moreover, since priority setting is inherent in all budget-making processes, and since the development of an annual or biennial budget has become a function of the executive at all levels of government in the United States, the combination of knowledge and opportunity to set budget priorities gives executives a powerful resource for influencing others, both inside and outside the government.

It may be objected that budgets are only recommendations, that the final decisions rest with legislators rather than executives. That is indeed accurate as far as it goes. But it fails to take account of the momentum generated by a budget, for the budget is an interlocking set of spending recommendations and revenue expectations that are reinforced by the extensive information resources developed through the central clearance process. It is, in short, an *agenda for spending,* and it is a well-known principle of decision making that the person who controls the agenda has a long head start toward controlling the outcome. Indeed, the three most important contrasts between the weak mayor form and the strong mayor form are to be found in the latter's power to appoint administrative personnel, power to veto legislation (usually including appropriations), and responsibility for development and presentation of budget recommendations.

To sum up, a full understanding of leadership should include formal powers, personal skills of the individual leader (especially communication skills with groups of all sizes), and central clearance.

COMMISSION FORM

In 1900, a devastating hurricane hit the city of Galveston, Texas, causing the deaths of several thousand people and catastrophic property damage. When the city government proved incapable of meeting the needs of the emergency, the state legislature appointed a commission of five local businessmen to run the city. The five men divided up their responsibilities and acted as heads of departments, but collectively they acted as a city council. The result of their efforts was so successful that the commission idea was widely adopted across the country. Unfortunately, what worked well in a crisis under the leadership of able and cooperative individuals failed to achieve the same results in other cities in the absence of crisis. The individual commissioners, with responsibilities as department heads, tended to focus their attention and energies on their departments. Thus the design of the commission plan tended to create rivalries and departmental parochialism, and it encouraged commissioners to run for reelection on the basis of their success as department heads. There was nothing in either the structure of the government or the process of administering the respective departments that would encourage a city-wide perspective.

Interest in the commission plan declined, and increasingly cities turned either to variants of the strong-mayor and council form or the council-manager form. Some cities retained the commission name but changed the way the plan worked, giving increased authority over the day-to-day administration of the city either to an independently elected mayor or, in other cases, to an appointed city manager.

COUNCIL-MANAGER FORM

The remaining form of municipal government is the council-manager plan. It too attempts to concentrate leadership responsibility, but unlike the strong-mayor and council arrangement, which concentrates leadership in the hands of an independently elected mayor, the council-manager form insulates the person exercising executive power in day-to-day administration from the direct control of the voter. This aspect is probably the form's greatest asset and greatest limitation. The voters choose, often by nonpartisan ballot, a city council in whose hands rests all legislative authority, whether it be approval of city ordinances, city budgets, or city planning and zoning. The mayor is a voting member of council and serves as presiding officer. The mayor also is the ceremonial head of the city and the legal head of the city for such purposes as official proclamations and receipt of legal documents.

It is the city manager who has the real executive and administrative authority in the city. Appointed by a majority of council, he or she serves at the pleasure of council. It is literally true that most managers can be fired by a majority of council at any time, indeed at any council meeting because few work under a contract for a fixed term. No notice need be given, unless the city ordinances or charter state otherwise. While it is not a common occurrence, it does happen that council will fire the manager without warning, as happened in the city of Cincinnati during the winter of 1993.

There are compensations, however. The pay generally is good. With a response rate of nearly 65 percent, an ICMA survey for the 1999 Municipal Yearbook[1] revealed that the average annual salary of city managers in 1997 was $70,541; for 1998 it was $73,002. And the job includes resources and the

---

1. *Municipal Yearbook 1999*, ICMA, Washington, D.C., Chapter C-1, "Salaries of Administrative Officials, 1998," by Evelina R. Mounder, pp. 79–80.

authority to get things done. True, there is no veto power over actions of council, but the manager can appoint and dismiss the department heads and his or her immediate staff (subject only to civil service rules), develop the city budget, and have a major role (if not total authority) in preparing council's agenda.

As an aside, there is another source of influence possessed by city managers that is not often mentioned. Councils constantly ask the managers to make recommendations concerning solutions to problems. The typical response of a manager is to collect appropriate information, sometimes through consultants, and then identify several possible paths toward solution, each of which has advantages and disadvantages. There is an old saying: "Whoever develops the options, rigs the game." The options described and evaluated by city managers cannot help but reflect their values and, implicitly (if not explicitly), their preferences filtered through those values and their professional judgments.

THE STRONG-MAYOR AND COUNCIL FORM VERSUS THE COUNCIL-MANAGER FORM

When the citizenry has agreed that their weak-mayor plan is no longer satisfactory, what factors may affect their choice between the strong-mayor and council form and the council-manager form? There is no hard and fast answer, but there are some generalizations one can suggest. The council-manager form is adopted more frequently by small and medium-size cities than by larger cities. Does this mean that the council-manager form cannot work successfully in truly large cities? Not necessarily, but it suggests that the citizens of the larger cities believe that the council-manager form will not meet their needs.

With the exception of Cincinnati, no city of more than 500,000 population when adopting the council-manager form continues to employ it today. Some (e.g., San Diego, Dallas, and Phoenix) adopted the council-manager form when they were smaller and retained it as they have grown. And in earlier decades a few cities having more than 500,000 adopted the council-manager form but later abandoned it. Cleveland in the 1920s is an example.

A recent effort in Cincinnati to blend the advantages of the council-manager plan with those of the strong-mayor plan seems promising, though a firm judgment would be premature. In May of 1999, Cincinnati voters approved a bundle of charter amendments, effective with the municipal election of 2001 that placed a strong mayor above the city manager. A nonpartisan primary election in September of odd-numbered years elects two candidates to compete in the November election for a four-year term as mayor.

Other changes are:

1. Mayor presides over council meetings but does not vote; can call special meetings of council; can propose and introduce legislation.

2. Mayor can veto legislation; veto can be overridden by six (of nine) councillors.

3. Mayor appoints and can remove council committee chairs and makes all assignments of agenda items to committees.

4. Mayor selects a member of council as vice mayor. Vice mayor will act in absence of mayor but will not have veto, appointment, or removal power.

5. Mayor reviews the annual budget estimate prepared by the city manager and submits the estimate, with comments, to council within fifteen days.

6. Mayor appoints city manager with approval of council majority (five members) after the mayor's recommendation for appointment. Before the vote, the mayor seeks the advice of council and gives council an opportunity to interview the candidates. Mayor has authority to initiate removal of manager with the advice of council. Council majority must concur in removal.

7. Mayor is ceremonial head and official representative of the city for all purposes, except as otherwise provided by the charter.

These amendments were adopted in an off-year primary election having a very low turnout (under 20 percent). Impetus for change seemed to come from two sources: Some council members, who perhaps harbored political ambitions and saw the new office as a stepping-stone, were joined by some neighborhood leaders who perhaps saw the proposed changes as opportunity for more access and influence at City Hall.

The U.S. Bureau of the Census published the following estimates of population (in thousands and rounded off) for the ten largest council-manager *central cities* as of July 1, 1997, in the *State and Metropolitan Area Data Book, 1997–98*. Data for the year 2000 are from the *2000 County & City Data Book, U.S. Census Bureau*.

	1997	2000
San Diego, CA	1,171	1,223
Phoenix, AZ	1,159	1,321
San Antonio, TX	1,067	1,145
Dallas, TX	1,053	1,189
San Jose, CA	839	895
Austin, TX	541	657
Fort Worth, TX	480	535
Kansas City, MO	441	442
Fresno, CA	396	428
Oakland, CA	367	399

Another generalization we can make focuses on the diversity and the socioeconomic traits of the population. As a general rule, (1) the more homogeneous a city's population and (2) the higher its educational achievement and income, the more likely is the council-manager form to be adopted and retained. The converse is equally true: where educational achievement and income level are lower and heterogeneity[2] is greater, it is more likely that a change will utilize the strong-mayor and council form. Why is this true?

Though there is no single, definitive answer to the question, one important reason pertains to the process of building a majority coalition in a democracy. In any representative democracy a majority coalition must be achieved within the legislative assembly on each issue, and this process of coalition formation seems to be facilitated when the legislative coalition is in turn supported by the presence of a large coalition of voters, preferably a majority. (In this connection, one should note that a political party, if available, can be an important instrument for building an electoral coalition and linking it to a legislative coalition.) It is worth emphasizing again that the task of electing a mayor, like the task of electing a U.S. president, is an exercise in coalition building. Mayoral candidates spend much of their energy and skill piecing together the largest possible electoral coalition. Thus it can be stated that some cities, because of their ethnic, economic, and social diversities, appear to *need* a mayor-council form of government to help build agreement on anything at all. Other cities, less divided on basic values and priorities, can devote relatively more attention to problems of means, implementation, and administration. It is a difference of degree.

A second possible reason has to do with the perceptions of the citizens concerning their ability to gain access to the political process. Because managers in council-manager cities are appointed by council rather than elected by the voters, various groups, whether religious, or ethnic, or class-based, may resent the apparent remoteness and insulation of the manager from the elective process. Perhaps they want an *elected* mayor in order to retain the sense that they have direct access to the chief executive they supported. But this is only speculation, not fact. Even though it is quite easy to demonstrate that managers are often better educated, better trained, and more skillful in obtaining compromise among contending groups than are most popularly elected mayors, it is nevertheless true that when there is conflict in a city, people seem more content with the system if they can go to the office and confront the person "they elected." This is true even if they didn't vote for the individual. It is also true that minority groups are likely to be particularly sensitive to this point. In a council-manager city, they seldom have the sense that a block of votes can be translated into a set of achieved goals.

Are council-manager cities more efficient than strong-mayor and council cities? Are they more businesslike? More professionally led? Less expensive? Are taxes lower? Services better? The council-manager form is often so advertised,

---

2. The term "heterogeneity" includes, but is not limited to, ethnic and racial diversity.

and there are examples of it being true. Yet perhaps the reason is attributable to the particular qualities of the citizenry rather than the political structure. It is government's job to reflect the values and aspirations of its citizens, and if efficiency is what they want, and if the community is relatively homogeneous, then that is what they probably will get. Communities will more likely use the council-manager plan as a means of gaining better services and leadership that is more professional. It is less likely that the council-manager plan will guarantee certain policy outcomes. A community divided over its goals and values will not suddenly become united just because it adopts the council-manager plan.

8

Land Use Planning, Planning Departments, and Planning Commissions

The purpose of this chapter is to describe and discuss briefly the structures and processes used to regulate land use within U.S. cities. Very sharp disputes can arise when the desire of a citizen to use his or her land in a particular way collides with the collective judgment of many citizens as has been expressed in local ordinances constraining the use of parcels of land within the city. Land use disputes can provide classic illustrations of the democratic problem of the one versus the many. At first blush, the dispute is likely to seem a matter of economics—pitting the potential gain of the landowner seeking change against the feared losses of landowners whose property might be less valuable or less marketable as a result of the change. But there may be another, very important dimension to the concerns of the opponents: They may see themselves as opposing a change that threatens the lifestyle of the neighborhood in which they have invested much thought, months or years of living and working, and a large portion of their emotions. Threats to dollar values may be secondary. Indeed, a perceived hazard to our preferred lifestyle may evoke some of the most intense feelings we possess. Thus, we should not be surprised to find that reverberations from a planning issue can include moral issues as well as important issues of taste and of judgment, along with the more obvious questions of economic impact on the neighborhood (or region) for which change is proposed.

LAND USE PLANNING

Although many city activities, such as police and fire protection, water supply, sewerage, and street maintenance, are carried out by administrative departments reporting to the chief executive, one important activity uses both a more complex process and a special commission to assist the city council. The process is called *land use planning,* and city council is assisted by the policy-making deliberations of the *city planning commission.*

Questions about how land may be used are important for everyone. Owners hope to maximize the income from their land in case of rental, or the capital gain from the land in case of sale. The more intensive the use of the land, the higher the potential rent or sale value. By "intensiveness of use" we mean the degree to which the value of a particular use for a parcel of land approaches the theoretical maximum value of any conceivable use of that parcel. Thus, duplex housing is a more intensive use than single-family dwellings, and a supermarket is a more intensive use than housing, even when that housing is a multi-family structure. Conflicts may arise when one owner sees opportunity for a more intensive use that would diminish the value of neighboring properties, such as a gas station being placed next door to your home. Economists would say that the gas station imposes "negative externalities" (i.e., undesirable spillover effects) on the properties around it.

Generally speaking, municipal corporations have substantial powers to regulate and influence land use within their boundaries, and substantial economic stakes can hinge on those decisions. To assist in the decisions, a city such as Camelot will have both a planning department and a planning commission.

PLANNING DEPARTMENT

The Planning Department collects and analyzes information about such matters as population trends, economic activities within the city and region, skills within the labor force, water supply quantity and quality, electricity costs, and proximity of the city to various types of markets within the region and the nation. Information of that sort can be useful in economic forecasting, helping to attract or retain jobs and investment capital for the city.

The department's professional staff also maintains data on the use of each parcel of land within the city boundaries. From data on the present uses of land, augmented by data on economic and population trends, the professional staff estimates growth rates and patterns. The city government then is in a better position to assist and shape the growth patterns.

The two most important ways of shaping growth and development are through *public capital investment* and through *land use zoning.* Public capital investment can be used for purposes that include upgrading of major streets, construction of new streets, improvements and extensions of water supply and sewerage, and locations for parks and recreation, sports arenas, convention centers, and schools.

Zoning

In addition to public capital investment, development patterns within cities are influenced through zoning regulations. The zoning code (i.e., the assembled land use regulations) describes the various ways in which land may be used within a particular sector, or "zone," of the city. Uses that are omitted from the description of a particular zone are, by implication, prohibited in that zone. In addition, to clarify meaning, the zoning code at times may explicitly prohibit a particular land use in a particular zone. Along with identification of the types of use permitted, zoning codes often specify minimum dimensions for lots, minimum and/or maximum dimensions for structures, minimum dimensions for yards in residential districts, required off-street parking spaces, and other desired matters.

Zoning codes inescapably restrict the "right" of property owners to use property in whatever way each owner may wish. The U.S. Supreme Court has upheld the reasonableness of most such restrictions against constitutional challenge by pointing out that zoning can stabilize property values within the zone by enabling all owners to ascertain the range of uses possible in the zone. Thus you can be assured before you break ground for your new house that the lot owner next door cannot construct or operate a laundromat there (unless, of course, you chose to build in a commercial zone). When each owner gives up some freedom, the remaining freedoms to use and enjoy one's property are reinforced.

Of course, there are limits to what lawfully may be done to restrict the use of a parcel of land through zoning. For instance, a zoning ordinance aimed at *who* may own land rather than regulating *how* the land may be used would be unconstitutional because of its potential for religious or racial discrimination. But very difficult problems can arise, leading reasonable persons to disagree in their assessment of which outcome is preferable. An example of this occurred in 1987 when Los Angeles County refused an application for a construction permit by The First English Evangelical Lutheran Church of Glendale, California, to rebuild a summer camp damaged by flood.[1] The church complained that the flood-plain regulations of the county effectively prevented *any* use of the land, thus violating the constitutional principle that government cannot take property without compensation. Thus, legal answers to questions about "inverse

---

1. *First English Evangelical Lutheran Church of Glendale v. County of Los Angeles, California* 482 U.S. 304 (1987).

condemnation" (circumstances under which government restrictions effectively convert private land to public use, thus requiring fair compensation by that government) continue to be difficult and elusive.

A similar constraint may arise from a community's interest in architectural and historic preservation. In 1997, the U.S. Supreme Court decided such a case that began when the City of Boerne, Texas, denied a building permit to enlarge St. Peter's Catholic Church by relying on a city ordinance governing historic preservation. The structure, constructed in 1923, replicated the mission style of the region's history. Seventy-four years later, the auditorium fell short of being able to accommodate the parishioners at Sunday masses. The case went to the U.S. Supreme Court. Attorneys for Archbishop Flores, the plaintiff, invoked the Religious Freedom Restoration Act (RFRA) passed by Congress in 1993. But the Supreme Court held that RFRA exceeded the Fourteenth Amendment authority given Congress.[2] Settlement was achieved, not by further litigation, but by negotiation between the litigants.

PLANNING COMMISSION

It is clear that the process of determining what types of uses should be permitted in which sectors of a city involves policy issues of great sensitivity around which may swirl strong interests and concerns. It is too important and sensitive to be left to the administrative professionals in the city's planning department. At the same time, the already crowded agenda of city council has little room for the numerous zoning and planning matters that come for resolution. Establishing a city planning commission is the response that has been most widely used in the cities of this nation. The planning commission, typically composed of citizens appointed either by the mayor or by the council, is in effect a screening committee for council. Through concentration on one type of issue, the citizens on the planning commission develop a degree of expertise and understanding that council, with its broader responsibilities, cannot attain. For that reason, planning commission recommendations to council are adopted much more often than not.

The process of planning for the city's future calls upon the resources of the Planning Department as well as the Planning Commission. The major tasks include (1) goal setting and standard setting and (2) application of those goals and standards to particular situations. The role of planning department staff is especially important in developing the information upon which *long-range goals* can be based. Those goals, and more detailed identification of means for attaining them, will go into the city's *comprehensive plan*. The comprehensive

---

2. *City of Boerne v. Flores, Archbishop of San Antonio, et al.* 521 U.S. 507 (1997).

plan includes a description and an assessment of present economic and social conditions, geographic circumstances, resources available and desired (such as those for commerce, culture, education, transportation, health), and any other matters that may be pertinent to the particular situation of the city. One important purpose of the comprehensive plan is to match those strategic resources to the goals of the plan and, in the process, identify other needed resources. The comprehensive plan includes a *zoning map*, which actually is part of the zoning code, showing the zone (i.e., land use category) for every portion of the city. Suggestions for alteration of the zoning map may develop as the master plan is considered and prospects for growth and change are identified.

ZONING ENFORCEMENT AND CHANGE

Enforcement of standards of the zoning code is an administrative process lodged somewhere within each city's administrative structure, though usually not in the planning department. The most important tool of enforcement is the requirement that a building permit be required for any construction or remodeling of any structure within the city. Because failure to obtain a permit may place both the property owner and the construction contractor at risk, and because the permit will not be issued by the city's permit office until the plans are checked against the zoning code for adequacy of lot dimensions and building dimensions, for legality of proposed use, and for any other pertinent constraints, the permit process is very useful for enforcement.

Finally, a word about possible exceptions to the operation of the zoning code is in order. Every piece of land on this earth is unique. No other parcel has precisely the same location, and few parcels have identical buildings placed on them. How then should claims for adjustment of the zoning code be handled when only a single parcel is affected? "Spot zoning," changing the zone boundaries for a single parcel, is widely condemned, for it undermines consideration of the collective good as a counterpoise to the individual benefit sought by the owner. An alternative procedure is to allow for the possibility of a *zoning variance* whereby a specific, narrowly defined adjustment of the zoning regulations, as applied only to that parcel, can be made. Such adjustments often are quite minor, as for example a reduction of the side yard minimum requirement by ten or twelve inches so that a carport of standard size can be constructed alongside the house.

A zoning appeals board (ZAB) is authorized to grant variances, at its discretion, upon petition by an owner. The appeals board may impose limits or conditions in any variance it chooses to grant. So long as the condition is not unreasonable, there are many possible adjustments that may be pertinent. A variance may be granted for a specified length of time or an unlimited time, depending on the judgment of the board or commission.

But some requests for a variance may be quite significant, even to the point of generating substantial opposition from owners or renters in the affected area. One of the authors observed closely a variance request resulting from destruction of a downtown business structure by fire. The cost of rebuilding to the former use as a restaurant did not balance the projected revenue stream to the owners, who insisted they could not afford to rebuild unless a variance allowed them to use a portion of their lot that was, under the zoning code, a required set-back from the lot line. After many months of a black hole in the ground, during which time considerable architectural ingenuity was applied to the problem, a compromise was achieved and a variance granted that allowed intrusion to the lot line in return for architectural concessions by the owners. The visual bulk of that intrusion to the lot line was reduced greatly by using a florist's greenhouse as inspiration for the dining area. The glass walls on one end and one side helped support a glass roof, and the room became the most popular portion of the restaurant.

In some smaller cities, applications for variances are reviewed and decided by a zoning appeals board.

Though either a zoning appeals board or a planning commission may consider other requests for variances because of hardship, the city charter usually forbids granting variances based on *economic* hardship. Thus, your request to turn your home into a duplex in order to ease an economic pinch after your retirement could not be granted by the zoning appeals board if your home is in an area zoned solely for one-family homes. Otherwise, the greed of some property owners and the economic need of others could give a zoning map the appearance of Swiss cheese.

PART II

Simulating Political Decision Making

WELCOME TO CAMELOT

You are about to enter a magic place. "That's ridiculous," say the cynics among you. "It is just a game of some sort. A mixture, no doubt, of the high school 'mayor for a day' and Monopoly." You may be in for a surprise. This is a simulation of a part of a city government. It has been developed and revised over more than a quarter century, and the consistent response has been enthusiasm by those who have participated. It is called *Camelot,* after the city of King Arthur legends, the difference being that it is a city of the present and future, not of the past.

A question frequently asked in any city is: "Who is running things around here?" During this simulation of local politics in Camelot, *you will run the government.* Within a few constraints to be described later, you can do as you think best.

9

Introduction to Simulation

WHY A SIMULATION?

A persistent student criticism is that the classroom does not seem to provide a sense of reality. "This theory is well and good, but what *really* happens?" is a familiar criticism. And that is exactly where a simulation comes in. It is the nearest thing we have to a laboratory. It is an attempt to create a situation that is like the real world, to simulate reality.

You may have had experience in a simulation before, or perhaps you have played a game that was an attempt to provide an illustration of the real world. But *Camelot* is different from a typical game and different from a gaming simulation: It is a role-playing simulation. It involves a city council and a planning commission in a medium-size city. The simulation requires you to play a particular role as realistically as you can. More on this topic is presented later in the instructions. For the moment, it is important for you to understand the difference between a game or gaming simulation and a role-playing simulation. In a game, there are prescribed boundaries, set rules, and winners and losers, each of whom knows what can be won or lost. The combination of luck and skill, used within the parameters and rules of the game, determines who wins. And winning is not ambiguous; one knows whether one wins or loses.

In a role-playing simulation, as in real life, things are never quite that simple. Sometimes it isn't clear who are the winners and who are the losers;

sometimes you lose by winning, or win by losing; sometimes you don't know whether you won or lost. It is this ambiguity that makes *Camelot* so realistic.

Of course, there are limits to what may be simulated. For example, most simulations rule out criminal behavior, as does *Camelot*. There really is no way to simulate the passions and intensity of fear that swirl around criminal trans-actions. Similarly, friendships and long-standing loyalties cannot match in the short span of a simulation the importance that they sometimes carry in real-life behaviors. Thus, although we cannot simulate passions, and although we choose not to try to simulate criminal behaviors, we can and do simulate the pursuit of interests and values by lawful and rational means. The interests, or stakes, will be varied, and the resources available to various members of the community as they pursue those interests and stakes will be diverse.

There is one other aspect to which we should alert you: *Camelot* is not only like reality, *it develops a reality all its own*. The decisions one must make, the responsibilities that come with the role, the duties of the office, the pressures of one's constituents—all are real. Truly real. You don't play at being a member of city council; you are, *in fact, a member of council,* and you have duties and obli-gations, just as everyone else in the simulation has. *Camelot,* you discover, *exists!* And the consequences of this discovery are always exciting and sometimes painful. There is no such thing as escaping from the pressures of a role.

Each year, the unanimous reaction of participants has been surprise at how much they learned about how city governments really operate.

The only constraints are the following:

1. One cannot violate the laws of the state and nation.
2. One is constrained by the city charter and city ordinances (especially the budget and zoning ordinances).
3. One must remain within the bounds of realism.
4. One must remain within one's role.

Thus, you cannot solve city budgetary problems by having the police agree to a pay cut or by winning the state lottery.

Your instructor serves as the judge at all times, to halt the proceedings if things become illegal or unrealistic. But fear not. These constraints only make the simulation more real, and the inventiveness of the human mind and the vari-ety of human activity are quite remarkable. Following are just a few illustrations to dramatize the kinds of things that have happened in previous simulations.

In one simulation, the city manager just disappeared—literally! It was the day the budget was to be presented to council, and there was no sign of the city man-ager. Council went on to other business while other members of the class made frantic phone calls, and the assistant city manager (understandably) even went to the apartment of the city manager. There was no sign of him. So the assistant city manager was named acting manager by city council, and then he struggled to become familiar with a budget from which the manager had excluded him during the preparation. Of course, the *Camelot Daily News* had headline stories, suggesting everything from foul play to embezzlement of city funds. But the assistant city manager had a learning and growth experience he will never forget. (The city manager, by the way, never did appear in class again. We later learned that he had withdrawn from school and didn't bother to tell anyone.)

In another instance, the newspaper reported that a councilwoman and the fire chief had shared a table for two at a local bistro. The councilwoman found to her surprise that she was quite angered by the story.

Still another time the police wanted a pay raise, and the chief reported a very high incidence of planned absenteeism. The newspaper then called attention to a wave of burglaries taking place in the central business district, with the merchants demanding more police protection, while at the same time the residents of the poorer neighborhoods were complaining about the inadequacy of police protection. Can you guess how that episode turned out? What would you have done if you had been on the city council?

These are just three examples of the kinds of unexpected events that occur in *Camelot*. There are dozens of other equally intriguing episodes created by class members. They reveal dramatically how unlike a game this role-playing simulation is. Remember the four basic constraints, and then use your imagination. The simulation will become very real for you if you work hard at playing your role.

WHAT TO LOOK FOR

Textbooks and lectures can never fully convey to you how things really work in a democratic society. All the words used to describe organized interests (or pressure groups), the role of mayor, powers of council, duties of the city manager, influence of key leaders, are just that—words. It is easy for citizens to view events in city affairs as all predetermined, or rigged, if you like. It is probably difficult for you to believe that planning commission recommendations and council actions are rarely predictable and may seem to defy explanation.

As the simulation progresses, there are several questions that you should ask yourself constantly, for they will help you to understand the process in which you are involved. Some, perhaps all, of these same questions may be asked by your instructor after the conclusion of the simulation, during what has been called "The Debriefing and Critique Session."

1. What surprised you?

2. In what ways was the simulation like real life? In what ways was it different?

3. Why was it different? What are the possible consequences of the difference?

4. As you think about an episode in your hometown, or where you now live, has the simulation given you a different understanding of the event?

5. Can you relate the words and the situations of the simulation to words and situations you have witnessed elsewhere?

6. In what ways has the simulation helped you to understand behaviors in other settings?

OTHER THINGS TO KEEP IN MIND

The most important ingredient in the simulation is you. The simulation is like life: It will be as good as *you* make it. If the simulation succeeds, it will be because you made it succeed. If it fails, you are the cause. You will, to your astonishment, make a difference. That is the most exciting, yet perhaps sobering, aspect.

It is absolutely essential that you stay within your role. You are not playing yourself; you are playing a role. Thus Camelot is not an upper-middle-class suburb. It is heterogeneous, especially in terms of socioeconomic class. In short, different kinds of people are living in one city, having to face the realities of conflict in values.

In order to dramatize this, there are various types of people in the simulation. *Read your role description very carefully.* Ask yourself how that person would think, how he or she would respond to the issues you have to face. Remember: You are *not* playing yourself. Read and reread the description of the person you are playing. You are constrained by that person's value system and by the responsibilities resulting from your official capacity, whatever it is.

The descriptions of each area in the city are very important, and so is the map. Read both of them carefully and refer to them. The newspaper will keep you informed about zoning changes proposed or under consideration. You must decide whether the proposed change will have an impact on where you live or work.

If you are chosen to play one of the more important roles, your presence in class is essential. As in real life, when key people are missing, things happen or sometimes fail to happen. A council member in one simulation was casual about attendance. A recall election was held, and he was voted out of office, but not before causing many problems for officials and citizens by his absences. The city charter, in fact, states that a council office is automatically vacated by two consecutive, unexcused absences by a member of council (Section 2.02). The excuse is in the form of a council action, recorded in the minutes of that meeting. It is a routine meeting action usually receiving unanimous consent.

As you plan your strategy to achieve some objective, whether it is to obtain increased funding for a city program, a revision in the zoning of an area, or approval to permit waitresses in your bar to be topless, you should ask yourself who might support you. Politics is the art of the possible, and what is possible is typically determined by coalitions. Think about who would be a logical ally, talk with him or her, and find out if support can be gained.

10

Starting the Simulation

HOW TO USE THE MATERIALS

1. Role Request Form (p. 195). Your instructor may ask you to fill out the form and return it in order to match student interests to simulation roles.

2. Role Descriptions (pp. 176–194). Become thoroughly familiar with the description of your role in the simulation. Look also at the descriptions of the other roles assigned to classmates to get a sense of what the other citizens of Camelot are like, where they live, and where they work.

3. Maps (inside the covers), Economic and Demographic Data (pp. 155–156), City Area Descriptions (pp. 156–160). Here you will find the basic information about the community, its geography, economic base, and social composition. You will note that the information is organized by named city areas and, of course, these areas are likely to have significance during the simulation.

    Before the simulation begins, you should read through the descriptions of each city area and find the map locations described. The map is drawn approximately to scale, and you will be able to use it to make rough estimates of distances and compass directions. You will want to be especially aware of the characteristics of your own area.

4. The Order of Business in a Sample City Council Meeting and How to Run a Meeting (pp. 94–99). These pages of information are of special importance to council members, the manager, and the clerk, all of whom should become thoroughly familiar with it. The pages will be of passing interest to

---

The Camelot Daily News

Your Independent Daily   *Yesterday*

Officer Dies in Shootout

For the second time in 18 months, a police officer was shot and killed in the line of duty yesterday. Officer Dennis Murphy, responding to a report of a robbery in progress at the College View Liquor Store, 1327 Robert Street, at 9:23 p.m., arrived just as the gunman ran into the street. In an exchange of gunfire, the robber was hit three times and died at the scene, but not before mortally wounding Murphy, who died of an abdominal wound five hours later while undergoing surgery at Camelot City Hospital.

Witnesses stated that when Murphy called for the gunman to halt, the gunman whirled and fired a shot that went wild, and in the exchange of gunfire that followed, Officer Murphy was struck once and the gunman was hit three times. The gunman emptied his six-shot, .32 caliber revolver at Murphy. Murphy fired only three times, wounding the gunman in the left arm, the left lung, and the abdomen.

Murphy, a four-year veteran of the force, is survived by his wife, Linda, a son, Kevin, age 5, and a daughter, Julie, age 2. The family resides at 3082 Westerfield Drive. Funeral arrangements were incomplete at press time.

This latest tragedy is expected to give new impetus to the drive of the Police Benevolent Association for greater protection for officers on duty.

Hotel Fight Looms

Crown Developers yesterday announced plans for Pioneer Plaza, a 20-story office and hotel complex along the west border of Pioneer Park. The multipurpose structure also will house restaurants, shops, and an underground parking garage. The president of Crown Developers emphasized the favorable impact this project will have on revitalization of the downtown business district. The hotel will offer first-class accommodations to business and university visitors, among others. Remaining floors will be devoted to business and professional offices. Crown Developers expects the development to attract additional business to the downtown area. In particular, they point to the attractiveness of the Plaza for headquarters operations that have been located at the edge of the city, near the interstate, in recent years.

The focal point of the project will be an eight-story, glass-enclosed atrium facing Pioneer Park. Plans call for purchase of a hundred-foot

---

council observers. Planning commission members probably will find them useful guides for their own meetings.

5. Nominating Petition (pp. 195–196). Your instructor will announce a date for elections to council and also will identify the council members whose terms are expiring. *Each candidate, whether incumbent or not, must be nominated by a properly executed nominating petition.* Information about eligibility and procedure can be found on each petition form. There is no limit to the number of candidates who may run for council or to the number of petitions a citizen may sign.

Petitions must be deposited with the city clerk no later than the close of the last simulation session before election day.

HOW TO BEGIN

To begin the simulation, the council members take their seats at the front of the council chamber and the instructor designates a mayor pro tem to preside until council has selected a mayor. The mayor pro tem calls the meeting to strip of the Pioneer Park border from the city in order to complete the project.

Alison Stanbaugh, vice president of the Camelot Historic Preservation League, criticized the project in a telephone interview yesterday. She pointed out that a strip of land 100 feet wide would encroach on land now occupied by First Presbyterian Church and its historic cemetery. To complete the plans as announced, the church would have to be demolished or else moved from its original, historic site. She estimated that as many as 25 graves of early settlers in the region also would have to be moved if the developer's wishes were met.

Crown Developers stated that the Camelot Planning Commission will receive the plans and a petition for the necessary permissions and land sale at its next meeting. Planning will consider the petition and report its recommendation to council.

Fairness in Housing and Employment Before Council Tomorrow
Selection of a mayor will be the first line of business as council meets for the first time since the recent election. Council is expected to turn

then to the following: the city attorney shall be directed to draw up legislation that will (1) prohibit in the renting, leasing, or sale of housing any discrimination based on sexual orientation or preference; and (2) prohibit in the employment, promotion, or dismissal of any person by any employer of ten or more persons any discrimination based on sexual orientation or preference.

Violation of the ordinance shall be a Class III misdemeanor, punishable by a fine of not more than Two Hundred and Fifty Dollars (for each offense, as a first offense).

An Editorial
As the Camelot City Council continues to wrestle with budget questions, it is worth remembering that the city's largest employer, the university, like almost every institution of higher education today, operates in a highly competitive environment. Today, each expenditure must be weighed not only for its impact on this year's budget but also for its impact on future budgets. In calling attention to this we take no position on any budget items. We wish only to counsel a careful and cautious approach to the budget in these highly competitive times.

order (see p. 94) and proceeds to follow the agenda (see p. 94) until he or she is able to transfer the gavel to a duly chosen mayor.

Agendas for the first two meetings of council are provided on pages 94–95. Thereafter, each agenda will be prepared by the clerk in consultation with the mayor and the manager and distributed to city officials and posted on the municipal bulletin board. (If no clerk has been appointed, the manager will prepare agendas.)

Simulation Time and Real Time

Two weeks are presumed to have elapsed between simulation sessions, regardless of how much real time has passed.

The newspaper's publication schedule requires the players to exercise their imaginations a bit. Since the newspaper can publish only one issue between council meetings, that issue must be presumed to cover all pertinent events and matters of the simulated fortnight, but the coverage is in the style of a daily paper.

The Order of Business in a Sample City Council Meeting

I. Mayor: "The Camelot City Council will please come to order."

II. Mayor: "Will the Clerk please call the roll."
Clerk: (Calls roll and announces number present and absent. A quorum is three councilors if council has five seats, or four councilors if council has seven seats.) "A quorum is present, Mr. (or Madam) Mayor." (If no quorum is present, your instructor will advise the class as to the proper procedure.)

III. Mayor: "Will the Clerk now read the Minutes of the previous meeting."
Clerk: (Reads Minutes.)
The Minutes should record:
1. Date of meeting.
2. Names of those on council present and absent, and who is presiding.
3. All actions taken. Thus all motions are included. No debate is ever included in the Minutes.
4. a. Motions such as close debate, amendments, adjournment, refer to committee, recess, etc., require a roll call vote.
   b. Procedural motions require a simple majority of those present and voting. Voice or hand votes are all that is required. The Minutes will simply say "motion passed" or "motion failed."
   c. All actions of council, including ordinances and resolutions, require

three [3] affirmative votes if council has five seats, or four [4] votes if council has seven seats. (Emergency ordinances require a larger majority. See the Charter of the City of Camelot, section 3.02.)
5. Announcements.
6. Time of adjournment.
Mayor: "Are there any corrections or additions to the Minutes as read?" (Pause) "Hearing none, the Minutes stand approved as read." (Note: Some councils will require the Minutes to be approved by a majority or even a roll call vote.) If there are corrections or additions, the mayor will then say ". . . approved as corrected."

IV. Mayor: "Are there any committee reports [such as treasurer or city manager]?"

V. Mayor: "Will the Clerk please advise us if there is any old business?" [This will be motions left on the floor at the time of adjournment at the last meeting, or previously tabled motions or motions scheduled to be discussed at this meeting.]

VI. Mayor: "Is there any new business?"

VII. Announcements.

VIII. Adjournment.
[The proceedings just listed are also applicable to a planning commission meeting.]

City of Camelot

Council Meeting

First Session of Simulation

Agenda
1. Call to order.
2. Roll call.
3. Minutes (explain what they should include).
4. New business:
   a. Election of a mayor.
   b. Election of a vice mayor.
5. Resolution of sympathy to the family of Officer Murphy.
6. City manager identifies budget items to be considered at next council session and warns council of deadline.
7. Resolution concerning fairness in housing and employment.
8. Other new business:
   [If time permits, the president of the Police Benevolent Association will ask for recognition at this point, concerning the officer protection issue.]

City of Camelot

Planning Commission Meeting

First Session of Simulation

Agenda
1. Call to order.
2. Roll call.
3. Minutes (explain what they should include).

4. New business:
   a. Election of a chair.
   b. Election of a vice chair.
   c. Appointment of a secretary by the chair.
   d. Beauty Salon Zone Variance Issue.
   e. Downtown Hotel Plaza Issue.

City of Camelot

Council Meeting

Second Session of Simulation

Agenda
1. Call to order.
2. Roll call. Mayor's warning to members of council regarding absence. (See Section 2.02 of The Charter of the City of Camelot.)
3. Minutes of meeting of first day of simulation.
4. Old business.

5. New business:
   a. Officer protection program issue. [If the Officer Protection Program Issue was introduced during the first council meeting, it should appear under "old business," above, at this second council meeting.]
   b. Consideration of budget items.
   c. Consideration of planning commission actions.
   d. Announcements.

City of Camelot

Planning Commission Meeting

Second Session of Simulation

Agenda
1. Call to order.
2. Roll call.
3. Minutes.

4. Old business:
   a. Beauty Salon Zone Variance Issue, petition to rezone from R-4 to C-1,_____ _____ , petitioner.
5. New business:
   a. Downtown Hotel Plaza Issue.
   b. Massage Therapy Facility Issue.

HOW TO RUN A MEETING

Rules of Parliamentary Procedure

You don't need to know Robert's Rules of Order in order to run a meeting, but you do need to know a few basic rules. And most of what you need to know are common sense principles upon which parliamentary rules of order are based. For example:

1. Organizations need rules of order so that the meetings are orderly. Except for those individuals who like to hear the sound of their own voice, most of us want to deal with the items on the agenda, solve the problems if we can, and go about our own business. We don't live to attend meetings.

2. Thus, if we want to have an orderly meeting:

   a. Only one person may (should) speak at a time.

   b. No one may (should) speak until recognized by the presiding officer.

   c. Only one motion may be considered at a time (parliamentarians refer to this as the "motion on the floor").

   d. Before a motion can be considered, we need to know that at least one other person wants to discuss it, which is why a motion requires a "second."

   e. Before a different motion can be discussed, the motion on the floor must be passed, defeated, sent to a committee, or postponed (to another time or date, or indefinitely).

3. Other things to keep in mind:

   a. A city council meeting is a meeting of those who were elected to council. It is *not* a meeting of the citizens in the audience. Therefore, although citizens have a right to speak at meetings of city councils, they may do so only at times designated by council.

   b. Our country is based on the principle that a majority rules. This means that 51 percent, or more than half, of the voters, or members of city council, make the rules, and the other 49 percent have to comply with those rules. This can be difficult for some individuals to accept when they are not among the 51 percent.

   c. However, although a minority of council does not have a right to rule, it has a right to be heard. The 51 percent of council are required to give the 49 percent, or any member of it, time to be heard.

   d. Parliamentary rules presume that some motions have greater immediacy than others, and so there is a rank order to motions. For example, a motion to adjourn has the highest rank, a main motion (that is, the "motion on the floor") has the lowest. Thus the motion to adjourn can be proposed any time during a meeting, and if it is seconded and a majority of council votes "aye," or "yes," all discussion ceases and everyone goes home. The motion that was being discussed now becomes the first item on the agenda of the next council meeting. Additional information on the rank order of motions can be found on pages 98–99.

How to Put a Motion on the Floor

Councilor 2:	"Mr. Mayor."	Councilor 1:	"Many people will be on vacation during the first week of August, myself included. I move to amend the motion by substituting 'the first week of October' for 'the first week of August.'"
Mayor:	"Councilor 2."		
Councilor 2:	"I move that council declare the first week of August be designated as Pioneer Week so that we may pay honor to those brave individuals who founded our city in 1802."		
		Mayor:	"You have heard the amendment. Is there a second?"
			(No one seconds the amendment.)
Mayor:	"You have heard the motion; is there a second?"		
Councilor 4:	"I second the motion."	Mayor:	"The proposed amendment dies for a lack of a second. Is there further discussion on the original motion?"
Mayor:	"It has been moved and seconded that the first week of August be designated as Pioneer Week. Is there any discussion?"		
		(Discussion follows, and perhaps other amendments will be proposed.)	
Councilor 1:	"Mr. Mayor."		
Mayor:	"Councilor 1."		

How to Get to the Vote on Any Debatable Motion

The simplest way to do this is for the mayor to sense that discussion has ended and say:

"Are you ready to vote?" or "Is there further discussion?"

The mayor then pauses and if no one says anything, the mayor continues by saying:

"Unless there is objection, the motion is [states the motion, or asks the clerk to do it]."
"All in favor say 'aye.'"
"Opposed 'no.'" [The mayor then announces the result of the vote.]

Another way is for one of the councilors, after receiving recognition from the mayor, to say:

"I move we vote immediately." (Or, "I move the previous question.")

This motion requires a second and a *two-thirds affirmative vote* of those voting on the motion. If the motion to "vote immediately" is approved by the required two-thirds affirmative vote, the mayor announces this fact and immediately states:

"The motion to vote immediately on the pending issue has been approved. We will now vote on whether the first week of August shall be designated as

Rank Order of Commonly Used Motions

Highest Rank on Top*	Needs Second?	Debatable?	Vote Required
1. To adjourn	Yes	No	Majority
2. To recess	Yes	No	Majority
3. To table (i.e., to postpone temporarily)	Yes	No	Majority
4. Previous question (i.e., to vote immediately)	Yes	No	Two-thirds
5. To limit debate	Yes	No	Two-thirds
To extend debate	Yes	No	Two-thirds
6. To postpone motion to particular day	Yes	Yes#	Majority
7. To postpone motion to particular time	Yes	Yes#	Two-thirds
8. To refer to committee	Yes	Yes#	Majority
9. To amend	Yes	Yes	Majority
10. To postpone indefinitely (i.e., to kill a motion)	Yes	Yes	Majority
11. Resolutions (proclamations, appointments, recognitions)	Yes	Yes	Majority
12. Ordinances	Yes	Yes	Majority
13. Emergency ordinances	Yes	Yes	Three-fourths

* Example: If a Rank 9 is "on the floor," only motions of higher rank can be proposed until the Rank 9 motion is disposed of.

Subject to restricted debate. That is, one can debate such items as limits on debate, or what day or time to which to postpone a motion, or special instructions to the committee (size, composition, and so on), but the main motion cannot be debated.

Pioneer Week. Because this is a resolution, not an ordinance, no roll call vote is required."

"All in favor of the motion will say 'aye.'"

"All opposed say 'no.'"

"The 'ayes' have it. The motion passes."

NOTE: There is a common misconception that when someone calls out "Question!" the mayor (or any presiding officer) is required to end the discussion. Not true! The mayor (or any presiding officer) has several choices:

1. Ignore the person who said, "Question."

2. Sense that the council is really ready to vote and say,

   "Question has been called. Are you ready to vote?"

   Or, "Question has been called. Is there further discussion?"

No vote is required. Asking council if they are ready for the question does not stop debate.

Incidental motions can be introduced at any time. They have no rank order. Examples are included below.

Incidental Motions	Needs Second?	Debatable?	Vote Required
Appeal the decision of the chair	Yes	Yes	Tie or majority
Point of order	No	No	No vote
Withdraw a motion	No	No	Without objection or majority if there is objection
Suspend rules of order (i.e., to revise agenda)	Yes	No	Two-thirds
Object to consideration (applies only to main motions)	No	No	Two-thirds-negative
Division of the question (into segments that will be voted on individually)	No	No	Decided by the chair. If there is objection, then majority vote.

If it is clear that council is indeed ready to vote, the mayor (or presiding officer) restates the motion to be voted on (or asks the clerk to do it) and calls for the "ayes" and "nos." It's that simple.

11

Issues

INTRODUCTION

It is a truism that life is an unending series of choices. For city governments this is a fact of daily life.

You will find two types of issues in this simulation: those involving money trade-offs and those involving people trade-offs. Both present difficult choices. Money trade-offs focus on the city budget. If you increase one service or program, you must either increase taxes or reduce another program, or do a combination of both.

The second kind of issue involves people trade-offs, such as when conflicts exist between and among people over lifestyle preferences or when people disagree as to how land shall be used. Only indirectly will the city's budget be involved. Shall a piece of land be zoned so that Mrs. Smith benefits by being able to use her property for a beauty salon, while her neighbor fears that his single-family home has lost value because no one wants to live next to a business? Or suppose developers want to build a strip mall on land currently zoned for residential use. All they ask is that the lot be zoned for commercial enterprise and they will pay for everything, plus generate additional property tax revenues for Camelot. Everyone benefits, no one loses. Or do they?

Some of the roles will provide clues as to what stand the individuals might take on certain issues. No one is precluded from taking positions, pro or con, on any issue. In fact, each of you, whether an elected official, an appointed official, or an ordinary citizen, is urged to consider every issue carefully in terms of whether you have some stake or preference involved. Whenever you find yourself concerned about how an issue will be resolved, it is important to speak up and attempt to convince others (council, planning commission, or fellow citizens) of the wisdom of your point of view.

As you read the issues and consider your involvement in them, there are three matters of law to be called to your attention. Additional details about each item are provided in the sections indicated.

1. *Initiative.* If there is an issue that has been ignored or defeated by council and you are not willing to accept this action, you can use the initiative petition procedure. If you obtain a sufficient number of signatures on a petition, the question will then be voted on by the citizens of Camelot. For details, see the Camelot Charter, Section 7.01 (Chapter 12). (If your instructor chooses to use the Smoking Ban Issue, you will experience the initiative petition procedure.)

2. *Referendum.* There may be instances when you are quite opposed to an action of council, in which case you have the option of forcing a referendum on the matter. This procedure requires the securing of a specified number of signatures on a petition, followed by the approval or disapproval of the voters. For details, see the Camelot Charter, Section 7.02 (Chapter 12).

3. *The sunshine law.* With only a few exceptions, all discussions and voting by elected or appointed public bodies must be carried out in public. For details and exceptions, see Chapter 12, pages 169–170.

RESOLUTION OF SYMPATHY

The councilor from Madisonville (the former chief of police) will present the following resolution immediately after the election of the mayor and vice mayor.

Resolved: That the City Council of Camelot express to the family of Officer Dennis Murphy its deepest sympathy and regret at the death of this brave member of the Police Force of Camelot, killed in the line of duty while attempting to arrest a robbery suspect.

That all flags on municipal buildings be flown at half-staff for seven days out of respect for Officer Murphy.

That an appropriate Certificate of Commendation of Officer Murphy be prepared and delivered to his family.

That these actions be recorded in the official Minutes of the City Council of Camelot.

THE FAIRNESS IN HOUSING
AND EMPLOYMENT ISSUE

This will be presented to Council on the first session of the simulation.

The councilor from College Town, a professor at Camelot State University, has requested that the following item be placed on the agenda for the first session of the simulation.

Resolved: That the city attorney shall be directed to draw up legislation that will (1) prohibit in the renting, leasing, or sale of housing any discrimination based on sexual orientation or preference; and that will (2) prohibit in the employment, promotion, or dismissal of any person by any employer of ten or more persons any discrimination based on sexual orientation or preference.

Violation of the ordinance shall be a Class III misdemeanor, punishable by a fine of not more than Two Hundred and Fifty Dollars (for each offense). The State has no parallel legislation.

THE OFFICER PROTECTION
PROGRAM ISSUE

This will be presented to Council on the first session of the simulation by the president of the Police Benevolent Association (PBA), time permitting (perhaps not sooner than the second session if class periods are sixty minutes or less).

As was reported in yesterday's issue of the *Camelot Daily News* a police officer was shot and killed in the course of responding to a report of a robbery of a liquor store. The president of the Police Benevolent Association will present the following demand to council on the date indicated.

Summary of Costs of Officer Protection Program

Shotgun Racks for Patrol Cars	
90 racks @ $180	$16,200
Kevlar Body Armor Jackets	
250 @ $420	$105,000
Taser Stun Guns, handheld, battery	
250 @ $205	$ 51,250
Safety Holsters	
290 @ $57	$ 16,530
Total	$188,980

Officers' Weapon Replacements (choose (a), (b), (c), (d), or (e))

(a) .357 Magnum stainless steel revolvers

290 @ $360	$104,400

(b) 9 mm parabellum Smith & Wesson double-action semi-automatic, 15 shot clip

290 @ $469	$136,010

(c) .40 S&W caliber, Smith & Wesson double-action semi-automatic, 13 shot clip

290 @ $480	$139,200

(d) 9 mm parabellum Beretta 92F, double-action semi-automatic, 15 shot clip (sidearm of the U.S. military)

290 @ $410	$118,900

(e) .40 S&W caliber, Beretta 96D double-action semi-automatic, 15 shot clip

290 @ $469	$136,010
Grand Total using .357 caliber Magnum revolvers	$293,380
Grand Total using 9mm caliber S&W semi-automatics	$324,990
Grand Total using .40 caliber S&W semi-automatics	$328,180
Grand Total using 9 mm caliber Beretta semi-automatics	$307,880
Grand Total using .40 caliber Beretta semi-automatics	$324,990

This is a one-time conversion cost. There will be additional ammunition expense each year to maintain officer proficiency.

Background Information

The present service revolvers are caliber .38 Special. One difference between the currently used .38 Special revolver and any of the other five choices—the .357 Magnum revolver, the two 9 mm semi-automatic, double-action pistols, and the two .40 S&W caliber semi-automatic, double-action pistols—lies in the shocking power (the stopping power) of the bullets. Much larger powder loads in the cartridges propel Magnum bullets, which in turn means that a person struck by a Magnum bullet is less likely to be able to flee or harm anyone else. The 9 mm bullets are nearly as fast, but they are lighter, thus producing less shocking power than the Magnum but significantly more than the .38 Special revolver. The .40 S&W caliber weapon fires a heavier bullet than the 9 mm bullet, with correspondingly higher shocking power. The contrast may be seen in the table that follows, which sets forth the comparative ballistics for the bullets usually preferred by law enforcement agencies in the various calibers. It should be noted that the .357 Magnum caliber has exceptionally high muzzle velocity and shocking power, but because of its higher velocity there is also a greater risk of the bullet penetrating and exiting beyond the target, to the possible injury of another person. The chance of a ricochet in combat is somewhat greater for the same reason.

Comparative Ballistic Data for Six Weapons

	Muscle Velocity Feet-per-Second	Muscle Energy Foot-Pounds (Shocking Power)

.38 Special (revolver)
  150 grain Super X + P
  (6-shot capacity)
    Cost: none (in inventory)
	910	276

.357 Magnum (revolver)
  158 grain Super-X
  Cost: $330
	1235	535

9 mm Parabellum (semi-automatic)
  115 grain STHP
  (15 shot magazine; quick-replacement
  of magazine clip)
  Beretta 92 F
    Cost $410
  Smith & Wesson
    Cost $440
	1225	383

A second difference is that a semi-automatic pistol has several points of superiority as compared to either of the revolvers. First, the semi-automatics have a larger magazine capacity—fifteen shots in 9 mm weapons, and either thirteen or fifteen shots (depending on the model) in the .40 S&W weapons—as against six shots for either of the revolvers. Second, a semi-automatic can be reloaded very quickly by replacing the magazine clip. This replacement can be accomplished in four or five seconds if the replacement clip is easily accessible to the non-shooting hand. Third, the pressure required to pull the trigger of a semi-automatic is much lighter (easier) than that of a revolver in rapid-fire situations, which means a greater chance of hitting the target with a greater number of bullets. Trigger pull is minimal (2 to 3 lbs. pressure), which reduces the risk that a trigger squeeze will pull the aim off target.

The recommended safety holsters are available to fit the weapons currently used or any of the proposed alternatives. The purpose of the safety holster is to prevent an officer's gun from being withdrawn by someone else, especially from behind the officer in the course of a struggle. The holster is designed so that the weapon can be inserted conventionally and easily, but in order to withdraw it the butt of the weapon must be pushed forward about one-quarter of an inch as it is withdrawn by lifting upward. Otherwise, the holster securely grips the gun and prevents its withdrawal. Inasmuch as officers are killed in the United States each year during struggles in which the arrestee pulls the officer's gun from its holster, this device will reduce the risks borne by officers in Camelot. The forward push and upward pull on the weapon comes naturally to the officer wearing the holster but is quite awkward for anyone else.

The body armor jackets are made of a densely woven fabric using incredibly high tensile-strength filament for the thread. These jackets are impervious to penetration by handgun bullets; they diffuse the force of the bullet's impact in such a way that, though a large and severe bruise will be inflicted, there will be no penetration of the body. They can be worn under regular uniform shirts.

The Taser stun guns are handheld devices about the size of a pocket transistor radio. Early versions of stun guns operated on a 9-volt transistor battery and produced a high-voltage crackling spark between two electrodes located about two inches apart. When the electrodes were pressed against a person's flesh or clothing and the switch button was activated, the resulting high-voltage shock incapacitated the target person for a period of several minutes. The voltage operated against major muscle groups to produce a temporary paralysis. Cardiologists tested and judged the stun gun to be completely safe, thus making it safer than chemical mace or a wooden nightstick, both of which pose some risk of injury. The obvious drawback to the stun gun was that the officer must be within arm's reach of the target in order to use the device, and some officers were injured as they tried to subdue an arrestee.

The Taser stun gun, a refinement developed in the past few years, now allows an officer to "shoot" from ten or twelve feet away from the target, and the Taser is very widely used among law enforcement agencies. The Taser shoots two small darts, each attached to twelve feet of very fine wire fastened at its other end to the box holding a battery and transformer. Though the incapacitation of the target is immediate and overwhelming, the effects are temporary.

If any of these proposed expenditures is authorized, you should note the implications for "The Budget Issue," which will be considered later.

This is a one-time conversion cost, not a recurring annual expense. There will be an additional ammunition expense each year to maintain officer proficiency.

THE BEAUTY SALON ZONE
VARIANCE ISSUE

This will be presented to the planning commission on the first session of the simulation.

A divorced mother of four children (Role 30) has just received her cosmetologist's license.[1] If she can open a beauty salon, even on a very small scale in her living room, she will be able to remain off welfare and be closer to her children. Otherwise, she will have to continue being a part-time waitress, leaving

---

1. Some states no longer permit beauticians to open beauty salons in private homes. Your state may have such a law, but for the purposes of this simulation, we have assumed that your state does *not* have such a law.

her children either with babysitters or by themselves. Her home (in an R-4 zone) is on a side street in North Madisonville, north of Woodworth Road. She seeks a variance allowing that commercial activity. Her neighbors are not sympathetic. An attorney (Role 49) will represent their interests before the planning commission and the council. The neighbors fear a loss in the value of their property if commercial activities are permitted in this residential area. Also, they are troubled by the absence of any off-street parking spaces in this older part of town. They already have problems finding a parking space on the street near their home. They fear that the additional traffic generated by the proposed beauty salon would make the problem even worse.

You should know that the citizens of Camelot approved by referendum a Charter Amendment at the last municipal election. The amendment authorizes the council to establish a zoning appeals board (see Sections 6.08, 6.09, and 6.10 of the Camelot Charter). However, the effective date of the amendment has not yet been reached, and so that amendment has no bearing on this issue. Your instructor will tell you whether upcoming council agendas will include a proposal to establish a zoning appeals board.

THE DOWNTOWN HOTEL PLAZA ISSUE

The following issue will be presented to the planning commission in the first session of the simulation, time permitting. If there is not sufficient time, it will be placed on the agenda for the second session.

The map of downtown Camelot (see inside covers) shows a small finger of land in the Central Business District (CBD) fronting on the north side of the river and abutting the east side of Robert Street. The space involved is approximately 315 feet on each side. Its southern boundary looks out on Camelot's Pioneer Park. (Figure 11-1 is a larger-scale map of the area.) The commercial area is filled with late nineteenth- and early twentieth-century buildings, housing some retail stores, several restaurants, a music store, a bank, two antique stores, an old hotel that rents by the week to single persons of limited income, and a large building, now vacant, that formerly housed a department store. The tallest building is the ten-story hotel. Thus none of the buildings exceed the height limits of the zoning code, which for the C-3 zone (the CBD) is twelve stories high. Most of the other buildings in the area are three to five stories high, with some as low as one story. With one exception, the buildings lack architectural grace or distinction. The exception is the bank, which dates back to the 1920s and is considered to be a fine example of the Italianate period, with its domed ceiling and elaborate brass interior railings and marble staircases. For years, there have been criticisms of the appearance of the area, but no renewal plan has ever come to fruition.

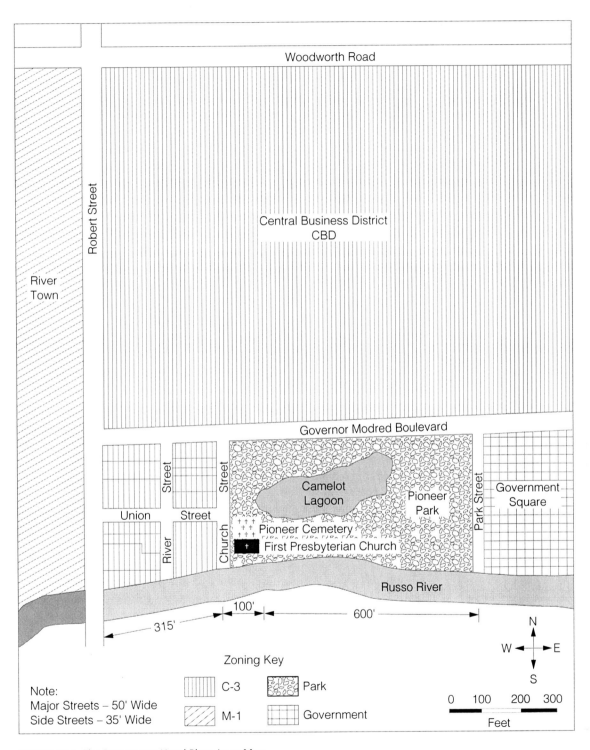

FIGURE 11-1 The Downtown Hotel Plaza Issue Map

Pioneer Park, on the other hand, is considered a green jewel surrounded by the concrete bulk of the buildings in Government Square and the Central Business District. The park's dimensions are modest, about 315 feet north to south and 700 feet east to west, comprising about five acres. Given the nature of the area, its chief use is during the day. Located at the southwest corner of Pioneer Park is the home of the First Presbyterian Church of Camelot, which was established in 1843. Though the congregation, which includes a considerable number of persons prominent in Camelot's social, business, and educational circles, enjoys much larger and more comfortable quarters today in another part of town, the historic structure, which measures only sixty-six feet in length by thirty-four feet in width, is maintained and supported by the congregation as a nonsectarian resource for the community. It may be the scene of a wedding one day, of a music recital the next, and of the meeting of a civic group the day after that. A small cemetery adjacent to the pioneer structure is believed to contain thirty-eight graves, though the condition of the parish records leaves the precise number in some doubt. Under the terms of an agreement made a half-century ago, the Pioneer Park land belongs to the city, but the Presbyterian Church pays a nominal $1.00 per year in rent to manage and use the building, and the congregation also has responsibility for upkeep and repairs to the building.

The Crown Real Estate Development Corporation, arguing that Camelot is overdue for a more effective use of the commercial area described, has presented an innovative proposal for a downtown hotel plaza. The developer's plan includes a twenty-story tower, featuring a glass-fronted hotel facing the park. The street level will contain shops, and the first seven floors will be commercial, including such activities as law firms, accounting firms, engineering consultants, brokerage offices, and regional offices of various corporations. The eighth and ninth floors will house the lobby and convention facilities for the hotel, and the top floor will house an upscale restaurant offering a panoramic view of Camelot. The hotel will occupy the remaining floors. A parking garage is included in the plan.

The developer's architectural team, one of the better-known commercial development firms in the United States, has submitted a design that requires more land than is available in the tract controlled by Crown Developers. More specifically, the plan calls for the acquisition and use of 100 feet of land to the east of the Crown tract, land owned by the city and managed under the agreement between the city and the Presbyterian congregation. The developer wishes to purchase the land on which sits the pioneer church, the cemetery, and a small portion (the westerly 20 feet) of the lagoon, which hosts skaters in winter and ducks in summer. The developer would pay the costs of moving the church and the graves to the eastern portion of the park or, in the case of the graves, to any other chosen site.

Other consultants have been called in by the developer and also by the city and the opinions of the consultants cast grave doubt on the economic viability of the project if it must be scaled back. Therefore, the Crown Development Corporation desires to purchase from the city, at a price that would be sufficient to include the cost of moving the church and cemetery to another portion of the park or to another location to be chosen by city officials, the western-most 100 feet of Pioneer Park. (See Figure 11-1.)

The planning commission and city council of Camelot now face a difficult decision. The decline of the downtown area has been apparent for many years. Regional malls located along the interstate highway to the north and south of Camelot, and outside its jurisdiction, have weakened the economic base of the Central Business District. Many of the buildings in the tract under discussion have been underutilized or empty for some time. It has been conservatively estimated that the real estate tax revenues from the plaza would be five or six times the revenues from the present structures. The plaza development, when finished and open, would provide employment for two hundred or more persons, and it would attract tourists, business travelers, and university visitors.

As can well be imagined, the proposed development has its detractors. Emotions are running high. There is a "Save Pioneer Park" group, headed by the minister of the First Presbyterian Church (Role 48), which has been outspoken in its opposition to "crass commercialism" that pursues its goals at the price of precious open space and the community's historical heritage. The group has many supporters, including the junior high school teacher (Role 43), whose grandparents and great grandparents are buried in the cemetery; the owner of the delicatessen (Role 26), who will be forced to relocate since the business would be unable to afford the much higher rent of the new structure; and the development editor (Role 45), an outspoken supporter of "Save Pioneer Park" and a persistent and staunch conservationist.

Supporters of the new development include the director of the Planning Department of Camelot (Role 33), the editor and publisher of the *Camelot Daily News* (Role 20), and the owner of the large business (Role 25), whose real estate holdings include the now-closed department store. Naturally, the developers (Roles 38, 39, and 40) are in the forefront of the struggle to get the high-rise approved.

Two individuals are finding the proposed development particularly troublesome. Both are members of the First Presbyterian Church and have ancestors buried in the cemetery, yet both also are concerned about the future of Camelot's decaying Central Business District and the resulting decline in employment opportunities and property tax revenues. The individuals struggling with the dilemma are the councilor who is vice president of the local chamber of commerce (Role 4) and the planning commissioner who favors the revitalization of the Central Business District (Role 13).

The planning commission and council have three decisions to make:

1. Should the city sell part of Pioneer Park to be used for the high-rise development? Neither body need concern itself with the amount of money involved, for if agreement cannot be reached between the parties on this aspect, the matter will be resolved in court. This is a land use issue, but one that has real costs involving loss of open space and dislocation of important human symbols and values. Yet these costs must be balanced against equally real benefits of increased employment opportunities and tax revenues, not to mention the revitalization of a declining Central Business District.

2. Should a zoning variance be granted to permit the construction of a twenty-story high-rise in this C–3 area? There is no question that this building would dominate the skyline of Camelot.

3. Will council approve vacating Union, River, and Church Streets? The automobile and pedestrian entrance to the hotel plaza, the office building, and the parking garage will be from Governor Modred Boulevard.

THE BUDGET ISSUE

At the first session of council, the city manager will alert council members that this issue will be on the agenda for the second session.

The following paragraphs include an abbreviated version of some aspects of Chapter 4, "Sources of Local Government Revenues and Their Constraints." The reader is urged to review that chapter in order to gain a fuller understanding of the problems surrounding the income generation side of city budgets. The emphasis of "The Budget Issue" will be on the expenditure side, with some necessary references to income generation aspects. However, the focus will be on questions such as: What services should cities provide? How should these services be paid for? No attempt will be made to review all the services that cities might provide. The problems presented here emphasize the difficulties involved in making decisions as to which services should be approved and paid for out of public funds.

Every year the city manager's staff (or the mayor's staff, depending on the form of city government) prepares a proposed budget for the following year, and the chief executive, whether mayor or city manager, submits the budget to the city council. A budget is a set of proposed expenditures for the next fiscal year. It is, in effect, a message from the chief executive officer to the legislative body (in this case the city council) requesting operating funds for the various municipal departments, and the response of that legislative body will be in the form of an appropriation for the coming fiscal year. For purposes of effective discussion and priority setting, budgets are subdivided into a section for each department (or activity) of the city government. The chief executive's staff must struggle to reconcile the proclaimed needs of city departments for staff and facilities (assertions of need often reinforced by demands of citizen groups for services from those departments) with the projections of revenues to be received by the city from various sources. Those sources include transfers of funds from the federal government and the state government as well as operating revenues generated by the water department, a city-owned electricity generating plant in some cities, and perhaps service charges for garbage and trash collection and disposal, plus charges for sewer maintenance and sewage disposal. (In many cities these latter charges are based on water consumption.) But most important are the funds derived from taxes on local citizens and businesses. More often than not, the perceived need for funds will exceed projected revenues: more police officers and equipment are desired; the streets need to be repaired or widened or rebuilt; the Health Department needs more staff and its equipment must be modernized. Citizens are asking for new services (a new swimming pool, additional recreational facilities); they also complain about the poor quality of existing services (inadequate refuse collection, potholes in streets, sediment in the drinking water, and storm sewer backup in rainy weather).

Of equal importance to the demands on government for services is the fact that city governments, unlike the federal government, are almost everywhere prevented from engaging in deficit spending. Expenditures for services cannot exceed income. Bonded indebtedness is permitted only for capital improvements, such as building a new city hall, a water treatment plant, or a swimming pool. A bond is essentially a promissory note issued by the city. The bond generates an annual payment of interest to the owner until the bond matures and the face value of the bond becomes due. This may require the levying of a special assessment or a special tax so that the bond purchaser (the lender) can be assured of repayment when the bond comes due.

The simplest response might be to tell citizens that they must pay for the services they demand. For some services this does occur, and a user fee is utilized. For example, in many, if not most, cities the resident pays for the water consumed, the swimming pool enjoyed, and the refuse collected. The persons using the service pay for all or most of the service. The city can estimate how much service is needed because use and users can be counted and then charged for the service.

Yet some services are what economists call "a public good," meaning that the service cannot be denied effectively to anyone. Police and fire protection exist all the time—are "consumed," if you will, constantly by everyone. In this case everyone pays for a service and everyone benefits from the availability of that service. But how do we know how much of this service to provide? Or how much to pay those who provide the service? Or what facilities are really needed? During recent periods of civil unrest, some police departments were of the opinion that armored vehicles were necessary. It was even suggested in some cities that tanks should be purchased. Currently, police departments regularly request protective body jackets and higher-powered weapons. While there may be honest disagreement among us as to what equipment, and how much of it, the police need, or how many officers there should be, or how much they should be paid, it is quite clear that we cannot leave the final decision to the police, nor can we limit the service to those who pay for it. (It is interesting to note that in some rural areas fire departments have a contractual arrangement with citizens. And if a property owner who does not pay an annual fee then has a fire, the fire department will limit its service to making sure no person is endangered. The buildings will be allowed to burn to the ground.)

For most of us, however, it is assumed that everyone will contribute through tax dollars for the police and fire services, and it is the elected officials, the city council members, who must make the final decisions as to what the proper balance between agency requests and actual agency needs shall be.

There is another important category of budget expenditure: Some expenditures have a *redistributive effect*. That is, the *costs* of a policy are borne disproportionately by one segment of the society and the *benefits* of the policy are bestowed disproportionately on a different segment. Though some examples are obvious, others are less so. Obvious examples are the free medical services city health departments may provide for those who cannot afford them and certain city services provided at no cost to those of low income, or at reduced cost to the elderly. Municipal transportation charges often are reduced for school children and/or the elderly, and rent subsidies may be provided to low-income families or individuals. The underlying assumption is clear. Certain services should be provided at little or no cost to those we believe less able to pay, and the cost difference is borne through tax revenues derived from those deemed more able to pay.

However, some cities also build marinas and golf courses with public funds, and often the user fees are not set high enough to cover the total cost of building and maintaining these facilities. Again there is a redistribution; in this case, tax money is taken from individuals who cannot or do not own a boat or play golf and the money is spent for the benefit of other individuals who do own boats or play golf. In such situations the governmental funds are used to subsidize the more affluent rather than the poor, which suggests that the more affluent among us are not without political influence.

Finally, there is one more category of city expenses—economic development. It is apparent that not all cities are at a similar stage of development. Some are stagnating and decaying; industries have moved or closed and have not been replaced by new enterprises. The Central Business Districts may look as though nothing has been built or renovated in the last thirty years. Yet other cities, perhaps in the same region, appear vibrant with new construction and new industry. Perhaps you can think of examples from your own travels. Clearly, many factors are at work, including the skills of city leaders, adequacy of water, quality of educational facilities and of city services, availability of skilled labor, proximity to markets, and attractiveness of the quality of life and climate, to name a few. But in addition there is the factor of willingness on the part of political leaders to attract new businesses with tangible enticements such as property tax abatement [reduction] or deferral, construction of access roads and water lines, sewer trunk lines to housing developments, or even free land upon which to build. Cities have been known to purchase land upon which stand old buildings, raze the existing structures at city expense, and then sell the cleared land at below cost to developers. The new developments, it is believed, will result in increased costs for the city in the short run but will increase tax revenues over the long run because of additional employment and establishment of new industries.

It is obvious that the simulation cannot include the entire process of budget preparation and approval, nor can all the preceding aspects be built into the experience. Therefore, in order to make the budget simulation more useful as a learning experience, certain simplifying constraints have been built into it so that your attention will be focused on a manageable number of decisions. Here are the constraints:

1. The entire city budget has been approved except for the following items that will be described. Though this may seem unrealistic, in fact the problems facing the council will be the same whether the entire budget is considered or only these few segments. Choices must be made; priorities must be set. If council does *x,* then there may not be enough money to do *y.* If the requests for funds are greater than the projected income, then some projects must be reduced or eliminated, or else more funds must be generated.

2. An uncommitted excess of income over expenditures for the next fiscal year is estimated at $475,500. This amount is available to council to fund some of the following proposals.

3. Council can only reduce or eliminate expenses from among the items presented. You cannot "invent" program savings by eliminating programs not listed. (One city manager in one of our classes announced that he had a buyer for the city transit system and that the proceeds from the sale would cover all the projected increased program costs. Needless to say, the instructor quickly suggested that while this was a very imaginative solution, it would not be permitted.)

4. The total program costs of the following items recommended for the next fiscal year exceed projected income, as will be noted in the discussion that follows. Depending on how many of the recommended programs are approved, all program costs that exceed the projected $475,500 excess must be paid for by funds generated by increasing taxes or by user fees. (Inventive solutions, such as winning the state lottery, are not permitted.) Council has authority

to increase user fees by ordinance. *A tax increase will require approval by the electorate.*

5. Action on the budget items listed must be completed no later than five minutes prior to the end of the third simulation session, assuming ninety-minute sessions. (Or no later than the fourth session, assuming fifty-minute sessions.)

6. The deadline listed in paragraph 5 includes *council approval* of the tax increase, if a tax increase is required. If council has indeed decided to increase taxes, the ordinance proposing the tax increase must schedule a special election for the next simulation session, to be held at the beginning of that session.

7. If the tax increase fails, council must again consider the proposed budget and determine before the end of the fourth ninety-minute simulation session (the fifth fifty-minute session) what must be eliminated or whether a different tax proposal is to be put before the voters at the beginning of the fifth ninety-minute session (the sixth fifty-minute session).

8. No deficit financing is permitted in the state. Thus, borrowing for the purpose of meeting current operating expenses is unlawful.

9. It is assumed that Camelot has sixty thousand families and that the median family income is $51,200, creating a total income base for tax purposes of $3,072,000,000. If the city income tax is increased, it will generate additional revenue as follows:

1/10% increase will generate $3,072,000.

1/4% increase will generate $7,680,500.

1/2% increase will generate $15,360,000.

An increase of one mill ($1 per $1,000 of assessed valuation) real estate property tax will generate $3,250,000 per year.

As an alternative to an increase in the real property tax, the Camelot city council may employ *either* a municipal income tax *or* a municipal sales tax, *but not both.* Your instructor will indicate which option is available in your simulation.

The city sales tax option: Retail sales constitute the tax base, but sales of the following are exempt from taxation: (1) groceries and/or food not consumed on the sale premises; (2) prescription drugs; (3) charges for labor or services; (4) any goods purchased for resale by a licensed vendor; (5) "intangibles" such as insurance protection. This means, in practice, that the taxable sales probably will amount to not more than 25 percent of the total wages/salaries earned in the city.

Taxation can be only in increments of one cent. Fractional increments are not available. (This accords with the practice of most cities having a sales tax.)

It is estimated that the annual revenue generated by a tax of one cent per dollar of taxable sales (1%) will be $7,061,000.

10. Council will concern itself only with the issues presented. Council may increase the amounts suggested, decrease them, or eliminate them entirely. Council may not revise the facts as given. That is, it cannot decide that it can acquire some of the items for less money than that stated in the proposed

budget. If, for example, council decides to replace police officers' weapons with a particular model of semi-automatic pistol or with .357 Magnum revolvers, it may do so, but only at the price stated per gun. Thus it may purchase fewer guns, or no guns (or more guns, for that matter), but the cost per gun may not be revised.

Following are some budget proposals from various departments for next year.

1. Police Department Proposal: New Programs—Drug Enforcement Unit
   In order to increase police capability to control the growing drug traffic in Camelot, the Police Department proposes the establishment of a Drug Enforcement Unit. The first-year start-up costs of this unit will be as follows: Personnel, equipment, and training for undercover drug investigations for four additional officers: $327,000.[2] In future years it is projected that the cost will be $247,000 each year (plus adjustments for inflation).
   Addition to chief's discretionary account: $80,000. This amount will cover supplies, payments to informers, and money for drug purchases during investigations. *This is a first-year cost and will be a continuing annual cost.*

Total first-year costs: $407,000.

Total cost each year thereafter: $327,000.

2. Health Department Proposal: Pediatrics Continuation and New Programs
   The present Health Clinic, based in the Madisonville section of Camelot, was funded under a five-year "demonstration grant" from a large charitable foundation as an experiment. The hope underlying the grant was that the clinic, which provides only pediatric services, would prove its worth to the community so that the city would take up the financial slack at the end of the grant period. That day of reckoning has now arrived.
   The clinic is open six days a week from 9:00 a.m. to 9:00 p.m. The services are for children and adolescents through age 16, and they include consulting, diagnosis, prescriptions, treatment of illnesses, referral, and physical examinations. Reimbursement for services is sought whenever possible, through health insurance of the family if coverage is available or through Medicaid. Contributions from the public also are sought and welcomed.
   The clinic is not equipped to handle trauma cases or other acute emergencies. Those cases go to the emergency rooms of local hospitals.
   This facility is located in an older house that has been converted to a clinic. The costs of the present facility are based on the assumption that it will be open to the public for 72 hours each week (six days times 12 hours each day), for 52 weeks each year, a total of 3,744 hours per year.

---

2. This figure assumes that the cost of one additional officer is about $78,750. This amount is based on a salary of $45,000 plus fringe benefits that amount to approximately 30 percent, uniforms, training, and equipment. The unit will consist of the equivalent of two full-time undercover agents (rotating) and two uniformed officers (specialists, supervisory level) who will be permanently assigned. The larger first-year figure will cover the costs of start-up training and equipment. Training is essential and includes an extended period at the officer training school of the U.S. Drug Enforcement Agency. In order for the city to retain its governmental immunity from lawsuits, it is essential to have evidence that the training is maintained at state-of-the-art levels.

Cost of Pediatric Services

Pediatricians (2) @ $90/ hour (inc. 25% fringes) x 3,744 hours	$336,960
Nurses (2 RN) @ $22.50/ hour (inc. 25% fringes) x 3,744 hours	$ 84,240
Receptionist/clerk (2) @ $17/ hour (inc. 25% fringes) x 3,744 hours	$ 63,648
Equipment (one-time cost)	$ 15,000
Supplies per patient (avg. 10 patients/hour x $6/patient = $60/hour) x 3,744 hours	$224,640
Fixed expenses (rent, utilities, janitorial service, maintenance) for an estimated 1,500 square feet: $2,000 per month	$ 24,000
Total cost for pediatric services	$748,488[3]

New Programs

    a. Proposal: Women's Health Program and Prenatal Services

        In order to meet the needs of women who cannot afford to pay for such services, the Health Department proposes the establishment of gynecologic and obstetric services for 36 hours per week, or 1,872 hours per year.

Cost of Women's Health and Prenatal Services

Gynecologist and obstetrician @ $95/hour (inc. 25% fringes) x 1,872 hours	$177,840
Nurse (RN) @ $22.50/ hour x 1,872 hours	$ 42,120
Receptionist (no additional costs)	–0–
Equipment (one-time cost)	$ 15,000
Supplies per patient (2 patients/hour x $15/patient = $30/hour) x 1,872 hours	$ 56,160
Fixed expenses (added costs for an estimated increase of 400 square feet, $540 per month)	$ 6,480
Total cost for gynecologic and prenatal services	$297,600

    b. Proposal: Planned Parenthood Services

        The increase in pregnancy among unmarried, very young girls has suggested the need for the availability of information and counseling. The Health Department is proposing the establishment of Planned Parenthood services. The minimum age for access to such services is 16, unless accompanied by a parent or guardian. The services will not include dispensing of contraceptives, nor will the services include any recommendation or referral concerning abortion. It is assumed that space will be made available within the present Health Clinic. The service will be available to the public for 72 hours per week, or 3,744 hours per year.

---

3. This amount is currently budgeted.

Cost of Planned Parenthood Services

Counselors @ $22/ hour (inc. 25% fringes) x 3,744 hours	$82,368
Nurse (none needed)	–0–
Receptionist (no additional needed)	–0–
Equipment (one-time only)—desk, chairs, files, answering machine, personal computer, and printer	5,500
Supplies (phone, postage, paper, pamphlets)	1,500
Total cost of Planned Parenthood services	$89,368[4]

3. Department of Development Proposal: Camelot Shores Project

The River Town side of the Russo River has been in a state of decay since the demise of the wheel foundry and other associated manufacturing plants. The rail siding is no longer used; the buildings are either unoccupied or used as inexpensive warehouses for marginal businesses. The Department of Development, in cooperation with the Parks and Recreation Department, has proposed that the land that abuts the river be developed into an attractive recreational area, with incentives to developers who would build upscale high-rise apartment complexes, restaurants, and marinas.

This would be a ten-year development plan. The G.&W. RR has agreed to remove the no-longer-used tracks and donate the former passenger station to the city. The city's Department of Development hopes to generate interest in developers to build a high-rise office building.

Cost of Camelot Shores—First Year

Purchase of privately owned land	$3,500,000
Razing of present structures	700,000
Total first year cost of Camelot Shores	$4,200,000[5]

4. Parks and Recreation Department Proposal: Camelot Marina Project

To make the shore area more attractive to both tourists and residents, the Parks and Recreation Department is proposing the development of a marina along the north shore line of the Russo River in River Town. This project is not meant to compete with Camelot Shores, but rather to make the entire area more attractive. It is planned that once the marina has been built, user fees will cover the cost of annual maintenance. Architect and engineering fees in the amount of $75,000 were funded last year.

---

4. This cost information was obtained from a medical consultant and represents costs in Midwestern cities of medium size. The authors are aware that regional variations occur in the United States.

5. It is estimated that this same amount will be needed each year for the next ten years, for land purchases and clearing, for installation of water and sewer lines, and for the building of streets, curbs, gutters, and sidewalks.

Cost of Camelot Marina Project for Next Year

Land acquisition		$ 750,000
Razing of present structures, grading, trash removal		135,000
Administration—service building, marina gas pump, sewage pumps, storage tanks, etc.		150,000
Docks: 200 for boats up to 20 feet long 100 for boats up to 25 feet long 50 for boats up to 40 feet long Construction cost of docks @ $2,700 average		945,000
Parking option for 100 more spaces		
Land acquisition	$ 550,000	
Preparation and paving	125,000	
Total cost, parking option	$675,000	$675,000
Total cost of Camelot Marina project next year		$2,655,000

Budget Worksheet

	Budgeted	Revision
Issue: Proposed addition of Drug Enforcement		
Unit: Four additional officers: salary and fringes, uniforms, equipment, training	$327,000	_____
Chief's Discretionary Account	80,000	_____
Total	$407,000	
Notes: _____		
Issue: Pediatric Services		
Pediatricians	$336,960	_____
Nurses	84,240	_____
Receptionist/clerk	63,648	_____
Equipment	15,000	_____
Supplies per patient	224,640	_____
Fixed expenses	24,000	_____
Total	$748,488	
Notes: _____		
Issue: Proposed addition of gynecologic and obstetric services		
Gynecologist and obstetrician	$177,840	_____
Nurse	42,120	_____
Equipment	15,000	_____
Supplies	56,160	_____
Fixed expenses	6,480	_____
Total	$297,600	
Notes: _____		

Budget Worksheet (*continued*)

Issue: Proposed addition of Planned Parenthood services

Counselors	$ 82,368	_____
Equipment	5,500	_____
Supplies	1,500	_____
Total	$ 89,368	

Notes: _____

Issue: Proposed Camelot Shore Project

Land acquisition	$3,500,000	_____
Razing of present structures	700,000	_____
Total	$4,200,000	

Notes: _____

Issue: Proposed Camelot Marina Project

Land acquisition	$750,000	_____
Razing of present structures, etc.	135,000	_____
Administration—service building, etc.	150,000	_____
Docks	945,000	_____
Total	$1,980,000	

Parking option for 100 more spaces

Land acquisition	$550,000	
Preparation and paving	125,000	
Total cost of option	$675,000	$675,000
Grand Total, with option		$2,655,000

Notes: _____

Total cost of all proposed programs and projects

Drug Enforcement Unit	$407,000	_____
Pediatric Services	748,488	_____
Gynecologic-Obstetric Services	297,600	_____
Planned Parenthood Services	89,368	_____
Camelot Shores	4,200,000	_____
Camelot Marina	2,655,000	_____

Officer Protection (if previously adopted)

Costs range: from $293,380 to $328,180, depending on weapon choice.

If .40 cal S&W double-action auto is chosen	328,180[6]	_____
Grand total	$8,725,636	_____
Minus surplus in current budget	$475,500	_____
Net cost of budget proposals	**$8,250,136**	_____

---

6. This figure assumes that the less expensive .357 Magnums were chosen. If .40 cal S&W double-action auto weapons were chosen, add $34,800 to expenditures.

THE MASSAGE THERAPY FACILITY ISSUE

This will be presented to the planning commission on the second session of the simulation (third session if class periods are sixty minutes or less).

The owner of Camelot Adult Bookstore (located in River Town on the southwest corner of Robert Street and Woodworth Road) is ambitious. Activities at the bookstore have been expanded, but there is a problem: The area is zoned M-1. Originally it was a religious bookstore, but as the character of the area changed, so did the kind of books sold. However, as long as it remained a bookstore there was no problem. The current owner of the bookstore has expanded the enterprise to include a "massage therapy" facility named Body Kneads. Opponents charge that it is nothing more than a "massage parlor." Although massage parlors have an unsavory reputation in some cities, the owner insists that Body Kneads is not a front for prostitution, as some have alleged, and points out that no arrests have ever been made for that charge or for similar charges. Critics concede that no arrests have been made but argue that male customers are given "massages" by scantily clad women, who are neither trained nor licensed. The owner's response is that no claim was ever made that the masseuses are trained and licensed, and that in fact, training and licensing are not required either by state law or city ordinance. Thus they are engaging in a lawful activity.

The zoning administrator has said this change is not lawful. As yet, the owner has not shut down the operation, nor has it been closed down by the city. The owner is now requesting a special use permit for the property from the planning commission and council, as is required by the M-1 section of the Zoning Code.

The question to be addressed by the planning commission is: Shall a special use permit be recommended?

When the issue reaches council, some councilors may wish to hear assurances from the city manager and the police chief that adequate investigation of the establishment has occurred and will continue to occur, and that illegal activities are not taking place.

The city manager and the police chief may wish to have council provide some guidance as to what priority should be given this investigation. Because police resources are limited, does council prefer that other activities, such as traffic enforcement or night patrols in the neighborhoods, be curtailed?

THE SMOKING BAN ISSUE

The following issue illustrates the procedure for an initiative petition. If your instructor decides to use this issue, he/she will appoint a member of the class to be the chairperson of an organization called "Smoke Free Camelot!"

The chairperson has several tasks:

1. Prepare an initiative petition (see sample on p. 197), and refer to Article VII, Sections 7.01–7.03, INITIATIVE, REFERENDUM, and RECALL, pp. 164–165.

2. The petition must state what is being proposed, which is: "Smoking of tobacco is hereby banned at any workplace, and any place where food and/or alcoholic beverages are sold for consumption on the premises within the borders of the City of Camelot."

3. This petition must be signed by 10 percent of Camelot citizens (students registered for this class).

4. The signed petition must be submitted to the clerk of council by a date set by your instructor.

5. Following submission of the petition to the clerk of council, a referendum on this issue shall be held at the next succeeding simulation session. The clerk of council will collect the ballots and announce the results.

In most cities where the banning of smoking is proposed, opposition comes not only from some smokers, but also from businesses whose clientele may include smokers.

Examples may well be:

Role 59, owner of the Topless Bar and Grill.

Role 70, Bartender, Mike's Bar and Grill.

Role 60, owner of the Firehouse Bookstore. While the owner may or may not permit smoking in the bookstore, he/she would, as a matter of principle, oppose the city attempting to ban smoking anywhere.

Support may well come from individuals in the medical profession, some non-smokers, or those allergic to cigarette smoke.

THE "OBSCENE PHOTOGRAPHS" ISSUE

The following issue will be presented to the council at the simulation session indicated by your instructor.

Ever since its establishment early in the twentieth century, the Camelot Art Museum has been well supported by the community. It has provided important leadership in introducing young people to the world of the arts. It has a governing board of ten individuals, nominated by the mayor of Camelot and confirmed by Camelot City Council. Board members serve for five years, with terms staggered so that two members are chosen every year. The art museum, a not-for-profit institution, has an annual budget of $1,850,000 and is funded by city tax dollars and by its endowment in nearly equal proportions.

Two years ago, the position of director became vacant when the director retired. The chair of the museum board was, and still is, one of the most successful attorneys in Camelot (Role 49). For a number of years the director has believed that any search for a new director must be national and open. As a result of the chair's efforts, a nationwide search was held and a person of out-standing credentials was chosen to be the new director (Role 61).

There have been no restrictions on the use of the endowment money, nor has there been any controversy in this respect. The citizenry in general, and council members in particular, have believed that support of the arts is a legit-imate use of public funds.

Two events created controversy that has brought a budget item to the atten-tion of the public. The first event was the arrival of an exhibit of more than 170 photographs by a now-deceased, famous artist/photographer, William James. The exhibit contains photographs—often of stark realism but almost uni-formly of exceptional beauty—of still life, nudes, and portraits. It is an impres-sive collection.

Included in the collection are five photographs, extreme in topic and exe-cution, that have triggered allegations of obscenity. The photographs are homo-erotic and use exclusively male models. The topics include a finger inserted into a penis; a fist, an arm, a cylinder, and a bullwhip (respectively) inserted into a rectum; and a man urinating into the mouth of another man. These pictures were displayed in the Camelot Art Museum separately from the rest of the William James exhibit, and viewers of the main exhibit were alerted to the subject matter by a sign suggesting that some might find the five photographs offensive.[7]

The second event was the reaction of the Presbyterian minister (Role 48) when given a description of the five photographs in question. The minister was outraged and communicated the outrage to council by calling a member of council (Role 3) who, it was believed, shared the minister's views. The min-ister also wrote a letter to the editor of the *Camelot Daily News,* spoke at a council meeting, and gave several sermons to the church's congregation.

One member of council (Role 3) does indeed share the minister's views and made these views known to council and to the public at a meeting of council. Both individuals believe strongly that the photographs are not art and should never have been included in an exhibit open to the public. The fact that the actual display of the five photographs in question was separated from the remainder of the exhibition was, to these critics, irrelevant. They are not art, these critics declared, and do not deserve to be seen. These five photographs

---

7. These descriptions of the homoerotic content are based on three articles that appeared in the *Cincinnati Enquirer:* "Seeing the Mapplethorpe Show," by William F. Buckley Jr., May 9, 1990; "Contested Pictures Described," by Ben L. Kaufman, September 26, 1990; and "After the Trial, Questions of Art," by Andy Grundberg, October 21, 1990. Thus descriptions are of actual photographs that were shown in the Contemporary Arts Center in Cincinnati, Ohio, and at several other galleries in the United States.

are evidence of the increasing corruption of American society and of the necessity to "draw the line."

The simulation should concentrate on the second issue, the issue of taxpayer support. Whether or not the five photographs are obscene, whether or not the entire exhibition is tainted by the presence of the five photographs, these and other possible legal questions will have to be decided by courts of law, not by this simulation. **However, the issue of the public funding of the museum is a matter for council to decide.** Although the Presbyterian Minister (Role 48) and the conservative councilor (Role 3) will lead the opposition, they will be joined by other concerned members of the community. However, the museum is not without its defenders. The new director of the museum (Role 61) and the chair of the museum's governing board (Role 49) will lead the defense, and they will be joined by those in the community who believe that any attempt to reduce the public funding of the museum because of disapproval of part of one exhibit is a not very subtle attempt by a minority of the community to censor the public's right of access to significant examples of artistic expression. **(Each member of the class has to decide how he or she stands on this issue and, having made a decision, has an obligation to defend that stand publicly.)**

Council and the public confront questions that include the following:

1. Should council continue to provide financial support for the museum?

2. If there is continued tax support for the museum, is it appropriate for citizens to participate in deciding what is proper to be shown in the museum?

3. If there is to be public participation, how should it be implemented?

THE STRIP MALL DEVELOPMENT ISSUE

The following issue will be presented to council at the simulation session indicated by your instructor.

The City of Camelot has been growing steadily in the last six years. The newest subdivisions, Camelot Acres and South Ridge, are located to the south of the University Park area, and are accessed from Robert Street. There is a vacant field of thirty-five acres immediately south of University Avenue and north of Camelot Acres (see map inside front or back covers). Camelot Acres is immediately south of University Park subdivision and is the site of moderately priced homes, ranging in price from $150,000 to $250,000. Although these are very nice homes, the lots are relatively small and modestly landscaped. About seventy-five homes have been built in this area, with space remaining for perhaps another twenty-five to thirty.

At the southern boundary of Camelot Acres is Lancelot Creek, which runs east-west in this location, and which separates the Camelot Acres subdivision from the South Ridge subdivision. Although the homes in South Ridge are not mansions, they are larger and more expensive, most of them falling in the $300,000 to $500,000 range. They are all very well landscaped. About fifty homes have been sited in the area, with the potential for more homes being built there.

Crown Development Corporation (Roles 38, 39, and 40) has proposed to build a 180,000-square-foot shopping center (in strip mall style, that is, not an enclosed mall). Because of the size of the proposed mall, two things are essential: (1) proximity to an interstate highway interchange and (2) a site of no fewer than thirty acres of open land. As is typical of land use around a city, especially near an access road to an interstate, much of the available space west of the interstate has been filled in with motels, gas stations, and fast food restaurants. Houses have been built along almost all the roads as farmers have sold off lots facing the roads in the area.

One piece of land meets the necessary criteria. It is near the interchange, and, at thirty-five acres, it is large enough to hold the mall and a parking area. *It runs east-west just south of University Avenue and north of the Camelot Acres subdivision. It can be reached from both University Avenue and Robert Street.*

Crown Development owns the land, having bought the former farmland three years ago, planning to build single-family homes. Crown Development requested an R-1 zoning for the land, which was approved by planning commission and council, but Crown Development did not proceed with the development because of uncertain economic conditions.

The developers now wish to have the zoning changed from R-1 to C-3. They believe that there is greater need for a shopping area that would be convenient to all the housing that has been built in the area south of town. In addition, they argue, the shopping area will reduce the amount of traffic now caused by shoppers who must go into town. The developers state that a mall of this size will be big enough for a large grocery supermarket, a major discount store, a hardware store, plus many smaller stores. Crown Development argues that a strip mall will be very beneficial to Camelot for several reasons:

1. It will benefit property tax revenues by increasing the amount of taxable property in the city. A firm figure is not yet possible; however, based on experience in similar locations, the developer estimates that property tax revenues will amount to between $150,000 and $180,000 per year.

2. Approximately four hundred jobs (some part time, some full time) will be created, which in turn will assist in reducing unemployment in Camelot. The additional jobs will reduce the welfare burden at the same time that $80,000 of income tax revenues would be generated, if Camelot were to adopt a 1 percent tax.

3. Perhaps the most appealing part of the proposal is that the city is not being asked to provide any tax funds to support the development of the strip mall.

Quite the contrary; the developers point out that building the mall will bring jobs and income to the city as a result of the construction of access roads, sidewalks, sewer extensions, and, of course, the buildings.

The city planning department director (Role 33) and the assistant city manager (Role 9) support the proposal.

The strip mall proposal is not without opposition. A coalition has been created by those who live in the newly developed Camelot Acres and South Ridge subdivisions. They have given their group the acronym S.O.S., for Save Our Subdivisions. These individuals feel threatened by the prospect of a strip mall built in an area not far from their homes. They foresee greatly increased traffic on both University Avenue and Robert Street, which will be the main access roads. Thus there will be a major increase in noise, dirt, clutter, and traffic congestion as a result of the mall, which in turn will increase the number of automobile accidents and pedestrian injuries, and will pose danger especially to the children in the area. In addition, mall parking lots are likely breeding grounds for drug traffic and crime, the critics argue. The residents have a very real fear that the property values of their new homes will be threatened.

Issues raised by opponents include the following:

1. Contrary to the statement by Crown Development, land already zoned C-3 is available to the west of River Town, and it is of an area sufficient for the strip mall. There is an interstate interchange at the northern boundary, and the mall could be accessed from both the interstate and Woodworth Road. (The developers object to this location because they feel the area is not as desirable and is not as well located for residents of the new subdivisions.)

2. Crown Development makes no mention of the cost to the city of sidewalk and road improvements required by the mall. For example, who will pay for the sidewalks that would enable pedestrians to get to the mall (estimated cost: $75,000), for widening the lanes on Woodworth road (estimated cost: $200,000), and for a new traffic signal (estimated cost: $60,000) that would be required?

3. The developers argue that Camelot needs the additional retail outlets, yet some opponents suggest that this is not true. Several apparel stores, restaurants, and a grocery store have closed in the past five years because of declining revenues. (The developers argue that the reason was lack of adequate parking, poor management, and inconvenient location.)

4. The developer did not submit the traffic impact analysis that is customary for regional shopping centers. Based on studies made by the planning department, it is estimated that traffic on Robert Street will increase 17 percent northbound and 22 percent southbound. The potential need for additional traffic control personnel is not discussed by the developer.

5. Finally, opponents claim that if the mall is a financial failure, not only will the projected increase in revenues not be forthcoming, but the city will also face the prospect of a decaying and empty shopping mall next to the newest

subdivisions. (The developers are particularly angry at this gloomy prediction, arguing that there is no evidence to support it.)

The S.O.S. coalition members include:

Retired Professional Football Player (Role 29)

Director, CSU Institute for Applied Gerontological Studies (Role 36)

Attorney (Role 41)

President, Right to Life Society of Greater Camelot (Role 53)

High School Teacher (Role 58)

Owner of the Firehouse Bookstore (Role 60)

As a result of the opposition, the planning commission split three to three, with one abstention, on the zoning change. Commissioners 10, 13, and 15 voted "yes"; commissioners 11, 12, and 14 voted "no," and commissioner 16 abstained. The tie vote means that the planning commission submitted the proposal to the council without a recommendation.

Other voices have been heard on the issue. Letters to the editor have appeared in the *Camelot Daily News* claiming that the opposition to the strip mall comes from the well-to-do who care only for themselves, not the unemployed. Minorities feel acutely the need for jobs created by the new retail stores. In addition to persons mentioned earlier, the following individuals have announced their support of the strip mall proposal:

Affirmative Action officer, city of Camelot (Role 31)

Minister of the A.M.E. church (Role 32)

Insurance Agent (Role 35)

Director of Urban Welfare Program (Role 37)

Minister of the First Presbyterian Church (Role 48)

Head of the Local Chapter of the NAACP (Role 50)

Executive Director, Camelot Chamber of Commerce (Role 62)

Chairperson of Camelot Hispanic Coalition (Role 72)

(Note: The list of proponents and opponents should not be viewed as exclusive. *Any citizen of Camelot is free to speak for or against this proposed zoning change.*)

The issue is: Should council change the zoning from R-1, single-family homes, to C-3, commercial? Since no city funds are involved, the council must weigh the possible increase in tax revenues and job opportunities against the threats felt by property owners in the Camelot Acres and South Ridge subdivisions to the potential loss in value of their property. Then council must decide whether approval of this new commercial facility is appropriate.

THE HOME FOR UNMARRIED
PREGNANT TEENAGERS ISSUE

The following issue will be presented to the planning commission at the simulation session indicated by your instructor.

Under the leadership of the minister (Role 48) and congregation of the First Presbyterian Church, and supported by several local foundations, it has been proposed that a residence be purchased and converted into a home to assist, at any given time, ten to fifteen unmarried pregnant teenagers. Sufficient funds have been raised to purchase the residence, pay for its upkeep and maintenance, and provide the necessary staff. The costs of medical service delivery will be borne by a combination of community organizations and such assistance as may be available from state and federal medical support programs.

The goal of the church is to provide an atmosphere for the young women that is homelike, rather than institutional. Thus a residential location is desired, and the house must have bedrooms and baths to meet the needs of the mothers-to-be, plus space for staff.

Just such a house is available. It once was the scene of a notorious crime, and because of its lurid history, it did not sell. The bank then foreclosed on the mortgage. The house has been on the market for fifteen months and the bank is willing to sell the house at a price within the budget of the church fund. There is a problem, however.

Camelot zoning laws require that the church must receive a conditional use permit in order to locate such an institution in any area of Camelot. And such a conditional use permit can be granted only after the Camelot Planning Commission gives its evaluation, followed by approval of Camelot City Council. The criteria applied by both bodies are whether such a use is beneficial and appropriate. There always will be concern for the reaction of nearby residents affected by the use of the property.

The residence is located in Forest Acres on Patricia Road. The houses are on large lots and set far back, with mature maple and oak trees providing a shaded canopy. Some Forest Acres property owners are quite concerned. At the next meeting of the planning commission, there is likely to be opposition. One concern may be that such a use of this property will have a serious impact on property values. As one person was heard to say, "Who will want to buy a house in a neighborhood full of pregnant teenagers? And what do I tell my children when they ask about it?"

The Presbyterian minister (Role 48) will emphasize the importance of the humane nature of the home and its importance in providing a haven. He or she will be saddened by the views of those who oppose it on the grounds of concern for property values.

The President of the League of Women Voters (Role 28) is expected to state that the local chapter of the League has studied the proposal and supports the home.

A social worker (Role 69) is serving as a consultant for some of the practical aspects of the proposed home. He/she supports the proposal because of (1) the availability of the property at a reasonable price and (2) the fact that, as proposed, there will be no cost to taxpayers.

Even before the proposal was placed on the agenda of the planning commission, it was reported in the *Camelot Daily News*. Residents of the Forest Acres subdivision began at once to organize opposition. However, some Forest Acres residents may not oppose the home.

Following is a partial list of the residents of Forest Acres:

Councilor (Role 1)

Member of the Planning Commission (Role 13)

Owner, Large Business (Role 25)

Insurance Agent (Role 35)

Real Estate Developers (Roles 38, 39, 40)

President, Data Tech Corporation (Role 47)

Attorneys (Roles 49 and 51)

ACLU Director (Role 73)

The planning commission and council face a clear choice: Shall a conditional use permit be granted the Presbyterian Church to establish a home for unmarried, pregnant teenagers in this location?

THE TOPLESS BAR AND GRILL ISSUE

The following issue will be presented to the planning commission at the simulation session indicated by your instructor.

When the Camelot Bar and Grill went bankrupt, it was purchased by Role 59. Then the menu was extended so that lunch was served on a regular basis, Monday through Saturday, and the hamburgers, chili, hot chicken wings, and other menu items became enormously popular, especially when an additional feature was provided—topless waitresses. Business boomed. The new owner found that by remodeling the interior he could increase the space available for tables, and thus increase the number of patrons. However, the additional space for patrons will require additional kitchen space, for the present kitchen is already inadequate for the volume of business.

When the owner sought a building permit to expand the kitchen by adding onto the rear of the building a space measuring fifteen feet by twenty feet, the application was denied because the restaurant does not conform to the zoning code. It now lacks five parking spaces that would be needed to bring it into conformity, and the kitchen expansion would take away three additional spaces.

A word of explanation about nonconforming uses is in order here. When a zoning code is adopted, or when it is amended in some way, there may be particular structures that fail to conform to the new standards. The nonconformity may be in the character of the current use—a rooming house in an area of single family homes, or a convenience store in a residential area. It may be in the dimensional requirements of the zoning code—a lot too small for a duplex, or side yards too narrow to meet the standard for single-family homes in that area. In such instances, the use may continue; the zoning code cannot extinguish an ongoing use that was lawful the day before the code (or its amendment) was adopted. *But a typical provision of zoning codes states that a structure that is nonconforming because of present use or because of dimensional inadequacies of the lot, or for any other reason, cannot be enlarged.* That is, whereas interior remodeling can occur lawfully, the external dimensions of a structure cannot be increased without a zoning variance. A *zoning variance,* which can be issued by the Camelot Planning Commission, is a special permission tailored to a specific property and circumstance. In most cities, a zoning variance request would be addressed to a zoning appeals board, established to relieve the planning commission of some of its burden of decision. However, for the purpose of the Camelot simulation, instructors have been given a choice. Where participants are numerous, a zoning appeals board is available within the simulation. But an alternative, especially where the number of participants is not large, is to have any request for a zoning variance heard by the planning commission. There is, however, one significant difference. A variance granted by a zoning appeals board cannot be overruled by the city council except by amending the pertinent section of the zoning code. But, as with all planning commission actions, council approval or disapproval is required for a variance granted by the planning commission.

The zoning variance requires one parking space for each 200 square feet of floor area. The current space available for parking is five spaces fewer than is required, but the building is considered a "non-conforming use" because it was built before the parking space requirement was established, and is therefore exempt from the requirement *as long as no changes are made in the size of the structure.* This addition would add fifteen feet to the building at the rear, in order to enlarge the kitchen and increase the seating capacity of the establishment. This addition would eliminate three more parking spaces. The building is already at the allowable front and side limits.

In addition to the problem of an insufficient number of parking spaces, there is the matter of the topless innovation, which has not been without opposition. Opponents include an unusual coalition: the head of the Camelot Chapter of the Feminist Majority (Role 54), the vice president of the Christian Revival Movement (Role 56), the development editor (Role 45), the junior high teacher (Role 43), and the minister of the First Presbyterian Church (Role 48). They have circulated a petition urging council to ban toplessness in food service establishments and then to order police action to close the restaurant. In addition, they have circulated a second petition that calls upon the planning commission and council to deny the restaurant owner's request for a zoning variance to enlarge the restaurant because of the restaurant's failure to have an adequate number of parking spaces. The city manager has referred the first petition to council and the second petition to the planning commission.

The immediate issue for council is whether to ban upper-body nudity in public places, in particular in food service establishments, when there is no suggestion that prostitution is involved. But council must face not merely the immediate problem of this bar and grill with topless waitresses but also what it forecasts. What if more bars decide to go topless? What if other businesses decide to have topless attendants? For example, the tiny New York State community of West Brighton, on Staten Island, once faced the prospect of a topless car wash. Does Camelot want to be in the same situation? The bar is located in the CBD, not far from the location of the proposed new downtown hotel plaza. The area is zoned C-3 (see page 168 for a description of this zone).

The question of topless bars has simply never come up before in Camelot. Since the waitresses are all members of a local union, their attorney (Role 51) will represent them.

1. The issue for the planning commission is whether or not to grant the zoning variance to permit the bar and grill to expand even though the expansion will eliminate more parking spaces. The planning commission does not have to deal with the question of topless waitresses, although the coalition opposing toplessness will urge a denial based upon this point. *Council must review the planning commission's recommendation on the variance issue.*

2. The second issue, that of permitting upper-body nudity in public places, does not require council to write a detailed ordinance. All that is needed is a resolution instructing the city manager to have appropriate legislation drawn up either to permit or prohibit upper-body nudity in public places. However, the resolution has to be specific about what is to be permitted or banned. State law prohibits lower-body nudity in all public places where food or beverages are served, so that is not at issue here.

It goes without saying that the petitioners are very upset. Equally concerned, because of the implied exploitation of women, are the female councilors.

The problem is not as simple as it may seem, for the laws of the state provide definitions and limits to actions council may take. Following are extracts from the relevant sections of the Revised Code of the state.

2907.01 *Obscenity.* A performance is obscene if the dominant appeal is to prurient interest. [Note: *Prurient* is that which tends to arouse sexual desire.]

2907.32 No establishment shall produce or direct an obscene performance for commercial exploitation. [Note: *Performance* is defined as any play, show, skit, dance, or exhibition performed before an audience.]

2907.37 The operation of an establishment can be enjoined if 2907.32 is being violated.

Arguments for the operation of a topless bar:

1. The waitresses are not performing, but are serving the customers.
2. The strong appeal of excellent food and a convivial bar contributes to the success of the enterprise. The restaurant's success is not due solely to the waitresses.
3. No sex acts are performed, nor is prostitution or solicitation permitted.
4. The laws prohibiting obscenity are not involved, for nudity, especially toplessness, is not in and of itself obscene.

Concluding remark from State *Jurisprudence,* Vol. 19, p. 493: "An employer's right to carry on a business in any manner that seems best so long as it does not violate any law or infringe upon the rights of others is a constitutionally guaranteed property right."

THE FIRE HOSE ISSUE

The following issue will be presented to the council at the simulation session indicated by your instructor.

The National Fire Protection Association,[8] the laws of this state, and the Procedure Manual of the Camelot Fire Department all require:

A. That fire hoses be maintained according to manufacturer's recommendations;

B. That all jacketed rubber-lined hoses be tested annually;

---

8. National Fire Protection Association (NFPA) is an international nonprofit membership organization (founded in 1896), with nearly seventy-five thousand members from one hundred nations. NFPA's three hundred safety codes are standards for fire prevention to save lives and protect property around the world.

C. That records be kept on each piece of fire hose used by the Camelot Fire Department;

D. That the officers-in-charge are responsible for ensuring that proper care and procedures are followed during the maintenance, use, and testing of fire hoses.

The Camelot Fire Department was testing fire hoses on campus at a hydrant on University Avenue when the president of Camelot State University, who was late for a meeting, refused to stop when directed to do so and drove his car over the department's fire hose. The fire department personnel, who witnessed the incident, were very angry and promptly radioed their fire chief about what had happened. The next day the chief called the president's office and was told by the secretary that the fire department crew had needlessly obstructed University Avenue with their fire hoses and the president had no choice but to drive over the hose. When, a week later, the chief finally talked directly with the president of Camelot University, the president reiterated that University Avenue was obstructed by the fire department hose testing crew and that the president acted appropriately in running over the hose. The chief reminded the president that the fire department was voluntarily providing fire protection to the university community and that the "agreement" renewal, which was due next month, might not be renewed unless the president formally apologized to the department and agreed to replace the damaged fire hose. The president responded by saying that the City of Camelot Fire Department was legally obligated, according to state law, to provide fire protection to all in need and that the service is not discretionary. However, the chief noted that the department personnel, because of the incident, had voted not to renew the agreement and Camelot State University accordingly will have to provide its own fire protection.

Setting: The issue as presented to council by the Chief of the Camelot Fire Department is whether or not the city council of Camelot will continue providing fire protection service to Camelot State University and accordingly renew, or terminate, the agreement.

THE NOISE ORDINANCE ISSUE

The following issue will be presented to council at the simulation session indicated by your instructor.

Camelot is not alone in its quest for quieter streets and neighborhoods. About one thousand other U.S. cities have noise ordinances, and more are considering drafting such legislation.

An average noise ordinance has a daytime maximum of fifty-five decibels, and an evening level of forty-five to fifty decibels. The level proposed for Camelot would be seventy decibels for the daytime and fifty for evening.

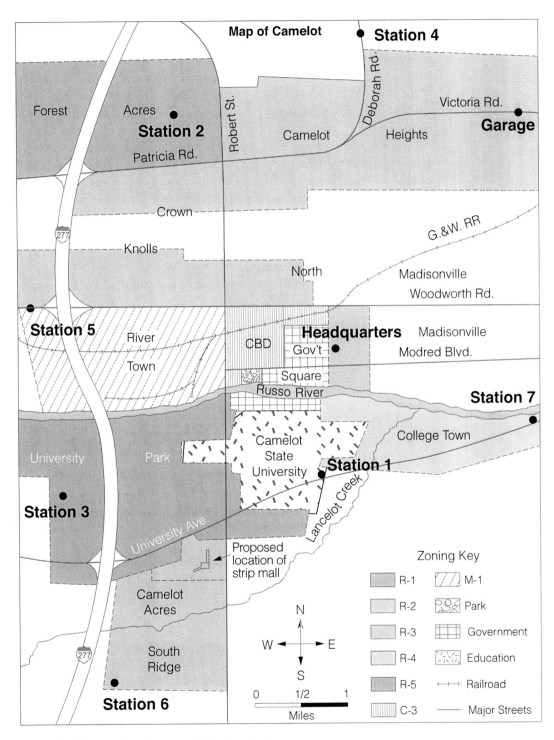

FIGURE 11-2 Camelot Fire Department Station Map

Noise ordinances differ among cities. While some stress vehicular and industrial noise, others have ordinances that focus primarily on noise in residential areas. Still others attempt to control loud radios or stereos.

The method of measurement differs also. For example, the ordinance in Akron, Ohio, states that if a police officer standing 80 feet away from a house can hear noise from that house, it merits a citation; if a police officer standing 100 feet from a car stereo can hear noise from that stereo, it merits a citation. No complaint is required. A North Olmstead, Ohio, ordinance restricts noise within places of entertainment. The level cannot exceed ninety-five decibels on a sound-level meter "at any point that is normally occupied by a customer." Richmond Heights, Ohio, sets the decibel level at fifty-five, measured at any lot line within a residential district. Industrial or commercial districts cannot exceed noise levels beyond sixty decibels at the lot line. Trotwood, Ohio, has an ordinance restricting the noise of motor vehicles. A level of eighty decibels cannot be exceeded at any time.

The legal justification for such ordinances is twofold: Excessive noise violates laws against disturbing the peace and/or violates road safety laws because individuals driving cars whose stereos exceed the prescribed limits cannot hear horns, sirens, or other warning devices.

The effects of noise levels on humans have been estimated and reported by the U.S. Environmental Protection Agency. At ten decibels, a noise is just audible. At fifty, the noise is described as quiet. (An average clothes dryer has a reading of fifty to fifty-five decibels from a distance of fifteen feet.) The noise becomes "intrusive" at sixty decibels, and annoying at eighty. Hearing damage may result from prolonged exposure to noise at the ninety-decibel level and beyond, according to the EPA. The report also said an increase in ten decibels doubles the perceived sound to the observer.

When drafting noise ordinances, cities take into account the nature of the population. A college or resort town sometimes legislates slightly higher noise levels than average residential areas. It should also be noted that when the federal Office of Noise Abatement and Control was abolished in 1982, due to federal budget cuts, its responsibilities were transferred to the states. Though there is no statewide law, cities where excessive noise has become bothersome have adopted their own ordinances.

Camelot citizens in College Town and University Park, in the area east and west of the university, are up in arms over the blasting stereos, the loud parties that often last all night long, and the impromptu parades of fraternity students in the middle of the night. The crux of the difficulty is that this area is undergoing change. It contains a variety of lifestyles and socioeconomic classes. The noise problem is more acute on the streets near the university. Many of the older homes are now crowded rental properties containing hordes of students, nonstudents, visiting transients, plus even some drifters. Interspersed with these buildings are extensively remodeled as well as new homes of young professionals, young faculty members, and clerical and technical workers connected with the university. On one street there are three fraternity houses.

A delegation of citizens, including the junior high school teacher (Role 43), the director of Public Health (Role 44), and the publisher of the *Camelot Daily News* (Role 20), will demand that council pass a noise ordinance and enforce it. The police chief supports such legislation because it will give a more easily enforceable standard than the disturbing the peace ordinance. The student newspaper has editorialized against such an ordinance, and several fraternities have hired an attorney (Role 49) to represent their interests.

Two types of noise ordinances exist, as discussed earlier in this section. One sets decibel levels and involves the use of devices that measure decibel level. The second type relies on a police officer's ability to hear sound beyond a set distance. Council thus has several decisions to make. Council may, if it chooses, do the following:

1. Ignore the demands of the citizens for a noise ordinance.

2. Pass a resolution that instructs the city manager to draft an enforceable noise ordinance that will apply to noise beyond a designated level. Council could include in its instructions to the city manager such items as:

   a. A recommendation concerning whether the ordinance will apply to audible sound from a residence and/or noise from a vehicle.

   b. Whether enforcement will rely on a device to measure decibel levels and/or on a human ear.

   c. The decibel level permitted at specified times of day or night, or on the allowed distance beyond which sound may not be audible.

If council agrees to pass a noise ordinance, then it should also add a penalty section. Following are two approaches, each of which is in use in some locations:

A. *Offenses Committed by Individuals*

   1st offense—Warning

   2nd offense—Minor misdemeanor, maximum fine of $200

   3rd offense—If within six months of previous offense, 4th degree misdemeanor, maximum fine of $250, maximum of 10 days in jail

   Offenses Committed by Organizations

   1st offense—Warning

   2nd offense—Maximum fine of $500

   3rd offense—Maximum fine of $1,000

B. *Offenses Committed in Vehicles*

   1st offense—Maximum fine of $200

   2nd offense—Forfeiture of stereo equipment if applicable

Council must decide:

1. whether a noise ordinance should be adopted,

2. what the penalties should be for violation of the ordinance, if adopted,

3. whether enforcement will be complaint driven or the product of routine enforcement patrols.

THE EMINENT DOMAIN ISSUE

"Nor shall private property be taken for public use without just compensation."

The following issue will be presented to council at the simulation session indicated by your instructor.[9]

The significance of the final clause of the Fifth Amendment to the United States Constitution is that a government [national, state, or local] may take private property only when (1) the property is to be used for a public purpose and (2) the owner, or owners, receive "just compensation" for the taking. This authority to compel the sale of land (and buildings thereon) to a government is called "eminent domain."

Few people would disagree with the basic premise of this section of the Fifth Amendment. It has been used to take land on which would be built railroads, highways, sewer lines, phone lines, electric power lines, water lines, and public buildings.

Recent extensions of the definition of "public use" have included parking lots for hotels, football stadiums, a private corporation, a racetrack, and a football team. (This topic is discussed at greater length on pages 30–33, "The Newer Uses of Eminent Domain.")

If those who oppose a particular instance of taking by eminent domain choose to challenge it by going to court, they are unlikely to prevail. Seldom will there be a middle ground on which to compromise, and the courts usually find that the taking is indeed for a public use or purpose, and therefore is lawful.

There is more variation on the issue of "just compensation," for that requires a decision setting a dollar amount rather than a simple "yes-or-no" answer to whether that government can compel the sale to it of a particular land parcel. (The issue of fair price can be decided by a jury after hearing evidence on the question.)

Crown Real Estate (Roles 38, 39, and 40) has planned a redevelopment of the northern portion of the bottom third of Crown Knolls to the east of Interstate 277 and the Woodworth Road exit (see p. 133, and the map on the

---

9. While this issue is located in Camelot, and the events described are unique to Camelot, the authors acknowledge the usefulness of an article entitled "Pushing the Limits of 'Public Use,'" under the byline of Dennis Cauchon in the April 1, 2004, issue of *USA Today*.

inside cover). This section of Crown Knolls contains working-class homes of similar small frame bungalow style; the post–World War II type of houses. These homes are not slums, but many need some repairs. On the periphery of the area are some older homes on larger lots. These houses also are not derelict, but they need repairs. A few small retail businesses in mostly small one-story structures, equally in need of repair, are located on side streets near the interstate entrance. A total of fifty properties are involved.

The Crown Real Estate development proposal is to buy all the properties, but only if the city agrees to use its power of eminent domain should any of the owners refuse to sell. The city would justify the forced purchase on the grounds that the properties in question are "blighted" and the increased city revenues from the taxes on the improved land use would fit the definition of "public use." The city would then sell the seized property to Crown Real Estate.

The Crown Real Estate plan is ambitious. In place of the blighted homes and businesses, the new development will include top-rated home furnishing retailers, which will bring other quality shops to follow its lead. Other companies of national reputation that currently have no outlets in Camelot are showing an interest in locating in this area: clothing stores, restaurants, and both of the large national bookshop chains have expressed interest in locating there. The nearness to the interstate access is clearly what draws them.

Five of the current owners have refused to sell; three are home owners, two are small businesses: a convenience store and a small hardware store. One of the home owners is a man in his seventies who has lived in the house for thirty years, and lives alone. At his age, he has said, "Where would I move to?" Another home owner is a single mother with two elementary school-age children. Her complaint is that she works full time and cannot find another house that she could afford. The third person refuses to sell on grounds of principle. No one, he says, has the right to take his home. The two small business owners say that there is no other place they can afford. They will be out of business.

All forty-five of the other property owners have agreed to sell; especially since the price they have been offered is significantly higher than their property's current market value.

The developers estimate that when finished, the new development will bring between 2,800 and 3,450 jobs and residents to Camelot. The economic benefit will be between $1.79 million and $2.79 million a year in earnings taxes. The school district would also receive an additional $300,000 to $400,000 each year.

The question for city council is, will they approve the use of eminent domain to purchase the properties of the five unwilling owners? Granted, the forced sale will be a hardship for five property owners. But failure to use eminent domain dooms the proposal, which means the city will lose the opportunity to increase revenues to pay for needed increase in city services: police, fire, assistance to the poor, and other current needs.

And it will be a loss of employment opportunities for some unemployed. Council members must decide whether the interests of forty-five property owners should prevail, or that of five property owners.

There is always the possibility that the five property owners whose property will be "taken" will take their case to court on the grounds that the use of eminent domain to seize the five pieces of property is not an appropriate "public use." It is rare that courts will rule against cities in their use of eminent domain. Where courts have objected, the reason usually has been that the proposed use of the seized property seemed to be primarily for the benefit of the developer, or, in one case, for a hotel that wanted to have more space for parking.

Four members of the class have a particular interest in this issue: two are members of city council who live in Crown Knolls (Roles 4 and 7), as do two members of planning commission (Roles 12 and 16). Roles 27, 43, 71, and 72 also live in Crown Knolls. Even though they do not live in any of the affected pieces of property, they may feel strongly either for or against the issue: for, because the proposed change will revitalize a dying area; against, because it will change it so drastically.

The decision, however, remains with the city council.

(For this simulation, your instructor will identify two members of the class; one to be a property owner who does not wish to see his or her home destroyed, and one to represent one of the small businesses.)

THE DRUG TESTING ISSUE

The following issue will be presented to council at the simulation session indicated by your instructor.

A small, but significant, number of employees of the City of Camelot are suspected by their supervisors of using substances prohibited by state or federal laws and by the personnel regulations of the City of Camelot. Several department heads have asked the city manager whether drug testing might be useful in pursuing the apparent problem. The manager has responded that such tests cannot be ordered without prior authority from council, and councilor (Role 3) has agreed to sponsor a proposed ordinance.

The proposal has the following provisions:

1. All successful applicants for employment by the City of Camelot must undergo testing for prohibited substances prior to appointment and assumption of duties.

2. Existing employees may be asked by their department head or director to undergo testing for prohibited substances if that person has a reasonable basis for suspecting such use.

3. Any person failing such a test may be suspended without pay for a maximum of ten working days.

4. Any person failing such a test for the second time may be discharged from his or her employment.

When the issue is considered, the city manager may ask the director of the Camelot City Health Department (Role 44) to explain the proposal and answer questions.

THE USA PATRIOT ACT ISSUE

The following issue will be presented to the city council at the simulation session indicated by your instructor.

The awkwardly titled *Uniting and Strengthening America by Providing Appropriate Tools Required to Intercept and Obstruct Terrorism Act of 2001* (USA Patriot Act or USAPA) was passed in response to the terrorists' attacks of September 11, 2001.[10] The act provides federal officials with greater authority to track and intercept communications from both domestic and foreign sources that are perceived as possible terrorist threats. The Patriot Act, which totaled 342 pages, made many changes and complex additions to existing laws. Among its provisions it created a new crime (domestic terrorism), made a federal crime of biological attacks on Americans, of attacks on mass transportation facilities, and of other support of terrorists, including money laundering. Additional provisions allow the federal government (FBI) to more easily engage in secret searches (with a warrant) of a home or office without notifying the suspect until much later. Also, the act makes it easier for the Central Intelligence Agency (CIA) and the FBI to share information. Finally, under the USA Patriot Act federal authorities are allowed to use "pen register" orders, which allow the FBI to monitor the who, when, and where of phone conversations, e-mail, and Internet activity. The idea of the "who/when/where" of a communication is to exclude the content, and the investigative agents must be trusted not to read the content. Although the USA Patriot Act passed through Congress by large margins in both houses only five weeks after it was proposed, there were a number of controversial provisions that have since been challenged by civil rights groups. In fact, some members of Congress predicted that parts of the Act will be tested in the courts.[11] Some of the criticisms of the Act follow:

> "It undermines vital checks and balances by expanding the use of secret courts and depriving judges of a meaningful role in ensuring that the law enforcement powers are not being abused."

---

10. See Charles Doyle, "The USA Patriot Act: A Sketch," *CBS Report to Congress, Congressional Research Service, The Library of Congress,* April 18, 2002, CRS, pp. 1–5.

11. www.aclu-wa.org; Peverell Squire, "The Pendulum Continues to Swing: Civil Liberties Two Years after September 11," in James M. Lindsay, editor, *American Politics after September 11* (Cincinnati, Ohio: Atomicdog Publishing, 2003), p. 31.

"It violates the First Amendment by allowing the FBI to easily obtain information about a person's reading habits, religious affiliations, Internet surfing, and other free speech activity if that activity can be tied somehow to intelligence purposes... Under Section 215 of the USA Patriot Act, the FBI can obtain records of the books people have checked out of libraries—even when there is no evidence that an individual poses a threat to national security. The Act imposes a 'gag order' that prohibits librarians from telling a person that the government has obtained information about his/her reading habits."

"After being charged with either an immigration or criminal offense, *noncitizens* (emphasis added) can be held indefinitely, with the Attorney General reviewing their certification every six months. Under the Act, their attorneys can initiate *habeas corpus* proceedings in federal courts to seek their release."

However, "they can remain detained if they have never been convicted of a crime and if the Attorney General certifies that he has 'reasonable grounds to believe' that their release will endanger 'the national security of the United States or the safety of the community or any person.'"[12]

Those who favor the Act generally are highly concerned with national security in these perilous times. In particular, the Act reduces the terrorists' ability to operate in the United States by allowing federal officials extra surveillance over, as President Bush says, "the evil doers." In addition, supporters claim that the Act creates a *culture of cooperation* between the FBI and the CIA that is desperately needed in fighting the "War against Terrorism." Proof of the Act's success is the fact that there have been no large-scale terrorist attacks since September 11, 2001. Finally, the supporters argue that although the Act does limit some freedoms, these limitations are necessary to provide a protective shield against terrorist organizations that are determined to destroy our way of life.[13]

Setting

Over 260 communities throughout the United States, following the lead of the national ACLU, have passed resolutions urging the U.S. Congress to repeal the USA Patriot Act. It is noteworthy that New York City, target of the 9/11 terrorist attacks, should resolve against the Act's infringement of its citizens' privacy rights. Other large cities, such as San Francisco, Oakland, Baltimore, and Philadelphia, passed similar resolutions expressing concerns that the Act is a serious threat to basic constitutional rights. The essence of the opposition to the Act is found in grassroots America, which the Bill of Rights Defense Committee estimates to be about forty-six million people scattered throughout the United States.[14]

---

12. www.aclu-wa.org/SafeAndFree/Patriot1FAQ.htm.

13. "Student Perspectives: Patriot Act: The Pros and Cons," www.news1.securesites.net/extras/patriotact.php.

14. Bill of Rights Defense Committee, www.bordc.org/.

A member of Council (Role 2), the ACLU Director for the state (Role 73), and a Camelot attorney (Role 51) wish to address the Camelot City Council concerning the adoption of the following resolution:

A Resolution of the City Council of the City of Camelot to Preserve Civil Liberties Endangered by the USA Patriot Act

WHEREAS, the City of Camelot is concerned with the security of our nation and the protection of civil liberties as found in our Constitution are the foundation of democracy; and

WHEREAS, in these dangerous times, it is the responsibility of local governments, at the grassroots level, to take a stand in support of our Bill of Rights which [is] threatened by the USA Patriot Act of 2001; and

WHEREAS, the citizens of Camelot believe that the actions of the Attorney General of the United States and the U.S. Justice Department since the September 11, 2001, attacks pose unacceptable threats to our constitutional freedoms; and

WHEREAS, the City of Camelot Library Board has expressed its concerns with the sections of the USA Patriot Act that [pertain] to public libraries and has requested that the Camelot City Council register its opposition to the USA Patriot Act; and

WHEREAS, the Fourteenth Amendment to the U.S. Constitution prohibits the government from denying "to any person within its jurisdiction equal protection of the laws"; and

WHEREAS, the First Amendment to the U.S. Constitution stipulates that no law be made, "respecting the establishment of religion, or prohibiting the free exercise thereof; or abridging the freedom of speech, or of the press; or the right of the people peaceably to assemble, and to petition the Government for a redress of grievances"; and

WHEREAS, the Fourth Amendment to the U.S. Constitution stipulates that "the right of the people to be secure in their persons, houses, papers, and effects, against unreasonable searches and seizures, shall not be violated, and no warrants shall issue, but upon probable cause, supported by oath or affirmation, and particularly describing the place to be searched, and the persons or things to be seized";

THEREFORE, BE IT RESOLVED that the City of Camelot affirms the rights of all U.S. citizens and non-citizens within the city as provided by the Bill of Rights and the Fourteenth Amendment of the U.S. Constitution; and

BE IT FURTHER RESOLVED that all city officials of Camelot respect the civil rights and civil liberties of all members of the city; and

BE IT FURTHER RESOLVED that the Camelot City Council affirms its opposition to all federal measures that violate the rights and liberties of members of our community, and

BE IT FURTHER RESOLVED that the Camelot City Council supports repeal of the USA Patriot Act, and

Accordingly, **BE IT RESOLVED** that the Camelot Clerk of Council communicate this resolution to all departments of the city, to the state legislature, the Governor, the Attorney General of this state, the state's Congressional delegation, the Attorney General of the United States, and the President of the United States.[15]

THE WILDFLOWERS ISSUE

The following issue will be used at the simulation session indicated by your instructor.

Role 62 (Executive Director, Chamber of Commerce) and spouse are justifiably proud of their beautiful front lawn. There is a bed of flowers next to the front of the house, and in the rear are large rose gardens and a vegetable garden. They have planted no trees; neither of them wants to rake leaves.

Role 45 (Development Editor) is not a single-issue person. She believes that if future generations are to inherit a decent world, we must all do our part to protect the environment, reduce air pollution, and save wildlife. She is particularly upset by the city ordinance that requires all yards to be mowed and gardens to be kept weeded, and especially to be kept free of dandelions, and that other weeds be eradicated from all lawns.

The present ordinance reads:

Section 27-835.1 Trees, Shrubs, and Bushes

No portion of any tree, shrub, or bush shall be allowed to block or impede pedestrian use of any sidewalk in the City of Camelot. No limb or branch over a sidewalk shall be less than 90 inches above the surface of the walk. Compliance with this provision shall be the responsibility of the owner of the tree, shrub, or bush.

Section 27-835.2 Lawns

a. All grass must be mowed or trimmed as often as is necessary to maintain a maximum grass height of four inches.

b. Clover, crab grass, plantain, mint of all varieties, and dandelions shall be eliminated from all lawns.

Noxious weeds, as defined by state law, are not subject to this ordinance.

Role 45 believes it is essential to stop the use of all poisons and that we should encourage the planting and care of trees, flowering plants, and shrubs. She argues that instead of polluting the ground with herbicides, we should grow more plants and trees to help replace oxygen. We should not endanger people, pets, and wildlife with countless poisons. Several times she has spoken at council meetings about her concerns. Each time, council members have listened politely and said they would take it under advisement. She decided it was time for direct action.

---

15. See "community resolutions" link, www.aclu.org/SafeandFree/SafeandFree.cfm?ID-11267&c=207.

An attorney (Role 49) and the owner of the Firehouse Bookstore (Role 60) have joined her in her rebellion against the lawn maintenance regulations. They have stopped mowing their lawns, and the owner of the Firehouse Bookstore has planted many kinds of wildflowers in the front yard, some reaching six feet in height. Neighbors have been particularly irritated by the clumps of goldenrod.

Role 45 has discovered that a citizen has the right of initiative petition. The Camelot City Charter, Article VII (p. 164) describes the petition procedure. (A sample nominating petition is provided on pp. 195–196. It can be modified, or the petitioners may wish to create their own, using the sample as a model. Your instructor can assist you by referring to the Instructor's Manual.)

Roles 45 and 60 begin the initiative procedure by gaining signatures of supporters.

Proposed Substitute Regulation 27-835.1: Lawn and Garden Maintenance

The purpose of the following regulation is to encourage, but not require, the development of lawns of wildflowers, planned or unplanned, for all residences and open land in zones R-1 and R-2. See Section 4 for exceptions.

Section 1: The provisions of Camelot City Code 27-385.1 shall not apply to owner-occupied residences in R-1 and R-2 zones as defined by the City of Camelot Zoning Code.

Section 2: Any portion of the yard of an owner-occupied residence may be used for flowers of all species, trees, and/or shrubs, except those poisonous to the touch (e.g., poison sumac, poison ivy, and poison cedar), and other noxious weeds as defined by state law.

Section 3: The owner of any vacant land or residential property in R-1 and R-2 zones that is not owner-occupied shall not permit grass to reach a height of more than four inches. Flower gardens are permitted, but must be maintained.

Section 4: These regulations apply only to R-1 and R-2 zones. All other sections of the existing regulations remain in force.

Role 45, with or without allies, must follow the procedure on p. 164. If there are sufficient valid petition signatures, the clerk of council will certify the issue to the board of elections for placement on the ballot at the next municipal election. [Your instructor will serve as the "board of elections," receiving the petitions, verifying them, and then transmitting the initiative petition to the city clerk for production of ballots. In a real-life setting, the board of elections would do all of this.]

THE PRIVATE USE OF PUBLIC SPACE ISSUE

One or more of the following issues will be presented to the city council at the simulation session indicated by your instructor.

Background

The phrase "freedom of expression" has always been understood to include the right to free speech, press, and performance. There are the usual limits, which include libel and slander laws, protection of minors, and a ban on public sexual activities.

Three different, yet basically related, types of activities have occurred in Camelot that have created problems for the city administration. (NOTE: All the activities listed in the following discussion have actually occurred in various American cities, including Philadelphia (PA), St. Augustine (FL), Cambridge (MA), Seattle (WA), Santa Monica (CA), and Cincinnati (OH)).

- One type of activity involves the homeless. But the term "homeless" includes several very different types of individuals. Some of the homeless have lost their homes as a result of unemployment, or have lost the family wage earner due to death, illness, divorce, or abandonment. Other homeless are victims of mental illness that prevents them from finding or keeping a job. But some are homeless either by choice or because they are alcoholics or drug addicts. A survey in Philadelphia, Pennsylvania, found that about half of the beggars downtown spent their "take" on drugs and alcohol, about half actually had homes, and at least one-third were scam artists. In Santa Anna, California, the "homeless" slept in the parks on blankets, cots, sleeping bags, hammocks, or mattresses; they set up tents or tarpaulins as cover from the rain; they cooked their meals on little stoves, entertained, had parties, got drunk, littered, stored their belongings, and raised their children, all in public parks. In fact they had appropriated public property for private use.

- Some beggars attempt to sell items in order to get money, or they beg for money. Some beggars sit silently on the sidewalk or in business doorways with a cup or plate in front of them and ask for help; some are more aggressive and will stand in front of people and beg, or use thinly veiled threats, or badger women while they are looking in their purses for parking meter change. At times they may block entrances to retail stores, making it difficult to pass them if they do not receive a gift.

- "Street entertainers" may be musicians providing noontime concerts, or groups playing wherever people gather. Donations are encouraged, although not necessarily insisted on. Or they may be individuals or groups who play every day, all day, immediately in front of retail stores, in the entrances to shops, in people's faces. Santa Monica, California, passed a law that outlawed chain saws, swords, and other noisy or dangerous objects as props for jugglers and street entertainers.

The Simulation

The struggle to find a balance between the preferences of the majority and the rights of the minority is familiar to us all. The U.S. Supreme Court has held that the constitutional guarantee of freedom of speech includes "freedom of expression." And who should determine what qualifies? Is it the right of each individual to define the term? At what point does one individual's freedom of expression conflict with another individual's right to be left alone?

The street entertainers claim that playing their music on public property is their way of expressing themselves. If they are prevented from doing this, then they are denied their right of free expression. The merchants and their customers should not be permitted to interfere with this right, street entertainers argue.

Much the same argument is offered by the "campers" in the park. The beggars argue that what they are doing is on public property and they have a right to be there, and they have every right to ask for donations or to sell their products or their services without interference. They, too, believe they are exercising their right of free expression.

The merchants in the business districts, the customers who want to shop at the stores, the many employees, and other business owners do not agree. There have been complaints that while going to and from their jobs, or while attempting to eat a quiet lunch in the park, or when entering or leaving restaurants, persons have found themselves harassed, or even threatened, by individuals who claim the protection of freedom of expression.

The matter has been brought (by Role 6) to the Camelot City Council to define "freedom of expression" more precisely and clarify what its limits, if any, may be.

The Issues

Three ordinances have been introduced by Councilor (Role 3). They state:

1. Regulation of Street Entertainers
   a. "Street entertainers" playing music, performing skits, or displaying feats of dexterity and/or athletic prowess in hope of receiving something of value from observers are not engaging in an activity protected as *freedom of expression*.
   b. Any person desiring to engage in any type of performance on public property, for which donations may be received, shall obtain a permit from the Director of Public Parks and Recreation.
   c. A reasonable fee may be charged for the permit to cover the cost of issuance.
   d. The Director shall have authority to set reasonable conditions regarding the performance.
   e. No performance which reasonably or foreseeably may pose a risk to the safety or health of other persons shall be permitted.

2. Regulation of Begging
   a. No person shall walk, stand, lie, grab, touch, or approach another person or vehicle in such a manner as to (1) block, interfere with, or impede the passage of that person or vehicle on a public street, sidewalk, or area, or (2) cause any person or driver to alter his or her intended route.

   b. No person shall request, solicit, or demand money, or other thing of
      value, in a manner which would alarm, intimidate, threaten, menace,
      harass, or coerce a reasonable person.

   c. Begging within six feet of a storefront, ten feet of an automatic teller
      machine, twenty feet of crosswalks or after 8 p.m. is prohibited.

   d. Begging from anyone getting in or out of an automobile is prohibited.

3. Prohibition of Camping on Public Property

   a. All camping on sidewalks is banned.

   b. It is unlawful to camp, occupy camp facilities, or use camping parapher-
      nalia in any public area that has not been designated for such purposes
      by the city manager, or the manager's deputy.

   c. The term "camp paraphernalia" shall include, but not be limited to, tar-
      paulins, cots, beds, sleeping bags, hammocks, and utensils for cooking
      and/or heating.

   d. No person shall leave unattended personal property in any park or street
      or sidewalk.

NOTE: For each of the preceding issues, the proposed penalty provisions
are identical:

lst offense—Warning

2nd offense—Minor misdemeanor, maximum fine of $200

3rd offense—If within six months of previous offense, 4th degree misdemeanor, maximum fine of $250, maximum of 10 days in jail.

Councilor (Role 2) strongly opposes the proposed ordinance(s); councilor
(Role 6) is especially concerned about the problems and plans to second such
motion or motions. The other councilors are as yet not sure whether they support or oppose the proposed ordinance(s).

Each person should read his or her role description carefully before taking
a position. Ask yourself: do you have a stake in the issue, perhaps because of
your lifestyle preferences, or your economic interests, or your views on the
protection of community values? Obviously, your support or opposition may
be based on other factors as well.

THE COUCHES IN THE YARDS
AND ON THE PORCHES ISSUE

*The following issue will be presented to council at a simulation session indicated by your
instructor.*

It has become a familiar sight in cities with residential universities, especially in areas where houses are rented by students: old, dilapidated couches,

often with fabric ripped and springs exposed, sometimes occupied, sometimes not, but often looking like the detritus of a lost battle. In residential neighborhoods, they bespeak student housing.

In an attempt to fight the practice, the city council of Athens, Ohio, the home of Ohio University, passed an ordinance that bans the placement of couches on porches. The rationale for the legislation is that couches on porches and in front yards detract from the city's appearance and sanitation (*Cincinnati Enquirer,* February 2, 1999).

The Athens, Ohio, action has come to the attention of Camelot's city manager, who frequently has received complaints from home owners, often with small children, next door to houses where mildewed and moldy couches are in the front yard or on the porch. Persuasion has failed, and the city manager has asked council to consider the type of legislation approved by Athens.

A proposed ordinance has been placed on the council agenda. It states:

Be it resolved that no upholstered furniture designed for interior use shall be located on the porch or in the front or side yards of any property within the corporate limits of the City of Camelot.

Penalty Section:

1st offense—Warning.

2nd offense—Minor misdemeanor, maximum fine of $200.

3rd offense—If within six months of previous offense, 4th degree misdemeanor, maximum fine of $250, maximum of 10 days in jail.

Council members are divided on this issue. Roles 2 and 3 are leaning toward supporting the proposed ordinance, although they can be persuaded otherwise. Roles 1 and 5 are inclined to oppose it because they do not like the city telling property owners what they can and can't do with their property. Roles 4, 6, and 7 have no strong views on the issue.

Within the community, the individuals who most strongly support the ordinance are those living in College Town. They are:

The Assistant City Manager (Role 9)

Director of Public Health Department (Role 44)

Development Editor, Megabook (Role 45)

Head of Local Chapter, NAACP (Role 50)

President, Camelot Chapter of Business and Professional Women (Role 52)

Opposition within the community may come from:

Reporter (Role 22) (thinks it is a stupid issue for council, but as a reporter may feel constrained about saying that in public)

Student Body President (Role 34) (his house has a couch on the porch)

Firehouse Bookstore Owner (Role 60)

ACLU Director (Role 73) has been approached by the Firehouse Bookstore Owner (Role 60) to represent him. The ACLU director has the matter "under advisement."

THE CURFEW ISSUE

The following issue will be presented to council at a simulation session indicated by your instructor.

Increasingly, Camelot has been plagued by unsupervised teenagers, as well as some pre-teens (eleven and twelve years of age), gathering in groups of varying numbers on street corners, in parking lots of shopping malls, and in downtown areas until midnight or later. At one time the problem was limited to weekend nights, but now that it is summer it occurs every night. And even during the school year it occurs almost every night. Articles in the *Camelot Daily News* have described drug deals in parking lots, drunkenness and vandalism, broken windows in downtown stores, and fights between individuals and between groups.

Questions have been raised at council meetings about why the police are not doing something about controlling the vandalism and violence, and the reply has been that there are not enough officers on duty to control the situation. At the first sign of a police car, drug dealers and their customers flee. In addition, the police chief has argued, much of the fault lies with parents who aren't maintaining control over their own children. If the police spend their efforts on controlling children, then they do not have sufficient personnel to combat adult crime effectively. The city manager has pointed out that budget requests for next year already exceed expected revenues, and the cost of adding more police officers to the force would fall between $500,000 and $700,000 per year. The councilor from Madisonville (Role 6), the former police chief, has offered an alternative solution: the following emergency ordinance. It has been placed on today's agenda:

> *Be it resolved: That a curfew shall be enforced for all individuals 16 years of age or younger, unless they are accompanied by a parent or legal guardian. The curfew shall be enforced Sunday through Friday of each week, to begin at 9:00 p.m. and last until 6:00 a.m. the following morning, and on Saturday to begin at midnight and last until 6:00 a.m. of the following morning.*

The councilor then read to council the following Associated Press news item distributed November 12, 1998.

PALMER, IL. There has been no more trash stuffed into the bank night deposit slot, no more burned flags thrown down toilets, no more chickens tossed to their deaths off the grain elevator. This farming town of 275 people is quiet again. Town officials believe it is attributable to the seven-day-a-week,

8 p.m. to 11 p.m. curfew (8 p.m. to midnight on weekends) imposed on anyone under 18.[16]

In March of 1999, the U.S. Supreme Court let stand a Charlottesville, Virginia, curfew for children under 17. The Supreme Court action was not a decision; that is, it did not discuss the issue, it merely did not rule against Charlottesville. (Richard Carelli, *Associated Press,* as reported in the *Cincinnati Enquirer,* March 23, 1999.)

Councilor (Role 3) will express strong support for the proposed curfew ordinance, as will the owners of the large and the small businesses (Roles 25 and 26). They may well be joined by the A.M.E. Minister (Role 32), the director of the Institute for Gerontological Studies (Role 36), possibly by one or more of the developers (Roles 38, 39, and 40), the police officer (Role 46), the Presbyterian Church Minister (Role 48), and the chairperson of the Hispanic Coalition (Role 72). Keeping your role description in mind, other participants in the simulation may wish to oppose or support the curfew proposal.

Council must decide:

1. whether a curfew should be adopted,
2. what hours each day and how many days each week a curfew should be enforced,
3. the ages of the minors who are affected,
4. the penalties for violations,
5. whether penalties shall apply to the minors,
6. whether penalties shall apply to the parents or legal guardian.

THE RIGHTS OF A HOME OWNER
ISSUE: HOME DECORATIONS

The following issue will be presented to the planning commission at the simulation session indicated by your instructor.

A person's home is his or her castle. Woe be to anyone who invades the rights of a home owner. But what about a home owner's preferences—color choice for example? Can you paint your house any color you wish, or in any style? What about the rights of your neighbors not to live next to a garish house?

The executive director of the Camelot Chamber of Commerce (Role 62) has lived in Camelot Acres for a number of years. It is a nice residential area

---

16. The *Cincinnati Enquirer,* Cincinnati, Ohio, November 12, 1998, p. A4.

developed about twenty-five years ago. The first homes built were modest in size, typically three bedrooms and one and a half or two baths. However, the lots are large enough to permit small additions, such as an additional bedroom and/or den. The lot widths vary between 100 to 120 feet, and the depth is typically 200 feet. Each side yard must be no less than twelve feet in width. The houses and lots are well maintained. Almost everywhere, the grass is mowed and the houses are nicely painted and kept in good repair. Every house has an attached garage for at least two cars. The area is not a tract in which the houses were all built by the same developer at the same time. As a result, there is considerable variety in the styles of the houses, of which the residents are quite proud.

The residential zoning regulations limit the type of use of property in the different zones, the minimum lot size, location, height, and fencing materials. No house may be more than two stories. All must be set back forty feet from the property line in front and at least twelve feet on the other three sides.

Over the last ten years, Role 62 has furnished and decorated his/her house with taste and at some expense. When the house recently was repainted, it was done in white. Role 62's neighbors also have painted their houses white or in various pastel colors. Typically, a single color has been used, though some have painted the trim a complementary color.

New neighbors (Role 36 and spouse) have moved into the house on one side of Role 62's house. Role 36 is director of the Institute for Applied Gerontological Studies, and his/her spouse is a photographer. Role 62 has met and talked to Role 36 and spouse. They have been pleasant to know. Already, the adults have shared coffee, dessert, and conversation several times. Despite differences in their occupations, they share a love of classical music, which they never play loudly. Role 36 is an academic who often works at home.

Role 36's house has for some time needed to be painted. However, Role 36 and spouse, especially the spouse, did not care for the pale colors chosen by the other residents on the street. The colors they chose were lavender, with chartreuse trim. Their objective was to bring visual vitality to what seemed a drab neighborhood. The neighbors of Role 36, and especially Role 62, are distressed by this departure from the white or pastels chosen by the owners of other houses.

In University Park, a more extreme example of the choice of house color has raised eyebrows and blood pressure. Role 76 is a freelance artist who works entirely at home. The artist is single with a son, age twenty, and a daughter, age seventeen, both of whom are hardworking and have part-time jobs. The artist has painted five-inch diagonal stripes on all the sides of the house.

Role 61, the director of the Camelot Art Museum, also lives in University Park, several streets from Role 76, and sees nothing wrong with stripes on a house. However, no support has come from Role 14, an urban planning professor at CSU, and a member of the planning commission, who happens to live just a few houses from Role 76's house. Role 14 believes that although urban planning should accommodate various lifestyles, diagonal stripes on a house go beyond the acceptable. There is every reason to believe, says Role 14, that to permit such deviation from good taste will have a negative impact on the property values of all other houses in the area. And it will encourage vandalism and graffiti.

The artist (Role 76) was surprised by the objections, saying that they had come from Los Angeles and enjoyed the beauty and the variety of color choices made by residents there. Role 76 has suggested that the opposition should lighten up.

A third example has occurred in South Ridge. The attorney (Role 51) recently made some changes in his/her life. Not long ago, he/she met and then married a retired, and very successful, attorney who had moved to Camelot from San Francisco to be nearer his/her children. Role 51's new spouse, with the enthusiastic support of Role 51, wanted to bring a little of San Francisco to their new $500,000 home and painted it in what Californians call the Painted Lady Style.[17] A typical Painted Lady will have two or more colors in combination, invariably bold, but not garish. Bright blue, red, and gray perhaps; or orange and green; or purple or yellow. The combinations are almost limitless. *Stunning* is the appropriate word to describe a Painted Lady.

However, the South Ridge neighbors of Role 51 are not impressed. In fact, some are outraged, for all the other houses are painted white or in pastel colors, or are faced with brick veneer or white or shades of red. The Painted Lady, sitting on its large lot, has created a sensation in Camelot. Every Sunday a constant stream of viewers will drive by, some to approve, some to scoff. The other owners of $300,000 to $500,000 houses are distressed beyond words.

Roles 18, 26, 29, 33, 36, 49, 53, 54, 57, 58, 61, 62, and 75 will appear before the planning commission and state positions that seem appropriate to their role descriptions. Role 51 will appear before the planning commission to defend the choice of striking, even if a bit daring, house colors.

The task for the planning commission is to determine whether, and how, restrictions on color choice can be added to the zoning regulations. Planning might recommend:

1. A list of acceptable color choices for outside painting of houses.

2. A ban on any kind of decorative pattern.

---

17. Students may wish to examine *The Painted Ladies Revisited* by Elizabeth Pomoda and Michael Larsen (New York: E.P. Dutton, 1989) for illustrations of this style of house decoration.

3. The creation of a public commission that would have the power to approve or disapprove color choices and/or decorative schemes for all outside house painting.

4. A standardized set of color choices for all houses, without any exceptions.

ZONING APPEALS BOARD ISSUES

One or more of these issues will be presented either to the zoning appeals board or to the planning commission at the simulation session indicated by your instructor.

Although the function of zoning appeals (determining whether a variance from the provisions of the zoning code should be granted to an individual who claims that distinctive hardship otherwise would occur) must be performed in some way, the use of a zoning appeals board for that purpose is optional in the *Camelot* simulation. Your instructor may choose whether to have a ZAB or use the Planning Commission for that function. If the class is not large, and if the instructor wishes, a board of three persons, rather than five, may be appointed.

The Zoning Appeals Board may attach whatever conditions, restrictions, time limit, or other stipulation to a variance that it approves. Of course, such conditions cannot be unreasonable if they are to survive a court challenge.

Issue 1: The Carport Variance Request

Role 52, President of Camelot's chapter of the Business and Professional Women's Organization, lives in College Town in an older house that has a wooden, single-car garage located at the left-rear corner of the lot (as viewed from the street), used for storage of garden tools, lawn mowers, lumber, and miscellany. The doors of that garage are too narrow to accommodate a full-size auto today. The petitioner owns a sport utility vehicle that is too large to pass through the doors. Thus she wishes to install a carport alongside the house, using the existing driveway. However, the petitioner has found that a standard size carport for a single vehicle will require two corner posts that would encroach fourteen inches into the minimum side yard required under the zoning code. The other two corner posts would touch the side of the house. The carport will be open on the other three sides.

The petitioner requests a variance to allow the corner posts and the prefabricated canopy of a single-vehicle carport to intrude not more than sixteen inches into the required side yard.

Issue 2: The Art Sale from the R-2
Zone Home Variance Request

Role 76 is an artist whose studio is at home. So long as the artist sold pictures through a local gallery there was no problem, for artistic endeavor carried on at home is not a violation of the zoning code. But the gallery owner chose to retire, and no buyer could be found to continue the business. So the gallery closed.

The artist then began to sell from home. Finished works, particularly landscapes, hang on the walls of the house, along with a few canvases of non-representational, abstract impressions. The artist has obtained a twenty-inch-wide by twelve-inch-high brass plate for the front door identifying the artist by name and adding the word "Gallery," and small advertisements appear from time to time in the *Camelot Daily News*. Prospective customers may come to the house by appointment, but more recently the advertisements have identified regular hours for Friday afternoons and Saturdays.

Several neighbors are displeased because the home is in R-1 zoning, where commercial activity is not allowed. (These include Role 4, councilor; Role 43, junior high school teacher; Role 71, public health nurse.) They believe that having shoppers drive to the house in response to advertisements, or to the recommendations of past customers, violates Camelot's zoning code. They complained to the zoning administrator, citing the impact on street parking and the adverse implications for the neighborhood in the future if the language of the zoning code need not be honored by citizens nor enforced by the city.

The zoning administrator mailed a notice to the artist, citing the pertinent provisions of the code and indicating that the artist is asserted by complainants to be in violation of the code. The administrator's letter, as is routine in such cases, called attention to the procedures for requesting a zoning variance if the artist desires.

The artist requests a zoning variance to permit the display and sale of the artist's work from the home.

Issue 3: "The Sideyard or Backyard?"

Several years ago the petitioner (Role 47, President of Data Tech Corporation) purchased a large home at 6123 Marilyn Drive, in Forest Acres. The house is on an exceptionally large lot, for the previous owner was the developer of the subdivision and kept the largest lot for himself. By keeping one large lot rather than trying to figure out a way to get two lots out of the large corner area, the developer solved the problem of having adequate street frontage for the property. And the developer used the lot to advantage by building the home at a forty-five degree angle, thus permitting a view down each street (see Figure 11-3).

The petitioner applied to the zoning administrator for a building permit to construct a large addition at the house's west corner (left rear, if viewed from the street). The administrator has been reluctant to grant the permit because of the need to interpret the zoning code. The minimum requirement for a sideyard is eight feet on either side, and the minimum required rear yard is thirty feet. The west corner of the proposed addition will be only eighteen feet from the west lot line.

However, there is uncertainty. If the west lot line defines the sideyard, the set back from the lot line is adequate. But if the west lot line defines the rear yard, then the set back is inadequate by twelve feet. The Camelot City Charter,

FIGURE 11-3 The Sideyard or Backyard Issue Map

Article VI, Section 6.09, provides (among other matters) that the Zoning Appeals Board may "hear appeals from any action of the City Zoning Administrator." If the administrator denies the building permit, the owner can appeal. If the administrator grants the building permit, owners on Maple Drive could appeal.

The home owner at 6118 Maple Drive (Role 35), whose backyard abuts the west lot line of the petitioner, opposes issuance of such a building permit, asserting that it would violate the zoning code. There is fear that granting the permit would depreciate the value of the Maple Drive home, the family's major capital asset. Moreover, a neighbor has heard "third hand" that the addition may serve as living quarters for the parents of the owner. Because the area is zoned R-1 (single family), a remodeling that creates a second dwelling unit on petitioner's property would violate the spirit, and perhaps the letter, of the zoning code.

The zoning administrator has denied the building permit, and the applicant now is appealing the administrator's decision to the Zoning Appeals Board pursuant to Section 6.09 of the Camelot City Charter.

12

Reference Materials

The City of Camelot is the state capital of the state. It is also the county seat and the home of Camelot State University.

CAMELOT: BASIC DATA

Population

Of 160,000 citizens:

90,500 are white and not students.

39,000 are minority (African American, Asian, Hispanic, Native American) and not students

30,500 are students

Camelot has an unusually high percentage of middle-class minorities and whites. There is an absence of depressing slums and a greater than usual degree of integration of the races.

However, there are many commuting, low-skilled, minority employees hired by the service and manufacturing businesses. Housing in Camelot tends to cost more than some of these people believe they can afford.

Because of the large number of undergraduate and graduate students living off campus, plus many young, and often childless, faculty members, apartment housing is widely used. However, there is much single-family housing, and some new housing developments are being built in neighboring and more distant suburban areas where less-expensive open land is available. There is a noticeable trend in Camelot to tear down older homes and replace them with apartments. Several luxury condominiums have been and are being built.

Although the presence of the university gives a strong middle- and upper-middle-class thrust to the employment market, as with any city this size, some portion of the population will be at the margins of employment possibility and mental competence. Every university community attracts numbers of hangers-on, some former students, some attracted by the variety of lifestyles to be found in such an area. Although there is no unusual source of poverty, there are some individuals who fall into the poverty range, some elderly, some physically or mentally infirm, some unemployable, some unemployed because of a closing within Camelot's small but old industrial base—the Camelot Steel Wheel Foundry.

Economics in Camelot

The major employer in Camelot is the university. It has a reputation for excellence, both in graduate and undergraduate programs. It has a policy of selective admissions with large, prestigious professional schools and many out-of-state and foreign students.

Quite a number of small- and medium-size high-tech industries have been developed in the last ten years as a result of the advanced research orientation of the science, medical, and engineering faculty of Camelot State University. This has been a rapidly expanding segment of the economic base of Camelot. The past decade also has witnessed the substantial growth of banking, insurance, and other service businesses. One national fast food chain began in Camelot and has its headquarters here.

Camelot is at a crucial point in its existence. The downtown area is slowly but surely becoming run down and dirty. Suburban developments and the Camelot Mall on the outskirts of the city have taken over the downtown's functions, the future of which will in large part be decided in the coming months through decisions of the Camelot City Council.

CAMELOT: AREA DESCRIPTIONS

Camelot Heights

This area of Camelot was built up after World War II. It is located east of Robert Street in the northeast corner of Camelot and is zoned R-2. The subdivision is basically working class to middle class. The homes vary in age from twenty to forty years and are modest three-bedroom homes priced 20 to 25 percent below the price of the average three-bedroom homes in the newer subdivisions of Camelot. The homes in the northeast corner of this subdivision are slightly newer and more expensive but are not priced as high as homes in the northwest corner.

The Central Business District (CBD)

The CBD is bounded by Woodworth Road on the north and Robert Street on the west. The east boundary of the CBD abuts Madisonville and Government Square. At the southwest corner is a finger of land that extends to the Russo River and has Robert Street to the west and Pioneer Park to the east (see The Downtown Hotel Plaza Issue map, p. 107). Except for this finger, the southern border of the CBD faces Pioneer Park and Government Square.

As you move north from Government Square, there are numerous banks and financial service offices, and then retail stores and restaurants, many of which occupy older structures. This area is zoned C-3.

College Town

The area east of the university is zoned R-4, and although there are some houses that rent to students, especially adjacent to the campus, this area is inhabited primarily by professors, clerical and professional workers connected with the university, and some government employees who commute to Government Square. The area includes many retired people. The streets are lined with trees, and the houses are fairly old but for the most part are well preserved and attractive. In some sections of College Town older houses are being renovated and extensively modernized; in other cases old houses are being replaced by architect-designed, modern homes. College Town is not the elite section of Camelot, but it is stylish and popular with younger individuals and couples. It is racially integrated.

Crown Knolls

The area north of Woodworth Road all the way to Patricia Road and west of Robert Street (and including the land west of the interstate highway) is known as Crown Knolls. In the portion immediately north of Woodworth Road, there are many old homes occupied mainly by lower-middle-class and low-income minorities and some low-income whites. In many cases, the homes are run down and dilapidated, in urgent need of repair. There are also many old garages and much refuse cluttering up the lots and alleys. This section is zoned R-4. The northern portion of this bottom third of Crown Knolls contains working-class homes of similar small frame bungalow style—the post–World War II type of home. With some exceptions, most are well kept. These homes are not derelict, but do need some repairs.

The next portion to the north, still to the west side of Robert Street, underwent urban renewal in the 1960s, and it now contains middle-class apartments and condominiums, as well as several fashionable townhouses. It has been zoned R-3.

The most northern third of Crown Knolls, just south of Patricia Road, has a higher proportion of middle-class residents, mainly white-collar workers. Lots here are of modest size, but the houses are neat and the streets tree lined. It is zoned R-2.

Forest Acres

Forest Acres, located west of Robert Street and north of Patricia Road, is zoned R-1 and is rather hilly terrain—hence its later development. This is a wealthy area, where the upper-middle class of Camelot live. The homes are big and expensive; they vary in age but are distinctive in architecture and landscaping. The lots tend to be large.

Madisonville

The area south of Woodworth Road and east of Government Square is a stable, older community. There are several small office buildings and retail stores, such as drugstores, barber/beauty salons, and newsstands, but the area is predominantly residential; zoning is R-4. This is an integrated, middle-class area. There are many small apartment buildings of four to six apartments, and the farther you are from the CBD, the more single-family homes there are, intermixed with small apartments. It is zoned R-3. The streets are lined with shade trees and are rather old but pleasant.

North Madisonville

This area of Camelot is north of Madisonville, with Woodworth Road as the dividing line. Its western boundary is Robert Street. Its characteristics are very similar to Madisonville. Almost all of it is zoned R-3. The only exception is the southwest corner just to the north of the CBD, which is zoned R-4. In the western part of North Madisonville, along the railroad tracks, there are some old multiple-family houses and small, older apartments occupied by low-income residents, many of whom feel threatened by the possibility that they will be evicted from their homes after the absentee landlords sell out to land speculators. This small neighborhood is disliked by its neighbors; the area has a bad reputation (middle-class residents tend to avoid the area at night). The remainder of North Madisonville is mostly white working class, becoming mostly white middle class as one goes north.

River Town

This entire area is zoned M-1. It used to be the traditional manufacturing and industrial area of Camelot. Some sections of it near the interstate highway have been cleared of the old structures, and those areas have been opened up for an industrial park. High-tech industries have been given incentives (tax abatements, cleared land, access streets) to locate here. Some have, although many have located outside the city limits. Other new businesses are light manufacturing, a truck terminal, and a regional warehouse for a large grocery chain. There continues to be a severe parking shortage in most of this area, although the program of razing old factories is easing this problem on some streets. The Camelot Steel Wheel foundry stands empty, a silent monument to the smokestack era.

University Park

Camelot State University is located with University Park to its west and south and College Town to its east. The majority of the residents of University Park, especially the first several blocks to the west of the university, are either students or are connected in some way with the university. All of University Park is zoned R-5. The area contains many apartments and rooming houses; the homes closest to the university are old and run down. As you move farther west, the buildings become newer; those farthest away from the campus (west of the interstate) are single-family ranch houses, many of which are owned by professors or administrators.

A large portion of the southwest corner of the city is undeveloped land.

Camelot Acres

This is a new subdivision, as is South Ridge. Camelot Acres is located immediately south of University Park subdivision, and west of Robert Street, which provides the means of access. Lancelot Creek's ravine separates Camelot Acres from the more expensive South Ridge subdivision. Camelot Acres is the site of moderately priced homes, ranging in price from $140,000 to $225,000. Although these are all very nice homes, the lots are not large and are modestly landscaped. About seventy-five homes have been built in this area, with space remaining for perhaps twenty-five to thirty more.

South Ridge

One of the newest subdivisions, it is situated west of Robert Street and south of the Camelot Acres subdivision. Lancelot Creek's ravine separates the two subdivisions. Access is available from Robert Street. The homes are upscale, ranging in price from a few at $500,000 to the upper end of the scale at one million or more. There are twenty-five homes already built, three more are under construction, and ten are in the planning stage.

The homes thus far range from 3,000 or 3,500 square feet up to 6,000 square feet. The typical home includes four bedrooms, a great room, a study, four bathrooms, and a fitness room. The usual public rooms may include an atrium. The rooms are spacious. The largest lot is only an acre in size, but all the homes are beautifully landscaped. The streets are cobblestone with European-style lamps.

The price range estimate is considered by a developer to be reasonably accurate for homes built in much of the United States, but for parts of the Southwest, the West Coast, and the Eastern corridor from Virginia to Maine the prices would be higher.

THE CHARTER

The City Charter (pp. 160–166) is the basic organizing document of the city. It establishes the city government in much the same way that a state constitution establishes the state government by providing for organization, powers, and duties.

You may find more details in the Charter than you use. Our purpose is to show you what a typical charter looks like, and what you read is based on a real charter. Thus, the "Powers of the Council" Section (2.11) lists all the powers a typical council might have, even though the Camelot council will not need to use all of them in this simulation.

In the simulation, as in life, knowledge of the Charter will be unevenly distributed among the citizenry. Those who wish to put it to use will become familiar with it.

THE CHARTER OF THE CITY OF CAMELOT

PREAMBLE

We, the people of the City of Camelot, in order to secure for ourselves the benefits of local self-government under the Constitution of this State, do ordain and establish this Charter for the government of the municipality of Camelot.

ARTICLE I

Incorporation, Form of Government, Powers
Section 1.02 Powers. Except as prohibited by the Constitution of this State or restricted by this Charter, the City of Camelot shall have and may exercise all municipal powers, functions, rights, privileges, and immunities of every name and nature whatsoever. The enumeration of particular powers in this Charter shall not be deemed to be exclusive, and in addition to the powers enumerated herein or implied hereby or appropriate to the exercise of such powers, it is intended that the City shall have and may exercise all powers which, under the Constitution of this State or under the laws of this State, it would be competent for this Charter specifically to enumerate.

Section 1.03 Manner of Exercising Powers. All powers of the corporation shall be vested in an elective Council which shall enact local ordinances and resolutions, adopt budgets, determine general policies, and appoint a City Manager, who shall see that the policies and legislation adopted by the Council are enforced. All powers of the corporation shall be exercised in the manner prescribed by this Charter, or if the manner be not prescribed, then in such manner as may be prescribed by ordinance or by general law.

Section 1.04 Form of Government. The form of government provided under this Charter shall be known as the "Council-Manager Plan."

ARTICLE II

The Council
Section 2.01 Number, Selection, Term. The City Council shall consist of five members,[1] elected at large, for four-year overlapping terms. All elections of Council members shall be on a nonpartisan ballot.

Section 2.02 Qualifications. Any qualified elector shall be eligible to serve as a member of Council, when elected as hereinafter provided. No member of Council shall hold any other public office. A councilor who ceases to be a qualified elector, or who accepts and enters upon the performance of the duties of an incompatible office, or who is absent, without excuse by the other members of Council, from meetings of Council during two consecutive meetings, shall automatically vacate the office on the Council.

Section 2.03 Vacancies, Filling of. Vacancies in the office of Council members shall be filled at the next simulation session by vote of a majority of the remaining members of Council, by the selection of a qualified elector. If Council fails to make this selection at the next simulation session, the Mayor shall make the appointment. Such person so chosen shall serve until the next regular municipal election. At such election a successor shall be elected to serve for the unexpired term, if any; if not, for a full term.

Section 2.06 Organization and Meetings. Following each municipal election Council shall meet for the purpose of organizing. At such meeting the newly elected members of Council shall take the oath of office and the Council shall proceed to elect a Mayor and a Vice Mayor and may transact such other business as may come before it. Thereafter, regular meetings shall be held as prescribed in the Council rules. All meetings of Council shall be open to the public. A majority of the members elected shall constitute a quorum at all meetings.

Section 2.07 Mayor and Vice Mayor. The Council shall select from among its own members one to serve as Mayor and one as Vice Mayor. The Mayor shall preside at Council meetings, when present, and shall have a vote on all matters which come before Council, but shall have no power to veto. He or she shall be the ceremonial head of the municipality, but shall exercise no administrative authority. The Vice Mayor shall preside over the meetings of the Council when the Mayor is absent and shall perform such other duties as may be assigned him or her by ordinance.

Section 2.09 Clerk of Council. There shall be a Clerk of Council, elected by vote of a majority of the members of the Council from outside its membership, to serve until a successor is chosen and enters upon the duties of the clerk's office. The Clerk may be appointed to serve full time or part time, and the Council may assign the duties of the Clerk of Council to any employee of the municipality as an additional duty. The Clerk shall give notice of Council meetings, keep the journal, advertise public hearings, record in separate books all ordinances and resolutions enacted by Council, and have the same published in the manner provided by this Charter. The Clerk shall perform such other duties as may be assigned by this Charter or by ordinance.

Section 2.11 Powers of the Council. Among other powers the Council shall have authority to:

Adopt ordinances and resolutions on any subject within the scope of its powers, and to provide penalties for the violation thereof.

Establish the internal organization, staffing and compensation of the departments, boards, and commissions created by this Charter; set up such additional departments, boards, or commissions as it may deem necessary and determine their powers and duties.

Adopt and modify the master plan and official map of the municipality.

---

1. May be enlarged to seven or more members by instructor.

Regulate the use of private real estate in the municipality by establishing zones, limiting the uses in each zone, and limiting the height of buildings and the intensity of land use.

Adopt a subdivision platting ordinance and approve subdivision plats which conform thereto.

Enact a comprehensive building code.

Authorize the levy of taxes and the issuance of bonds as provided in this Charter.

Adopt an annual appropriation ordinance based upon the annual budget.

Appoint and remove the City Manager, establish his or her salary, and appoint an Acting City Manager when necessary.

Inquire into the conduct of any municipal officer or employee in the performance of his or her public functions.

Make investigations of any office, department, or agency of the municipality.

Grant public utility franchises by vote of two-thirds (2/3) of the members of Council.

Provide for the employment of engineering and other professional services on a consulting basis when deemed necessary.

Issue subpoenas for witnesses and to require the production of books and papers which may be necessary in the conduct of any hearing or investigation.

ARTICLE III

Ordinances and Resolutions

Section 3.01 Action of Council. The action of Council shall be by ordinance or resolution. On all matters of a general or permanent nature, or granting a franchise, or levying a tax, or appropriating money, or contracting an indebtedness, or issuing bonds or notes, or for the purchase, lease, or transfer of property, action shall be taken formally, by ordinance in the manner hereinafter provided. Action on all other matters of a temporary or informal nature may be taken by resolution.

Section 3.02 Enactment of Ordinances. Each proposed ordinance shall be introduced in writing by a member of the Council, and in addition to the title shall contain an opening clause reading as follows, "Be it ordained by the Council of the City of Camelot." The action proposed to be taken shall be fully and clearly set forth in the body of the ordinance. Each ordinance shall contain one subject only, which shall be stated clearly in the title. No ordinance shall be passed without the concurrence of a majority of all members elected to Council, except that emergency ordinances, as hereinafter provided, shall require concurrence of three-fourths (3/4) of all the members elected to Council for passage. Final passage of all ordinances and resolutions shall be certified by the Mayor or Vice Mayor and the Clerk of Council.

Section 3.03 Effective Date. Ordinances providing for appropriations for current expenses of the municipality, or for raising revenue, or ordinances wherein an emergency is declared to exist, shall become effective immediately upon passage or at such later date as may be provided therein, and such ordinances shall not be subject to referendum. All other ordinances shall take effect thirty minutes after passage. An emergency ordinance as referred to herein is one which must be passed and made effective at once or in less than thirty minutes to meet an emergency in the operation of the city government, or which is necessary for the immediate preservation of the public peace, health, safety, morals, or welfare. Each emergency ordinance must contain therein a separate section setting forth the reason for the emergency. No ordinance granting a franchise or fixing a rate to be charged by a public utility shall be passed as an emergency measure.

ARTICLE IV

City Manager

Section 4.01 Appointment of Manager. The Council shall appoint, by majority vote of all members elected thereto, an officer of the City who shall have the title of Manager. The Manager shall be chosen solely on the basis of executive and administrative qualifications, as judged by the adequacy of training and experience. At the time of appointment the Manager need not be a resident of the City or State, but during tenure of office shall reside in the municipality. No Council member shall be eligible for appointment as Manager during the term for which that councilor has been elected.

Section 4.02 Manager's Duties. The City Manager shall be the chief executive and administrative officer of the municipality; shall be responsible to the Council for proper administration of all affairs of the municipality, and to that end, subject to the provisions of this Charter, shall have authority and shall be required to:

1. See that this Charter and the ordinances and resolutions of the City are faithfully observed and enforced.

2. Appoint and remove all officers and employees of the City except those selected or appointed by Council, or as otherwise provided in this Charter.

3. Prepare the tax budget and annual budget, submit them to Council for approval, and administer the appropriations made by Council.

4. Prepare and submit weekly reports to the Council. Prepare and submit to the Council and the public annually a complete report on the finances and administrative activities of the municipality for the preceding year. Such annual report shall be published and distributed in the manner provided by ordinance.

5. Formulate and arrange contracts, franchises, and agreements subject to the approval of Council. Sign all contracts, bonds, and notes on behalf of the City.

6. Attend meetings of Council, and shall have the right to take part in the discussion of all matters coming before Council, but shall have no vote.

7. Serve as an ex officio member (without vote) of all boards and commissions authorized under this Charter, except the Civil Service Commission.

8. Delegate to subordinate officers and employees of the municipality any duties conferred by this Charter or by action of Council, and hold them responsible for the faithful discharge of such duties.

9. Perform such other duties, not inconsistent with this Charter, as may be required by the Council.

Section 4.04 Removal of the Manager. The City Manager shall serve for an indefinite term, subject to removal by the Council at any time by a majority vote of all members elected thereto. The Council shall adopt a resolution stating the reasons for the removal. The Manager may reply in writing and may request a public hearing. After such public hearing, if one is requested, and after full consideration, the Council may adopt a final resolution of removal.

ARTICLE V

Taxation and Borrowing
Section 5.02 Submission of Extra Levy to Vote.
The Council may at any time declare by resolution, adopted by a vote of two-thirds (2/3) of all the members thereof, that the amount of taxes which may be raised within the limitations of this Charter will be insufficient to provide an adequate amount for the necessary requirements of the City for current operating expenses, and other expenses payable from the general fund of the City, and such permanent improvements and equipment as shall have an estimated useful life of five (5) years or more, and that it is necessary to levy taxes in excess of such limitation, in addition to the levies authorized and limited by this Charter, for the municipal purpose or purposes specified in such resolution. Such resolution shall specify the additional rate which it is necessary to levy, the purpose or purposes thereof, the number of years during which such rate shall be in effect and the date of the proposed election thereon. Such resolution shall be effective upon its adoption and shall be certified thereafter to the election authorities, who shall place such question upon the ballot at the next succeeding simulation session. If a majority of the electors of the municipal corporation voting thereon vote for the approval of such additional levy, the Council shall, for a period not in excess of that prescribed in such resolution, make such levy, or such part thereof as it finds necessary, pursuant to such approval and certify the same to the County Auditor, to be placed on the tax list and collected as other taxes.

ARTICLE VI

Boards and Commissions

Section 6.06 Planning Commission. There shall be a City Planning Commission consisting of five[2] members appointed by Council from among the qualified electors of the City.

Section 6.07 Powers and Duties. The Planning Commission may act as the Platting Commission of the municipality. As such, it shall provide for planning, zoning, and regulations covering platting of all lands which are subject to control by the municipality, and shall cause an official map of such territories to be made. The Commission shall carry out the municipal planning function including the preparation of a master plan, and make such investigations, reports, and recommendations relating to planning and the physical development of the City as it finds necessary and desirable.

Section 6.08 Zoning Appeals. The Planning Commission shall hear and decide all requests for a zoning variance unless Council shall have exercised its authority under Section 6.09 of this Charter by establishing a ZONING APPEALS BOARD and appointing members thereto.

Section 6.09 Zoning Appeals Board. The Council may, at its discretion and by ordinance, establish a ZONING APPEALS BOARD, consisting of five persons appointed by Council from among the qualified electors of the City, to hear appeals from any action of the City Zoning Administrator and to hear requests by property owners for Variances from the Zoning Code of the City of Camelot in cases where the application of the Code has caused, or would cause, hardship to the petitioning property owner.

Economic hardship to the petitioner is not a sufficient basis for granting a variance.

Section 6.10 Zoning Variance Hearings. No Zoning Variance shall be granted on the basis of economic hardship alleged by the petitioner. Other reasonable criteria may be applied according to the best judgment of the hearing body.

No hearing on a request for a zoning variance shall be held prior to thirty (30) days after the mailing, to every owner of property adjacent to the property that is the subject of the variance request, of a notice (1) stating that a variance request has been filed, (2) providing an accurate summary of the contents of that request, and (3) stating the date, time, and location of a hearing on the requested variance. For the further benefit of interested persons, the Zoning Administrator shall cause a sign to be placed on the petitioned property, for thirty (30) days preceding the hearing, stating that a hearing is pending and specifying the date, time, and location of the hearing.

Section 6.12 Manager—an Ex Officio Member. The City Manager, or an official so designated by the City Manager, shall be an ex officio member without vote of all boards and commissions created by or under authority of this Charter, except the Civil Service Commission.

ARTICLE VII

Initiative, Referendum, and Recall

Section 7.01 Initiative. Ordinances and other measures providing for the exercise of any powers of government may be proposed by initiative petition. Such initiation must contain the signatures of not less than ten (10) percent of the number of electors of Camelot. The petition must be filed with the Clerk of Council (or your instructor, if you have no Clerk) no later than the close of the simulation session preceding the date set for the general election. The Clerk must certify that there are a sufficient number of valid signatures, and then submit the proposed ordinance or measure for approval or rejection of a majority of the electors of the municipal corporation voting on this issue at a special election to be held at the next succeeding simulation session.

Section 7.02 Referendum. Any ordinance or other measure passed by Council shall be subject to referendum, except as provided by Section 3.03. No ordinance shall go into effect until the simulation

---

2. Your simulation may have more members, at the discretion of your instructor.

session immediately following its passage by Council, except as provided by Section 3.03. A referendum petition must contain the signatures of not less than ten (10) percent of the number of electors of Camelot. The petition must be filed with the Clerk of Council (or your instructor, if you have no Clerk) no later than the close of the first complete simulation session immediately following the passage of said ordinance or other measure. The Clerk must certify that there are a sufficient number of valid signatures, and then submit the ordinance or other measure referred to in the referendum petition for approval or rejection by a majority of those voting on this issue at a special election to be held in the simulation session immediately following the passage of said ordinance or other measure.

Section 7.03 Recall. Any elective officer of Camelot may be removed from office by the qualified voters of the city. The procedure to effect such removal shall be:

1. A petition signed by qualified electors equal in number to at least fifteen (15) percent of the number of electors in Camelot, and demanding the election of a successor to the person sought to be removed, shall be filed with the Clerk of Council (or your instructor if you have no Clerk). Such petition shall contain a general statement of not more than 200 words of the grounds upon which the removal of such person is sought.

2. If the person whose removal is sought does not resign by the end of the simulation session in which the petition is certified by the Clerk as containing a sufficient number of valid signatures, the Council will instruct the Clerk of Council to prepare a ballot to be submitted to the electors at the next simulation session to determine the question of removal, and for the selection of a successor to each officer named in said petition.

3. The nomination of candidates to succeed each officer sought to be removed shall be made by filing a petition proposing a person for each such office, signed by electors equal in number to ten (10) percent of the electors of Camelot.

4. The ballots at such recall election shall, with respect to each person whose removal is sought, submit the question:

"Shall (name of person) be removed from the office of (name of office) by recall?" Immediately following such question there shall be printed on the ballots these two propositions in the order set forth: "For the recall of (name of person)."

   "Against the recall of (name of person)." Under each of such questions shall be placed the names of candidates to fill the vacancy. The name of the officer whose removal is sought shall not appear on the ballot as a candidate to succeed him/herself.

5. In any such election, if a majority of the votes cast on the question of removal are affirmative, the person whose removal is sought shall be removed from office upon the announcement of the official canvass of that election, and the candidate receiving the plurality of the votes cast for candidates for that office shall be declared elected. The successor of any person so removed shall hold office during the unexpired term of his or her predecessor.

ARTICLE VIII

General Provisions

Section 8.01 Oath of Office. Every officer and employee of the City shall, before entering upon his duties, take and subscribe to the following oath or affirmation which shall be filed and kept in the office of the Clerk of Council:

   "I solemnly swear (or affirm) that I will support the Constitution of the United States and of this State and will obey the laws thereof and that I will, in all respects, uphold and enforce the provisions of the Charter and Ordinances of this City, and will faithfully discharge the duties of which I am about to enter."

Section 8.03 Personal Interest. No member of the Council or any officer or employee of the City shall have any financial interest, direct or indirect, in any contract with or sale to the City of any materials, supplies, or services, or any land or interest in land. A person who knowingly and willfully violates this section shall be guilty of malfeasance in office and, upon conviction thereof, shall be removed from office. Any contract or agreement made in violation of this section shall be voidable at the election of the Council.

Section 8.05 Amendments to the Charter. Any section of this Charter may be amended by submission of proposed amendments to the electors of the municipality. Such amendments may be initiated either by two-thirds (2/3) vote of the Council or by petition to the Council of ten (10) percent of the electors of Camelot.

ZONING REGULATIONS AND LAND USE

An important tool for influencing the ways in which land is used in the different sectors of a city is the city's zoning code. The zoning code describes the various uses to which land in a particular sector, or *zone,* may be put. Uses that are omitted from the description of a particular zone are, by implication, prohibited in that zone. In addition, the zoning code at times may explicitly prohibit a particular land use in a particular zone. Along with the types of use permitted, the zoning code often will specify minimum dimensions for lots, structures, yards, and parking spaces.

The Camelot zoning code, which follows, is sketched rather than fleshed out, but it is sufficient to give you a good understanding of how such a code operates. In particular, you will notice that the zones are "nested" to a substantial degree. That is, R–1 (a residential zone) is the most restrictive. R–2 zone includes all the permissions of R–1 plus some additional permissions (sometimes these permissions allow smaller lot sizes). An R–3 zone includes all the permissions of R–2 plus still more permissions. And so it goes. When you get to commercial zones, the nesting is apparent to some degree but is less pronounced.

A zoning map is an integral part of the zoning process; the code would be worthless without a map to indicate where the zones are located. A concern for printing simplicity led to the development of a Camelot zoning map that omits any designation of C–1 or C–2 areas. The issues work quite satisfactorily without this added complexity, and we believe that you will find sufficient challenge in comprehending the various residential zones.

Zoning codes are not retroactive. A use that becomes "nonconforming" through adoption or amendment of a code may be continued, the language of the code notwithstanding. Often, however, the structure housing the nonconforming use cannot be enlarged or replaced. An example of this occurs in the "Topless Bar and Grill Issue." Once discontinued, a nonconforming use cannot be reinstated.

CAMELOT: ZONING REGULATIONS[3]

No land or structure shall be used and no structure shall be erected within the City of Camelot except in conformity to the following requirements and limitations:

R-1 RESIDENTIAL ZONE:
PERMITTED USES

Single-family residence.

$2\frac{1}{2}$ story height limit or 35 feet.

Lot size—minimum 30-foot yard in front and back; side yards—minimum of 20 feet total; not less than 8 feet on either side.

Minimum lot area of 12,000 square feet.

Minimum lot width of 90 feet.

Special uses (permit required).

Park, playground, community building (public).

Public school.

Church or temple.

Structures used for charitable purposes.

R-2 RESIDENTIAL ZONE:
PERMITTED USES

Single-family residence.

Any of R-1 uses.

$2\frac{1}{2}$ story height limit or 35 feet.

Front and back yard restrictions same as R-1; side yards—minimum total of 15 feet; not less than 6 feet on either side.

Minimum lot area of 7,500 square feet.

Minimum width of 70 feet.

Special uses (permit required).

Any of R-1 Special Uses.

R-3 RESIDENTIAL ZONE:
PERMITTED USES

Any of R-2 uses.

Two-family dwelling.

A multiple-family dwelling that is designed for or occupied exclusively by not more than six dwelling units.

$2\frac{1}{2}$ story height limit or 35 feet.

Front and back yards of no less than 30 feet each; side yards not less than 10 feet on each side.

Minimum lot area of 8,000 square feet for single family dwelling.

Minimum lot area of 9,000 square feet for two-family dwelling.

Minimum lot area of 12,000 square feet for multiple-unit dwelling or 3,000 square feet per dwelling unit, whichever is greater.

Minimum width of lots—65 feet for single dwellings, 75 feet for two-family dwelling, 90 feet for multiple-unit dwelling.

Special uses (permit required).

Any of R-1 Special Uses.

R-4 RESIDENTIAL ZONE:
PERMITTED USES

Any use permitted in R-3.

$2\frac{1}{2}$ story height limit or 35 feet.

Lot size—minimum 25-foot yards in front and back; side yards—minimum total of 15 feet; not less than 6 feet on either side.

Minimum lot area for single-family dwelling 5,000 square feet.

---

3. The Zoning Code, while somewhat simplified, closely parallels many zoning codes now in use. The simplification is most apparent in the commercial zones, where illustrative uses have been identified but where there has been no effort made to list the full range of possible commercial uses.

Minimum lot area for two-family dwelling 7,000 square feet.

Minimum lot area for three- or four-family dwelling, 2,500 square feet per dwelling unit.

Minimum lot width of 60 feet.

Special uses (permit required).

Hospital, clinic, nursing home, club, lodging, or boardinghouse.

Multiple-family dwellings having not more than 100 dwelling units and not more than 10 stories in height. Any such dwelling shall be equipped with an elevator if more than 2 stories in height and with not fewer than two elevators if more than 3 stories in height and containing more than 20 dwelling units.

R-5 UNIVERSITY DISTRICT: PERMITTED USES

Any use permitted in R-4.

Dormitory, sorority, fraternity.

Professional office building, drugstore, barber and/or beauty shop, restaurant, food and/or beverage store, bookstore, apparel store, bank.

Minimum lot area and width and minimum yard sizes are the same as in R-4.

Minimum lot area for sorority, fraternity, or dormitory is 15,000 square feet.

Special uses (permit required).

Any Special Use permitted in R-4.

C-1 LIMITED COMMERCIAL: PERMITTED USES

Uses permitted: bank; art, gift, or jewelry store; offices; drugstores; automotive repairs; apparel stores; food stores; hardware, appliance, and music stores; restaurants; optical services; theaters; barber shops and beauty salons. [Authors' note: this list is illustrative, not exhaustive. Certain uses will be added to this list in C-2.]

Any use permitted in R-4.

Special uses (permit required).

Gasoline service station.

Motel, hotel.

Drive-up window for sales or service (e.g., banks, food).

Any Special Use permitted in R-4, except that no structure may exceed four stories in height.

C-2 GENERAL COMMERCIAL: PERMITTED USES

Any use permitted in C-1.

Warehouses.

Automobile sales.

Bowling alleys.

Gasoline service station.

Motel, hotel.

Any use permitted in R-5 except sorority house, fraternity house, or dormitory.

Height limited to six story maximum.

Area regulations are the same as in R-5.

Special uses (permit required).

Drive-up window for sales or service (e.g., banks, food).

Any Special Use permitted in R-4.

C-3 BUSINESS DISTRICT-GENERAL: PERMITTED USES

Any commercial use permitted in C-1 or C-2, except the following Special Uses.

Any residential use permitted in C-2.

Height limited to 15 story maximum.

Special uses (permit required).

Gasoline service stations. Drive-up window for sales or service.

M-1 INDUSTRIAL DISTRICT

A building or premises may be used for any purpose except as listed.

Residential uses are not permitted; however, existing residences in place may be repaired and structurally altered, and enlarged where such enlargement is made within ten (10) years after passage of this Zoning Code and does not constitute more than a ten (10) percent increase in the cubical contents of the building existing at the time of the passage of this Zoning Code.

Any use, change of use, or additional use of land or the structures thereon must be authorized by a Special Use Permit.

SPECIAL USE PERMIT

Where so authorized in this Code, a Special Use Permit may be granted for one or more of the special uses permitted in that section of the Code. A Special Use Permit is obtained by application to the Camelot Planning Commission. If the application is approved by a majority of the members of the Commission, the permit becomes effective in thirty (30) days unless rejected by a majority of the members of the Camelot City Council. The Planning Commission may impose, as conditions of the permit, minimum lot size requirements, minimum yard requirements, and/or minimum parking space requirements.

ZONING VARIANCE

A zoning variance (i.e., permission to deviate in some specified way from the terms of the zoning code) may be issued by the Zoning Appeals Board (ZAB), at its discretion, in response to a petition asserting a case of individual hardship. That hardship, according to the Camelot Charter, shall not be economic in character. See the Camelot City Charter, Article VI, "Boards and Commissions," for pertinent information. If the simulation does not have a ZAB, the instructor may designate the Planning Commission to act in that capacity under the terms of the charter. Decisions of the ZAB are final, provided that due process of law has been accorded.

DEFINITIONS:

Dwelling unit—a "dwelling unit" is space within a dwelling, comprising living, dining, sleeping room or rooms, storage closets, kitchen area with sink and hot and cold running water, and full bath containing a bathtub or a stall shower, toilet stool, and lavatory sink, all used by only one family.

Family—a "family" is either an individual; two or more persons who live together in one dwelling unit and maintain a common household, related by blood, marriage, or adoption; or not more than four persons unrelated by blood, marriage, or adoption.

THE "SUNSHINE LAW"

All local government councils, boards, and commissions, whether elected or appointed, must conform to the state's "sunshine law," which stipulates that all meetings of such public bodies must be:

1. Open to the public.
2. Announced by public notice at least twenty-four hours in advance of the meeting, which notice shall specify the date, time, and location of the meeting.

A meeting is defined as any occasion on which 50 percent or more of a public body's members are present for the purpose of discussing topics of potential concern to that body.

Executive sessions (closed to the public) may be held only for the following purposes:

a. Discussion of pending litigation.

b. Discussion of personnel matters.

c. Discussion of land acquisition.

The penalty for violation of this section may include removal from office.

13

Elections

ELECTION PROCEDURES—CITY OF CAMELOT

There will be an election on the sixth (or eighth) session[1] of the simulation. On the fourth or fifth day of the simulation the instructor will inform you about two questions: First, which are the seats to be filled; whose term of office is expiring? Second, if you are a candidate, will you be running for a designated seat (and running against one or more other persons who have filed their candidate petitions for that same seat), or will you be running in a popularity contest in which the vacant seats are filled by ranking all candidates according to number of votes received, then counting down from the top of the list until each vacant seat has been filled? Any duly qualified elector of the city of Camelot may run for a seat on council. Nominations are made by depositing with the city clerk a nominating petition containing the signatures of eight duly qualified electors of the city. (For a margin of safety, in case a signature or two should be challenged, most candidates try to have a few more signatures.)

---

1. If your class period is sixty minutes or less in length, your instructor may schedule the election for the eighth session of the simulation rather than the sixth, as just described. However, you should confirm the date with your instructor to be certain.

City of Camelot

Sample Nominating Petition
[Use tear-out located on pages 195–196.]
The undersigned, duly qualified and registered voters of the City of Camelot, hereby nominate
_____ for the office of council member, City of Camelot, seat number
_____. (Ask your instructor whether seat numbers are to be used.)

NAME	ADDRESS	DATE
1. _____	_____	_____
2. _____	_____	_____
3. _____	_____	_____
4. _____	_____	_____
5. _____	_____	_____
6. _____	_____	_____
7. _____	_____	_____
8. _____	_____	_____
9. _____	_____	_____
10. _____	_____	_____

Attestation by Petition Circulator
I hereby affirm, subject to the penalties for perjury, that the above signatures were recorded in my presence and that the names and addresses are accurate to the best of my knowledge.
Date: _____   Name _____
                                             (Signed)
             Address _____
This document was received at _____ o'clock _____ m. _____

                                    _____
                                    Clerk,* City of Camelot

Petitions must be filed with the City Clerk (*your instructor, if there is no clerk), City of Camelot, not later than 5:00 p.m. of the last simulation session preceding the election.

The sample nominating petition form is printed above. Be sure to note the deadline for submission. If your instructor has chosen the "designated seat" method of election, be sure that your nominating petition (or any such petition you sign) designates the seat that is being sought. A tear-out form is on page 196.

Elections are at large. In other words, all citizens of Camelot are eligible to vote for each contested seat, and each councilor represents the entire citizenry.

On election day, the Camelot League of Women Voters will sponsor a candidates' meeting, open to the public, to which all candidates will be invited for

---

Sample Ballot, to Be Prepared by Clerk: Designated Seats

Ballot

For the Camelot City Council, four-year term beginning immediately after announcement of election results:

Seat Number 2 (Vote for one)

_____ Charles Sullivan

_____ Louise Vance

_____ Philip Russo

Seat Number 4 (Vote for one)

_____ Katherine Hartman

_____ Alan Engel

Seat Number 5 (Vote for one)

_____ Janice Calder

_____ Peter Franconi

_____ Dora Garcia

_____ Clyde Brown

Sample Ballot, to Be Prepared by Clerk: The [insert number] Highest Votegetters Will Be Declared Winners

Ballot

For the Camelot City Council, four-year term beginning immediately after announcement of election results:

(Vote for not more than three)

_____ Clyde Brown

_____ Janice Calder

_____ Alan Engel

_____ Peter Franconi

_____ Dora Garcia

_____ Katherine Hartman

_____ Philip Russo

_____ Charles Sullivan

_____ Louise Vance

---

the purpose of brief (up to five minutes) statements of their qualifications and their objectives if elected. The meeting will be held in the council chamber. A representative of the League of Women Voters will chair the meeting.

14

Role Descriptions, Settings, and Lists of Duties

HOW TO USE THE ROLE DESCRIPTIONS

The pages immediately following describe the roles used in the simulation. Because the simulation has been designed for classes of various sizes, you may discover that some roles are not used for your simulation. Your instructor will decide, for example, whether there are to be five or seven members of council. The same will be true of the planning commission. Neither the usefulness of the simulation as a learning experience nor the reality it conveys is affected by deleting some roles to fit class size.

Let us remind you again that you are not playing yourself: *You are playing a role*. It is essential that you read your role description carefully and that you remain within your role. One of the purposes of the simulation is to demonstrate to you how conflicts develop in a democratic society when citizens with different values must live and work together. You also will come to understand how these conflicts can be, and are, resolved.

CAMELOT CITY GOVERNMENT AND LISTS OF DUTIES OF SOME OF ITS OFFICERS

Camelot has a council-manager plan of government.

The Mayor

The mayor is a member of council, elected for a one-year term by a majority of council. The mayor's authority is limited to:

1. Preparation of council's agenda (external events can determine items for agenda) in consultation with the manager and the clerk of council. The actual production of the agenda is handled by the clerk of council.

2. Presiding officer of council.

3. Ceremonial functions (cutting ribbons at opening of new bridges, roads).

4. Calling special meetings of the council.

5. Serving as legal head of the city by signing and receiving legal documents pertaining to the city.

6. Issuing proclamations (such as state of emergency, curfew, in times of stress).

For additional information see Camelot City Charter, Article II, Section 2.07, in Chapter 12.

The Council, City Manager, and Assistant Manager

There are five members on council (unless your instructor has specified a seven-member council). Elections are nonpartisan.

Term of office for all councilors is four years; staggered terms.

All of the councilors are elected at large.

An election will occur later in the simulation. Several councilors are coming up for reelection. We do not know if they plan to run, but the media reporters will be pressing them for a decision.

All who plan to run for office will receive further information later.

Council's authority is almost entirely legislative. It has power to enact ordinances, adopt resolutions, and appropriate monies by adopting the budget, in whole or in part. Council also has the power to appoint members to various boards and commissions and to appoint (and remove) the city manager. It has no executive or administrative responsibility.

Council, by majority vote, may revise the agenda.

There is no such thing as a veto power.

Council members are:

1. Required to be present at all meetings of council (according to the charter; two unexcused absences can result in having council declare your seat vacant. An excuse is granted by council by means of a motion duly seconded and approved by a majority of those present and voting).

2. Authorized to vote on ordinances, budgets, and resolutions, and to approve minutes.

3. Empowered to approve appointments (manager, members of special boards, commissions, and so on).

For additional information, see Camelot City Charter, Article II, Sections 2.01, 2.02, 2.03, and 2.06 in Chapter 12.

Role 1.   Councilor, Camelot City Council   *age 45, Forest Acres*

Is owner of a very successful catering business, and has served on council for nine years. Has a reputation for fairness and avoiding extreme positions, and has announced candidacy for the position of mayor. Spouse is a successful lawyer. They have two children and live in a large, architect-designed home within city limits. Supports the Downtown Hotel Plaza Issue, and opposes any new taxes, especially property taxes. Is inclined to oppose the Couches in the Yards and on the Porches Issue because he/she does not like the city telling property owners what they can and cannot do with their property.

Setting: Moderate members of council often find themselves playing the crucial role of trying to find the middle ground around which a consensus can be developed; the Police Protection Issue is an example. The police representatives and their supporters on council may well be urging maximum protection and firepower for the police; those who identify with minority groups (who often believe they are treated unfairly by the police) sometimes are outraged by any attempt to give the police more-powerful weapons. The moderate may feel the criticism of both sides and be tempted to either remain silent or to choose sides, rather than hold out for fair procedures or search for a compromise position.

Role 2.   Councilor, Camelot City Council   *age 34, College Town*

Is a professor at Camelot State University whose reputation on the council and in the press is that of a vigorous supporter of feminist causes. This is first term on council. Is a strong advocate of day-care centers and of increasing the number of women in executive positions in city government, and of social welfare issues in general. Lives near the university. Will present the Fairness in Housing and Employment Issue to council on the first session of the simulation. Strongly opposes the proposed ordinance(s) in the Private Use of Public Space Issue. Leans toward support of the proposed ban on couches in yards and on porches, but can be persuaded otherwise. Will present the Officer Protection Issue to council.

Setting: The difficulty this person will experience is that the image conveyed will probably either repel or attract possible allies in a limited sphere. Thus the necessary search for a coalition will be inhibited—the image of having too narrow a range of concerns might get in the way. The dilemma will be that councilor 2 might feel the need to be consistent on all issues, which might further alienate possible allies or attract opportunistic allies. For example, on the Fair Housing and Employment Issue, won't councilor 2 likely support the principles of "rights"? To do otherwise might seem to be a contradiction. Can one support only feminist causes? The same would be true of issues about which minorities feel strongly. But if one becomes labeled as being "far left," will moderates perhaps be reluctant to be allies even on less-controversial issues?

Role 3.   Councilor, Camelot City Council   *age 60, North Madisonville*

Is a strong conservative, divorced, and believes that his/her voice on council is the voice of the common people. As self-appointed representative of all conservatives, believes that the only way to prevent corruption of city council by the more liberal members is to get elected as mayor. Is a hard-line advocate of strict enforcement of the law against all criminal activity and believes that increasing the strength of the police force is necessary to protect the homes, persons, and children of honest citizens. Lives in an older neighborhood of small homes that are well kept. Is outspoken in support of a "workfare" program, which requires welfare recipients to perform assigned tasks in order to receive financial assistance. Will introduce and support the proposal to eliminate city financial support for the art museum (see the "Obscene Photographs" Issue). Leans toward support of the proposed ordinance banning couches in yards and on porches, but can be persuaded otherwise. Will express strong support for the proposed curfew ordinance. Supports the drug testing issue.

Setting: It is important to realize that councilor enjoys the certainty of fixed attitudes. Having worked hard for as long as he/she can remember, and having treasured self-reliance, there is understandable anger toward "the desire of liberals to use tax money to help those who seem unwilling to help themselves." It is not so much racial or ethnic prejudices that motivate councilor 3, but rather an unwillingness to see and acknowledge the full range and depth of disadvantages and discrimination experienced by some people in our society. This unwillingness to see prevents the councilor from perceiving and understanding the changes that are occurring in our society. The dilemma faced by the strong conservative will tend to parallel that of the most liberal members of council. It may not be easy for any of them to take less than an extreme position on sensitive issues.

Role 4. Councilor, Camelot City Council   *age 54, Crown Knolls*

Is vice president of the local Chamber of Commerce and believes that the way to a healthy city government is through friendly attitude toward business, which means low taxes. Is also a vice president of the Galahad Biotech Corporation. Often, but not always, goes along with law-and-order proposals. Lives in a new luxury apartment building. Has no strong view on the Couches in the Yards and on the Porches Issue. Has not yet decided whether to support or oppose the Downtown Hotel Plaza Issue.

Setting: Councilor 4 can best be described as "successful." This is not likely to be an angry person, as councilors 2 and 3 may be. Although there will tend to be a probusiness outlook, decisions probably will be pragmatic, nonideological. It seems likely that on sensitive issues, such as police protection, councilor 4 will attempt to find middle ground, but there will be less willingness to compromise when the issues involve new construction, revitalization of downtown Camelot, and jobs. Councilor 4, therefore, could easily experience personally the phenomenon of shifting alliances and coalitions, depending on the issue.

Role 5. Councilor, Camelot City Council   *age 50, South Ridge*

Recently became head of accounting for a large downtown business firm. Has an ethnic/racial minority heritage that makes for great sensitivity when any issue or argument seems to suggest ethnic or racial prejudice or discrimination. Recently bought a home in one of the new subdivisions. Although no longer living near the central city, is still concerned about the decay of the central city. Is open to suggestions of means of reversing this trend. Increased employment for minorities and increased support for day-care centers and financial assistance of some kind for single parents were campaign promises, as were means to revitalize the CBD. Inclined to oppose the Couches in the Yards and on the Porches Issue because he/she does not like the city telling property owners what they can and can't do with their property.

Setting: Being a member of an easily identifiable racial or ethnic group creates special problems for the council member, and this may be particularly true for an educated, successful professional. "Who am I?" is a question often asked by such individuals, and councilor 5 is no exception. The minority community is likely to see this person, an executive in the business world and a city council member, as both a symbol of success and a representative of minority interests. Yet such a professional may discover a greater identity with upper-middle-class values than with the working class or the poor. This conflict of community expectations versus personal values, when combined in the fishbowl of council politics, can easily inhibit alliance making for minority group representatives. The reality for minority group representatives is a world that may have a narrower range of alternatives from issue to issue. Regardless of personal feelings, how much freedom, for example, does this person have on an issue as sensitive for minority communities as greater firepower for police weapons?

Role 6. Councilor, Camelot City Council   *age 66, Madisonville*

Former chief of police, now retired. Came up through the ranks, and while a young member of the force, took courses at night at Camelot State University, finally earning a degree in criminal justice studies. Had a reputation for firmness but fairness as chief. Ran for council on a platform of increasing the number of police, improving the pay and fringe benefits of police and fire personnel, and getting more and better weapons for the police. Favorite quote is "the criminals are better equipped and armed than the police." Is proud of police professionalism and thus is no simple-minded law-and-order hard-liner, but nevertheless is firmly committed to increasing the percentage of the budget allocated to police. Would be willing to accept the mayor's position, especially as a compromise candidate. Will present the Resolution of Sympathy to council immediately after the election of the mayor and vice mayor. Strongly supports the proposed ordinances in the Private Use of Public Space Issue. Has no strong view on the Couches in the Yards and on the Porches Issue. Will ask the mayor to put the curfew ordinance on the agenda and will support it vigorously.

Setting: Little deviation from a pro-police position is to be expected on the Officer Protection Issue or on the police portion of the budget. But the growth that comes with advanced education, and wisdom resulting from the responsibility of having been chief, have made councilor 6 an enigma to supporters. If it is necessary, in order to win support for police issues, this individual would be in a position to take surprisingly liberal stands on moral issues and on community growth issues. Individuals whose conservative credentials are widely acknowledged have a freedom of movement on issues that most other citizens can only envy.

Role 7. Councilor, Camelot City Council   *age 47, Crown Knolls*

Works for Huron Electric Power Company at their regional office located in Camelot. Has a supervisory role, but not at a high level. Has a high school education and is an electrician by trade. At one time was active in the unionization of Huron Electric and has strong working-class convictions. Has a fundamentalist Christian commitment and is an active member of the church. Also is an active fund-raiser for the United Appeal and a high school athletic booster. Is strongly against any increases in property taxes or public funding of recreational programs, such as marinas and golf courses, but is a great supporter of Little League. Is skeptical about the growth of welfare programs, but maintains a strong sense of Christian responsibility and believes that the family unit is the key to the solution to present-day problems. Lives in a modest working-class neighborhood. Would love to be mayor. Has no strong view on the Couches in the Yards and on the Porches Issue.

Setting: The description of councilor 7 gives the impression that this is a person of firm convictions whose political judgments will be based on deeply rooted religious beliefs. There still is the possibility, however, of position variation on issues of community growth and some zoning questions. For example, it is not certain what position will be taken on the hairstylist's request for permission to have a home business in an area that does not now permit this. The desire to protect a neighborhood will be in conflict with the self-improvement aspiration shared with the hair stylist.

Working-class people are at times conservative on social or moral issues, yet liberal on economic issues. What this suggests is that such individuals may be interventionist and change-oriented in their desire to assist working (especially blue-collar) people and to penalize business. Thus they may tend to be supportive of such antibusiness legislation as special taxes on business or regulation of working conditions (especially worker safety laws). On the other hand, on social or moral issues, they may or may not want government to get involved, depending on the issue. They may want local governments to censor the books in local libraries and to close down topless bars; yet they may not want local governments to ban prayers in public school or discrimination based on sexual preference.

Role 8. City Manager   *Age 37, Madisonville*

Is in first post as city manager and wants to do a good job to prevent city council from finding another manager. Is a graduate of the University of Kansas, with a master's in public administration

(M.P.A.), and lives with spouse, who is an attorney, in a condominium near Government Square. Tries to be nonpolitical, but tends toward the liberal side of the political spectrum. Wants to increase taxes to maintain city services and to initiate such projects as the development of the downtown Hotel Plaza. Will take no position on the Strip Mall Development Issue. **At the first session of council, will alert council members that the Budget Issue will be on the agenda for the second session.** Supports the Officer Protection Issue.

Responsibilities: The city manager is appointed by council (requires affirmative votes by a majority of members), and serves at their pleasure. He/she may be removed at any time (requires the same majority for removal as for approval).

The city manager is in complete charge of the city administration. He/she has:

a. Power to appoint or remove all department heads, including the assistant city manager. Although council may criticize (or applaud) any such appointment or removal, its actual administrative authority is limited to the appointment or removal of the city manager.
b. Responsibility for the preparation and presentation to council of the city budget.
c. Power to appoint (and remove) any employee of the city (subject to limitations of civil service).
d. To respond to council requests for information.
e. To provide suggestions and supporting information to council concerning municipal administration.
f. To execute council instructions.
g. To administer according to the laws of the state, the Camelot Charter, and the ordinances of Camelot.
h. To attend council meetings.
i. To attend planning commission meetings, or send the assistant city manager if council meetings conflict.
j. To assist in preparation of council agenda (in consultation with mayor and clerk of council).

Setting: The city manager serves at the pleasure of a majority of council. To forget this may result in instant unemployment. The point is stressed here because at times a manager may be tempted to act as if he/she possessed authority independent of that granted by the city charter and the council. It is a high-risk strategy, therefore, for the manager to engage in brokerage politics or coalition formation. A quite acceptable and proper strategy for the manager, however, is to alert council to issues that ought to be considered. Equally appropriate for the manager is to suggest, when this is requested, alternative solutions to a problem. What the manager may not do is initiate programs without council approval, spend money without authorization by council, or tell council what to do. Council members, after all, are elected by the people, and the council has merely hired someone called a city manager to carry out their directions.

Role 9. Assistant City Manager   *Age 27, College Town*

Has been working for the City of Camelot since receiving a master's degree in city planning three years ago. Is a native of Madison, Wisconsin, married, no children. Would like to be the city manager of a city after picking up a bit more experience. In Camelot, the assistant manager is appointed (and may be removed) by the manager.

The assistant city manager has duties and responsibilities assigned to him/her by the manager. These duties may include serving as staff aide to the planning commission and filling in for the manager at planning commission meetings when schedule conflicts prevent the manager's presence. Supports the Strip Mall Development Issue. Strongly supports the Couches in the Yards and on the Porches Issue.

Setting: Whereas the city manager is directly responsible to the city council, the assistant city manager is directly responsible to the manager. The assistant city manager is typically younger and less experienced than the manager, although that need not always be so. What is more likely is that the day will come when the assistant must step into the boss's shoes. It may only be while the manager is on vacation, or because the manager has succumbed to the blandishments of a better position; but in either event, the assistant city manager is instantly in charge, even if the position is not a permanent one. Loyalty to one's superior is essential, and it behooves the young assistant city manager to learn the job as quickly as possible. Lightning may strike sooner than expected.

The Planning Commission

The five members of the planning commission (or seven members if the instructor chooses) are appointed by council to five-year, staggered terms.

Responsibilities are advisory only. Council tends to give substantial weight to planning's reports and recommendations because of planning's expertise, developed through length of service and through large amounts of time (as compared to council) spent on each matter. Nevertheless, council may decide any matter contrary to planning's recommendation.

The chair is chosen by majority vote of the commission. **It is the responsibility of the chair to report or to cause to be reported to council all actions of the commission. Usually this report will be in the form of an oral presentation at a council meeting. But a written report may be submitted if preferred.**

It will be the responsibility of the chairperson of the planning commission to notify the clerk and the city manager whenever a place on the next session's agenda of council is desired.

Because the planning commission's work is advisory only, decisions can be made by a majority of a quorum.

See also the last section of Chapter 8 and the Camelot Charter, Sections 6.06 and 6.07.

Role 10.   Member, Planning Commission   *age 35, Camelot Acres*

Is a graduate of Penn State with a master's degree in geography. By occupation is a corporate land-use planner, and is a strong advocate of regional land-use planning and stricter zoning regulations. Feels that appropriate planning could lead to solving the city's land-use and traffic congestion problems. Will be opposed to house color regulations (Rights of a Home Owner Issue).

Setting: This planning commission member will tend to solve difficult zoning questions by focusing on the needs of the community as a whole, rather than on the rights of an individual. This is a quite legitimate position to take, but it is not always a popular one. The assumption underlying this member's attitudes is that the community's needs take precedence over the right of an individual owner to use property as the owner sees fit. To put it another way, this commissioner tries to use the "big picture" as the principle in making recommendations for land use, not what will most benefit the owner of the land in question.

Role 11.   Member, Planning Commission   *age 62, North Madisonville*

Is an integral part of the movement to revitalize Camelot's central city. Agrees with the idea of greater land-use planning, but opposes the concept of decentralization. "Freeways will only worsen urban sprawl; we should be promoting the public transit system instead" is a frequently stated position at planning commission meetings. A vigorous supporter of Downtown Hotel Plaza Issue.

Setting: Role 11, planning commission member, appears to have a definite goal in mind for Camelot. City government intervention in land use is probably quite desirable, in member 11's mind, if the authority can be used to achieve the goals described in the role description. Thus, member 11 will likely be more concerned about revitalizing the central city and less concerned that achieving such goals may mean restrictions on an individual's use of private property.

Role 12. Member, Planning Commission   *age 40, Crown Knolls*

Is a "housespouse" at present, with two daughters, and was an urban studies major in college. Has a deep interest in the future of downtown Camelot, where he/she has always lived. Wants to abolish all vehicular traffic in a six-square-block area of Camelot's CBD, except for commuter buses and trucks at certain prescribed hours. Is as yet undecided about the Home for Unmarried Pregnant Teenagers Issue.

Setting: Although the goals of commissioner 12 may seem radical, they are in fact more likely to be aspirations than ideological commitments. This person may have a tendency to be idealistic rather than practical. At times, this can create dilemmas, but there is sufficient flexibility in point of view to permit listening and compromise.

Role 13. Member, Planning Commission   *age 47, Forest Acres*

Is a local real estate agent who is divorced and supports two children in their late teens while still finding time to be actively involved in the United Appeal, the Chamber of Commerce, and the CSU Alumni Association. On land-use questions, stresses the right of the property owner to use the land in any way to maximize profit. Supports the revitalization of the CBD. May favor freedom of the home owner, but is not sure. Faces a dilemma on the house decoration issue.

Setting: Commissioner 13 has strong convictions, as stated in the role description. For this individual, all zoning questions tend to be decided on the basis of the rights of the individual property owner. It is not that this commissioner believes the community has no rights; rather, it is that the community as a whole is best served when the individual is given the greatest freedom to use property (buy, sell, or develop) as the owner desires.

Role 14. Member, Planning Commission   *age 38, University Park*

Is employed in the Bureau of Governmental Research at CSU. Has a Ph.D. in urban planning and taught at another college for three years before coming to CSU. Is sensitive to the need to plan for a variety of lifestyles in a city such as Camelot. Wants to postpone the house color issue. Would like to abstain, but knows he/she ought to take a stand.

Setting: Given the training and professional interest of Role 14, it is probable that planning decisions will be temperate and that the emphasis will be on making deliberate decisions based on factual evidence. Hasty conclusions and rash actions will more than likely be discouraged.

Role 15. Member, Planning Commission   *age 38, Camelot Heights*

Is a college graduate and, as a member of a minority group, is interested in equal opportunities for minorities. Is employed as a stockbroker in downtown Camelot. Feels that the key to Camelot's future is farsighted city planning and hopes that efforts by the planning commission will assist the various minorities in the community. Supports the Downtown Hotel Plaza Issue because it will mean a possible increase in jobs for minorities. Will be supportive of the Home for Unmarried Pregnant Teenagers Issue.

Setting: Educated members of minority groups discover, when placed in representative positions, the extent to which community decisions are often in fact special interest decisions. Thus commissioner 15 will learn very quickly the advantages of coalition formation in order to achieve minority group objectives. The old saying "politics makes strange bedfellows" will probably be understood better at the end of the simulation than at the beginning.

Role 16. Member, Planning Commission   *age 50, Crown Knolls*

Is chair of the Small Business Association and, needless to say, is probusiness. Is a liberal and believes in enlisting the help of government to assist small businesses. Is pragmatic and a strong lobbyist. Feels that as crime rates rise, business will rapidly decline, and supports any measure that promises to obtain security for downtown shoppers.

Role 17. Police Chief   *age 52, Camelot Heights*

Is a hard-nosed, law-and-order policeman. However, grew up in an ethnic neighborhood and has worked up through the ranks to present position—started as a patrol officer at twenty-one. Is a frequent critic of the city government and has predicted a general police strike if there is not more money for equipment and personnel. (See Officer Protection Program Issue and the Budget Issue.) Supports the passage of a noise ordinance and, after attending a "Securing the Homeland Conference," supports the director of the Camelot Office for Homeland Security.

Responsibilities: Is the head of the Police Department of Camelot and enforces all Camelot ordinances and laws of the state. The chief of police has responsibility to maintain the public peace, suppress riots, and other disturbances. Additionally, the chief has the power to appoint and remove subordinates in the department and make rules and regulations of the department in accordance with city ordinances and state statutes.

Setting: The city of Camelot Police Department currently employs 360 sworn police officers, 90 civilians, and 30 reserve officers. The department's mission is to provide a high level of service, and is headed by a chief who has the latest equipment and specialized personnel at his disposal. The department is undergoing the rigors of accreditation (Commission on Accreditation for Law Enforcement Agencies, Inc., CALEA) and anticipates successful completion of the program. The City of Camelot is divided into eleven patrol teams that, for security reasons, rotate among the eleven subdivisions of the city.

Role 18. Clerk of Council   *age 29, Camelot Acres*

This is his/her first public office, after teaching in the local school system for three years. Quit because the system "was simply inadequate. Not enough money or teachers. I had to get out before I went up the wall." Spouse still teaches at a local high school and hopes for a raise in teachers' salaries.

Responsibilities: The clerk shall give notice of council meetings, keep the Minutes of every meeting of council, advertise public hearings, and record all ordinances and resolutions enacted by council. The clerk shall perform such other duties as may be assigned by the Charter or by ordinance. The Minutes should record:

1.   Date of meeting.
2.   Names of council present and absent, and who is presiding.
3.   All actions taken. Thus *all* motions are included. *No* debate is ever included in the Minutes.
4.   a.   All motions requiring a two-thirds majority vote (see tables on pages 98–99) require a roll-call vote.
     b.   For motions requiring only a simple majority vote of those present and voting (see tables on pages 98–99), a voice or hand vote is all that is necessary. The Minutes will simply say "motion passed" or "motion failed."
     c.   *All actions* of council, including ordinances and resolutions, require affirmative votes of majority of members.
5.   Announcements.
6.   Time of adjournment.

Role 19. Fire Chief   *Age 45, Camelot Heights*

Born and raised in the City of Camelot, and has been a member of the Camelot Fire Department for twenty-three years. Resides in Camelot Heights along with his wife and three children. Was especially upset by the terrorist attacks of 9/11 and strongly supports the Director of Homeland Security for the City of Camelot.

Responsibilities:

a.   Serves as head of the fire department of Camelot and has responsibility and supervisory authority over all activities relating to the extinction and prevention of fires necessary for the protection of life and property within the corporation limits of the City of Camelot.

b.   The fire chief shall appoint and remove all personnel in the department as necessary and according to the rules of the city, and applicable state and federal laws.

c.   During fires the fire chief shall have complete authority over the property involved and all persons in the immediate vicinity of the fire.

Setting: The City of Camelot Fire Department employs 154 professionally trained persons who provide fire, rescue (including water), and emergency medical services. The department has in service six pumper engines, five ladder trucks, one heavy rescue truck, two rescue boats, two hazardous materials units, and eight paramedic squads. These units operate out of eight fire stations. For the location of these eight stations see Figure 11-2.

The Newspaper Roles

The *Camelot Daily News* is published every day of the simulation. The reporter and the editor have very important roles to play. They have the following obligations (*in addition to preparing a paper for each day*):

1. To make sure the citizenry know what went on at council and planning commission meetings (typically, the editor covers council meetings and the reporter covers planning commission meetings).

2. To alert the citizenry to forthcoming deadlines, meetings, hearings, issues, council and planning commission agenda, if known.

3. To make certain the citizenry are aware of the significance (as the editor sees it) of issues and decisions.

4. To be alert to any wrongdoing on the part of public officials, including possible conflicts of interest involving public officials (consult with instructor concerning invented stories and events).

5. To editorialize as desired and deemed appropriate.

6. To report community happenings, problems, and the like that have clear or potential relevance to city government and its policies. An illustration is a bad fire that killed a firefighter and injured two others. Investigate? Question departmental efficiency?

7. To keep in mind the risks of libel. Consult with the instructor if desired.

8. To print anything else you wish—movie reviews; wise sayings by Ben Franklin, A. Lincoln, or your instructor; quotes from Shakespeare; horoscopes; advice to the lovelorn; and so on.

Role 20. Editor and Publisher, the *Camelot Daily News*   *age 39, Camelot Heights*

The editor is deeply concerned by the lack of political responsiveness evident in city government, and he/she deplores meetings closed to the public. Believes that "secrecy breeds conspiracy." The paper does not aim for complete objectivity but tries to present an open forum for debate, an in-depth look at local affairs, and exposure of political wrongdoing. Conservative council members criticize the paper for being too liberal and more interested in raking up dirt than in constructive reporting. The editor admits to a liberal philosophy, feeling that the paper is the means to keep city government active and honest. Regular assignment is to cover every council meeting.

Role 21. Editorial Writer, the *Camelot Daily News*   *age 55, University Park*

Started as a reporter at the *Camelot Daily News* twenty-seven years ago. Has been an editorial writer for ten years. With the passing of the years has come wisdom. Tries to see beyond the obvious, the blatantly political or ideological. Prefers to call the readers' attention to that which is praiseworthy in both politics and life, as well as to predatory human behavior and observed injustice. Is quite willing to take controversial stands if necessary. Supports the Downtown Hotel Plaza Issue and the Officer Protection Program Issue.

Role 22. Reporter, the *Camelot Daily News*   *age 27, College Town*

The reporter stayed on in Camelot after graduating from CSU with a degree in journalism. Is unmarried and has been covering the city hall beat for the past two years. Regular assignment is to cover planning commission meetings. Thinks city council is stupid even to consider the Couches in the Yards and on the Porches Issue, but as a reporter may feel constrained about saying that in public. May slant the article, however, to reveal his/her views.

Involved Citizens

Role 23. Owner-Operator of Camelot Adult Bookstore and Body Kneads (Massage Facility)   *age 31, Madisonville*

Lives in an old loft apartment near the central city, south of Woodworth Road. Distrusts government (of any kind), but voted in the last election for individuals who would be most likely to leave small businesses alone. Opposes increase in funds for police (see the Officer Protection Program Issue and the Budget Issue, Chapter 11). "All they do is try to hassle people in business." Will present the Massage Therapy Facility Issue to the planning commission in the second simulation session (third session if class periods are sixty minutes or less).

Role 24. President, Camelot State University   *age 43, University Park*

Defines the job as fundamentally being a PR person for CSU; it is his/her job to influence the government and the people to adopt laws and policies favorable to the university. Graduated from Camelot University and is a strong advocate of the status quo. Favors the Officer Protection Program Issue, but opposes the noise ordinance, especially on weekends. "Let young people be young" is the president's motto.

Role 25. Owner, Large Business   *age 60, Forest Acres*

Owns the now-closed Merchandise Mart, Camelot's largest downtown retail establishment. Inherited the business. Plans to build a large discount outlet in the proposed strip mall. Very supportive of police. Will express strong support for the proposed curfew ordinance.

Role 26. Owner, Small Business   *age 69, Camelot Acres*

Has operated a delicatessen in the same place for the last thirty years, but is now encountering financial difficulties. Many of the customers in the past lived in buildings that have been torn down to make parking lots. This small business owner's fate lies with the central city. If Camelot's downtown continues to deteriorate, there will not be enough customers, and the delicatessen will go bankrupt. Is very supportive of police. Will express strong support for the proposed curfew ordinance. Opposes the Downtown Hotel Plaza Issue because it will require relocation. On the Rights of a Home Owner Issue, will take a stand appropriate to the role description.

Role 27. President, Police Benevolent Association, Local 402   *age 57, Crown Knolls*

Is a former Camelot police officer who was elected PBA president ten years ago. Has been a very successful, very aggressive spokesperson for the police. In bargaining sessions, has a reputation for bluntness, and has insisted on getting better salaries and more fringe benefits for the police. Has been neutral on the NAACP demand for more black police officers. (See the Officer Protection Issue and the Budget Issue.) Will present the Officer Protection Program Issue to council at the first session of the simulation, time permitting, or the second session at the latest.

Role 28. President of League of Women Voters   *age 39, Camelot Heights*

Has a Ph.D. from a prestigious university and is a tenured member of the English Department faculty. Uses position to try to elect council members who advocate increased city services. As parent of three children, she believes the quality of the Camelot school system is of great concern. In the last election, the LWV succeeded in defeating an initiative petition to cut the school budget; is pledged to continue League action to achieve "a quality environment." Lives in a nice home on Patricia Road, east of Robert Street.

Although this individual is not part of the official city administration, **it is her responsibility to chair the candidates' meeting that is held the day before the election.**

Role 29. Retired Professional Football Player   *age 34, South Ridge*

After a successful and lucrative career as a quarterback for one of the NFL teams, he retired last year. Since then, he has not been employed full time but has engaged in some television work, appearing as a guest commentator when one of the major networks broadcasts football games. This has not been completely satisfying, and now his goal is to get into politics, using the name recognition that has come to him as a result of his many years as a football star and his current exposure in television. He has begun to attend regularly the meetings of council in order to understand local politics and to find his own set of political values. He has a strong desire to run for local office as a means of gaining experience in getting elected and in holding office. His political inexperience will force him to choose carefully the issues on which he will take a public stand. However, it is very important that he be seen and heard, for it will not serve his ambitions at all to be viewed as merely a quiet observer. Opposes the Strip Mall Development Issue. Strongly opposes the proposed curfew ordinance. On the Rights of a Home Owner Issue, will take a stand appropriate to the role description.

Role 30. Hair Stylist   *age 30, North Madisonville*

Is divorced and has four children. Is learning to be a hairstylist, recently received cosmetologist license, and now wishes to open a beauty salon in his/her home. In this way, will be able to remain off welfare, yet be closer to children. He/she will present the Beauty Salon Zone Variance Issue to the planning commission at the first simulation session (or perhaps the second session if class periods are sixty minutes or less).

Role 31. Affirmative Action Officer, City of Camelot   *age 36, University Park*

Has been in the present post for eighteen months and is the first affirmative action officer the city has had. Came to Camelot after college in another state, obtained a job as caseworker in the welfare department, became a supervisor there, transferred to the Department of Public Housing when it was established in Camelot, went from there to the personnel office of the city, and now has responsibility for implementing federal and state prohibitions against discrimination on the basis of race or sex in hiring, compensation, promotions, and terminations. Supports the Strip Mall Development Issue.

Role 32. Minister, African Methodist Episcopal (A.M.E.) Church

age 59, Madisonville

The reverend is a man of moderate views. He reminds people of Martin Luther King Jr.— sensitive to racial injustices and working for their elimination, but always doing so in a reasonable way and in a spirit of Christian charity. He tries to inspire others by his example of dignified civility; he is not a table thumper. Some of his younger parishioners criticize him for not doing enough for the cause of racial equality. Has some political ambitions and has contemplated running for council. Will be upset by Officer Protection Program Issue because of allegations it is an anti-minority program. May choose to join the support for the proposed curfew ordinance. Supports the Strip Mall Development Issue.

Role 33. Director, Planning Department, City of Camelot

age 41, University Park

Was appointed to the planning department twelve years ago and became its director just recently. Is a professionally trained planner, a member of the American Planning Association (www .planning.org), a certified planner with a master's degree from the University of Virginia. Is more than a "mortar and bricks" physical planner and thus is interested in preservation—of green space; of graceful old buildings; of neighborhoods—and land use for people, as well as being concerned (as must be all planning directors) with maintaining the city's economic base. Supports the Downtown Hotel Plaza Issue and the Strip Mall Development Issue and the Rights of a Home Owner Issue. Recently returned from a Comprehensive Planning Seminar in Chautauqua, New York, and advocates a Comprehensive Plan for the City of Camelot. Comprehensive plans generally include: maps, charts, studies, resolutions, reports, and other materials that identify the goals and policies affecting the long-range growth of a city. He/she expects to work with the planning commission and community leaders to develop a Comprehensive Plan for the City of Camelot.

Role 34. Student Body President, CSU

age 20, College Town

Takes pride in being independent; sometimes makes considerable effort to remind others of those traits. Won office by a wide margin, and sometimes toys with the question of whether the student body has the potential to be welded into a strong political force in Camelot. Very much opposed to the restrictions on placing couches on porches and in front yards as a matter of principle. His house has a couch on the porch. Strongly opposes the proposed curfew ordinance.

Role 35. Insurance Agent

age 55, Forest Acres

Served a term on council and then declined to run for reelection because of illness in the family. Since the graduation of the youngest son from college, friends have urged him/her to consider running again. Appears not to have decided the question, but maintains a lively interest in local affairs. As an occupant of a downtown office, is especially sensitive to the quality of the CBD. Views him/herself as a moderate Republican, rather than as a conservative. Supportive of police on all such issues. Role 35's backyard abuts the west lot line of Role 47's lot, and Role 35 opposes the issuance of the building permit for an addition to Role 47's house on the grounds that it would violate the zoning code. See Zoning Appeals Board (ZAB) Issue 3. Supports the Strip Mall Development Issue.

Role 36. Director, CSU Institute for Applied Gerontological Studies

age 47, Camelot Acres

Although primarily an academic, also regards Camelot as a prime setting for the application of gerontological information and ideas. In practice, this means concern with such matters as transportation for the elderly, the relation of housing to shopping, to part-time employment opportunities, and to amenities. Problems of crime, which especially victimize the elderly, are of special concern. Believes that academics have a duty to intervene in civic affairs and to offer their advice and expertise on current problems. His/her spouse is an artist. Opposes the Strip Mall Development Issue. Will support the Officer Protection Issue and the police items in the Budget Issue. He/she and spouse have decided to paint their house lavender with a chartreuse trim (note the Rights of a Home Owner Issue). May well join those who support the proposed curfew ordinance. On the Rights of a Home Owner Issue, will take a stand appropriate to the role description.

Role 37. Director of Urban Welfare Programs *age 34, Madisonville*

This is his/her second position as a professional since graduating from college. Worked as a retail clerk after high school, then later entered evening classes at CSU; but after graduation could not find employment other than a sales position for quite some time. Has considerable empathy with Camelot's poor. Although believing in the central city, believes also that housing for the poor must be near employment opportunities. If Camelot's industry moves to the suburbs, is committed to locating low-cost housing there, too. Supportive of health department proposals (see the Budget Issue). Supports the Strip Mall Development Issue.

Role 38. Real Estate Developer *age 52, Forest Acres*

Is one of three partners in Crown Real Estate Development Corporation. Believes that the trend toward suburbanization is the way to make money. Has a large interest in the downtown Hotel Plaza that he/she proposes to build, and frequently attends planning commission and city council meetings to push views. Is a very smooth representative for this successful firm, Crown Developers. Very much favors the Downtown Hotel Plaza Issue. Roles 38, 39, and 40 will work together to decide who will be the spokesperson (or spokespersons) for the Downtown Hotel Plaza Issue to the planning commission at the first simulation session, or the second session at the latest. They will also introduce and support the Strip Mall Development Issue.

Role 39. Real Estate Developer *age 32, Forest Acres*

Is the young, ambitious partner in the very successful development firm Crown Real Estate Development Corporation. Is active in planning many new projects. Politically is conservative, wants council to stay out of private affairs and to play a supportive role in improving the city's tax base. Very much favors the Downtown Hotel Plaza Issue. Will join those who support the proposed curfew ordinance. Roles 38, 39, and 40 will work together to decide who will be the spokesperson (or spokespersons) for the Downtown Hotel Plaza Issue to the planning commission at the first simulation session, or the second session at the latest. They will also introduce and support the Strip Mall Development Issue. Opposes the Officer Protection Program Issue.

Role 40. Real Estate Developer *age 50, Forest Acres*

Took over spouse's interest in Crown Real Estate Development Corporation after his/her untimely death three years ago. Spouse was one of the three founders of the firm. He/she had begun as an accountant with the firm, thus is very familiar with every aspect of the business. With death of the spouse, is now a one-third owner of the company. Very much favors the Downtown Hotel Plaza Issue. Roles 38, 39, and 40 will work together to decide who will be the spokesperson (or spokespersons) for the Downtown Hotel Plaza Issue to the planning commission at the first simulation session, or the second session at the latest. They will also introduce and support the Strip Mall Development Issue.

Role 41. Attorney *age 32, Camelot Heights*

This young attorney, only two years out of law school, decided to hang up a shingle to see if it is possible to find enough clients to keep food on the table. He/she is willing sometimes to offer services at little or no charge to deserving groups (and perhaps individuals) in order to become better known and to build a law practice. Has been retained by those opposing the proposed strip mall developments.

Role 42. Lancelot PTA Vice President
age 40, North Madisonville

Is a graduate of CSU, an art designer for a local publishing company. Now divorced and is raising two daughters, ages eight and six. Is concerned about the quality of education in Camelot, thus has been deeply involved in the PTA. Although city council has no control over the school system, Role 42 is concerned about taxes, crime, and any issue that involves the future of Camelot.

Role 43. Junior High Teacher
age 43, Crown Knolls

Is a math teacher in a junior high school, unmarried, and an active member (born again) of an evangelical Protestant church. Has become disturbed by the opening of a massage facility west of the CBD and has been searching for allies so that an effective complaint can be made to the council, the manager, perhaps the planning commission, or anyone else who might be able to help close what is suspected to be a front for prostitution. Has joined a delegation of citizens who will urge that council pass a noise ordinance. Has joined the "Save Pioneer Park" group, which opposes the Downtown Hotel Plaza Issue. Is opposed to granting a zone variance in the case of the Topless Bar and Grill Issue.

Role 44. Director, Public Health Department
age 39, College Town

Is an M.D., and very "middle class" in attitude. Frequently one finds that the scientific or technical training of persons whose profession is an "applied" endeavor (as, for example, a physician) produces training experiences that tend to create an intolerance for mistakes and errors. This intolerance also can form the foundation for an exaggerated confidence in their own analyses. Persons accustomed to working in a black-and-white world, even a complex one, do not always adjust easily to the rich coloration and vibrant diversity of matters outside their field of expertise. One also may expect this individual to support such legislation as compulsory drug testing (proposed by the Public Health Department). Strongly supports the Couches in the Yards and on the Porches Issue. Has joined a delegation of citizens who will urge that council pass a noise ordinance. Has been asked by the city manager to explain the drug testing proposal to council and answer any questions that arise.

Role 45. Development Editor, Megabook Publishing Company
age 35, College Town

She has been employed by this nationally known college textbook company for eight years. Several times has felt the sting of discrimination because she is a female, and has been quite active in feminist causes. She views with contempt such exploitively sexist events as beauty pageants, and she is equally hostile to all other aspects of the "skin trade." This young woman is not a single-issue person. She is an outspoken supporter of "Save Pioneer Park," and, as a persistent and staunch conservationist, she is opposed to the development of the Downtown Hotel Plaza Issue. She is particularly upset by the city ordinance that requires all yards to be mowed and gardens to be kept weeded. Strongly supports the Couches in the Yards and on the Porches Issue.

Role 46. Police Officer
age 32, Madisonville

Is a five-year veteran of the Camelot Police Force after serving in the U.S. Marines for four years, has been going to the CSU evening program and working toward a two-year certificate in the criminal justice program. Is married, has a child. Ranks third on the civil service examination, and strongly believes that if a vacancy occurs or if an increase in the strength of the force is authorized, will be promoted to sergeant. Will support all police-related issues. Supports the proposed curfew ordinance.

Role 47. President, Data Tech Corporation
age 35, Forest Acres

A product of Camelot State's information technology department and an inventive genius. Has successfully developed and marketed new software programs and is already a multimillionaire. Is a solid Republican of a conservative sort, but is quite practical. Has little use for ideologues, whether conservative or liberal, but does favor keeping government out of business. Believes that what this country (and this community) needs is more people who think that government should be run on sound business principles. Supportive of police on all such issues. Has been denied a building permit by the zoning administrator to build an addition to his/her house. Has appealed to the zoning appeals board (ZAB). See Zoning Appeals Board Issue 3. Because of membership on the City Betterment Committee of the Chamber of Commerce, he/she supports the ban on couches in yards and on porches.

Role 48. Minister, First Presbyterian Church   *age 44, Camelot Heights*

The reverend's church probably is the most fashionable church in town, drawing heavily from Forest Acres for its congregation. Wants to avoid becoming insulated from the larger problems of the times; recognizes the risks of insularity as one ministers to an affluent congregation. Consequently, has established close ties with the United Campus Ministry at CSU, and the reverend's church extends a friendly welcome to students each Sunday. Is concerned with social questions, but is practical enough to believe that he or she must appeal to the more traditional views among communicants as well as to the more liberal views of some. As a result, his or her desire for racial equality and for urban renewal coexists with a strong opposition to vice and organized crime. Is especially embarrassed by the continuing presence of the massage therapy facility, which, it is alleged, has been visited occasionally by CSU students. The historic pioneer Presbyterian Church and neighboring cemetery are threatened by the downtown Hotel Plaza. Is very supportive of the proposal to eliminate city financial support for the art museum (see the "Obscene Photographs" Issue). Supports the proposed curfew ordinance. Heads the "Save Pioneer Park" group who oppose the downtown Hotel Plaza plan, which requires moving the church and cemetery. Supports the Strip Mall Development Issue. Is opposed to granting a zone variance in the case of the Topless Bar and Grill Issue.

Role 49. Attorney   *age 43, Forest Acres*

Is a very successful attorney with a lucrative private practice. As a result, has become increasingly able to pursue an interest in causes. Is chair of the Camelot Art Museum's governing board and often acts as representative for groups such as welfare mothers and environmental groups. Often represents neighborhood groups on zoning change issues. Is a member of the First Presbyterian Church, and has ancestors buried in the cemetery there. Especially interested in causes involving women. Thus can be counted on to be a willing representative for women's groups on the issues described in Role 45. Has been hired by the neighbors of Role 30 to oppose the Beauty Salon Zone Variance Issue. Has joined Role 45 in her rebellion against the lawn maintenance regulations. Has agreed to represent several fraternities who oppose the passage of the noise ordinance. On the Rights of a Home Owner Issue, will take a stand appropriate to the role description.

Role 50. Head of the Local Chapter, NAACP   *age 42, College Town*

Feels that the way for an African-American community to advance is to secure governmental positions. Has a reputation for being a powerful orator and an effective organizer. Has stated publicly that if any more African-American homes are torn down for highways or parking lots, the city of Camelot is in for the hassle of all time. Is very supportive of the downtown Hotel Plaza, and bitterly opposes the Officer Protection Program Issue (the more-powerful weapons, not the body armor). Strongly supports the Couches in the Yards and on the Porches Issue. Supports the Strip Mall Development Issue.

Role 51. Attorney   *age 60, South Ridge*

Is very likely the highest paid attorney in Camelot. Lives in South Ridge in the most exclusive section. Represents the interests of the waitresses in the request for a zone variance for the Topless Bar and Grill. Has been hired by a group of residents to resist the locating of the home for unmarried pregnant teenagers in their neighborhood. Role 51 will appear before the planning commission to defend the choice of unusual, if a bit daring, house colors.

Role 52. President, Camelot Chapter of Business and Professional Women's Organization

age 46, College Town

An energetic, successful female executive. She is a vice president in charge of research and development for one of the largest home products manufacturers in the nation. The research center is located in a lovely wooded section approximately ten miles out of town. She has a Ph.D. in chemistry from an Ivy League university, but her academic passion is concern about protection of the environment, including preservation of our architectural heritage. She is single and lives in one of the restored older homes in the trendy area of College Town. She is self-confident and assertive, but her experience as a successful administrator has made her a skillful mediator of conflicting interests and personalities. She takes frequent stands on public issues, and her independent attitudes make it difficult to predict her positions in advance. Has requested a zoning variance from the zoning appeals board. See the Zoning Appeals Board Issue 1, the Carport Variance Request. Strongly supports the Couches in the Yards and on the Porches Issue. Because she is a strong supporter of neighborhood community and endeavors, she believes residential property should be attractively maintained.

Role 53. President, Right to Life Society of Greater Camelot

age 40, Camelot Acres

A well-educated professional who in the past was not interested or involved in political activities. However, as a result of a profound religious experience five years ago, he/she suddenly felt compelled to take strong stands on moral issues, in particular those involving children and human life. On the Rights of a Home Owner Issue, will take a stand appropriate to the role description. Supports the Home for Unmarried Pregnant Teenagers Issue. Opposes the proposed allocation of funds for the Planned Parenthood program (see the Budget Issue). Fears it will use the funds to support abortion, in spite of denials by Planned Parenthood supporters.

Role 54. Head of Camelot Chapter of the Feminist Majority

age 38, Camelot Acres

A very successful executive of an advertising agency. Is bright, articulate, and assertive. She is supportive of a feminist political agenda and committed to confrontational tactics. Will take a strong stand on any issue where she senses women have a stake. Is not known for her readiness to compromise. Will strongly oppose the Massage Therapy Facility Issue. Is opposed to granting a zone variance in the case of the Topless Bar and Grill Issue. On the Rights of a Home Owner Issue, will take a stand appropriate to the role description.

Role 55. Student Body Vice President, CSU

age 19, Camelot State U.

Lives in a university residence hall. Is a born-again Christian and opposed to almost all of the liberal causes of the day. Will oppose massage parlors and any similar issues that come before council. Opposes ban on couches on porches and in yards because he likes to sleep on one. Opposes the noise ordinance.

Role 56. Vice President, Christian Revival Movement

age 22, Camelot State U.

Lives in a university residence hall and is a history major at CSU. Views are similar to those described in Role 55. Is opposed to granting a zone variance in the case of the Topless Bar and Grill Issue.

Role 57. Director, Camelot Public Library

age 49, University Park

Has built the library into one of the best in the state by aggressive advocacy of its importance. Is proud of the advanced information retrieval system adopted by the library and the high level of professionalism of its staff. Is concerned about the implications for the library of the attack on pornography and the call by some elements of the community for more careful screening of acquisitions and allocation of shelf space. Will defend the First Amendment with great vigor. On the Rights of a Home Owner Issue, will take a stand appropriate to the role description.

Role 58. High School Teacher

age 42, Camelot Acres

A social studies teacher, married, politically active on social issues—but careful not to get too controversial. Is very concerned that minorities, especially Hispanics, get fair treatment in terms of access to housing and employment. Wants the council to put more teeth into its present antidiscrimination laws so that violators, especially real estate agents, will be subject to severe fines for "steering" clients into segregated areas. Has been known to urge friends that what Camelot needs is a strong rent control law. Opposes the Strip Mall Development Issue. On the Rights of a Home Owner Issue, will take a stand appropriate to the role description.

Role 59. Owner, Topless Bar and Grill

age 50, River Town

Is very angry that the press seems to be against what he/she sees as a legitimate business. Started as the bartender, and as a result of very hard work and a shrewd business sense, was able to buy the bar at a good price and build it into a successful enterprise. Has stated publicly that he/she sees nothing wrong with a public display of the human body, although is firm in opposition to anything beyond toplessness at the bar. Is responsible for supporting the request to the planning commission for a zone variance.

Role 60. Owner, Firehouse Bookstore

age 58, CBD

After graduating from CSU as a philosophy and English major, used a modest inheritance to buy an abandoned fire station in the Central Business District close to the university and convert it into a bookstore. The bookstore has become a legend in its time, for the owner has accumulated a vast collection of new and used books. Is sympathetic to a Libertarian viewpoint, but not aggressive on the subject. Views government's domestic role as limited to protection of an individual's person and property, and other basics, such as street maintenance, sewage disposal, trash collection, and an adequate supply of safe water. Believes people must take care of themselves, and help others when they are in dire need. Every effort should be made to keep government out of people's lives.

Will take active stands on many issues: all issues that involve expenditures of taxpayer money (the marina, Camelot Shores Project, gynecologic and obstetric services, Planned Parenthood); restrictions on individual rights (such as the color of one's house; laws that restrict the rights of property owners to decide who they should rent apartments to, whether the art museum can display controversial pictures, whether students can put couches on their lawns, or the beauty salon owner's rights to use his/her house as a business); the right of a citizen to own a gun; and the curfew ordinance.

Has joined Role 45 in her rebellion against the lawn maintenance regulations. Has stopped mowing the lawn and has planted all kinds of wildflowers in the front yard, some reaching six feet in height.

Role 61. Director, Camelot Art Museum

age 55, University Park

Lives in an expensive condominium near the university. Last member of Camelot's founding family. His/her great-great-grandfather was first preacher of the First Presbyterian Church; family plot is in that cemetery. Educated in eastern schools; travels yearly to Europe. Believes no one should censor art. Collects art prints. Strongly opposed to the proposal to eliminate city financial support for the art museum (see "Obscene Photographs" Issue). On Rights of a Home Owner Issue, will take a stand appropriate to the role description.

Role 62. Executive Director, Camelot Chamber of Commerce

age 52, Camelot Acres

Married; three children in college, two at CSU. Began business career in real estate development with first cousin, Role 38. Was one of the founders of the Chamber of Commerce ten years ago; owns several pieces of rental property; is a part owner of two retail businesses in Camelot, a restaurant and a wine shop. Became very disturbed when Role 36 and spouse decided to paint their house lavender with a chartreuse trim. Has joined with other outraged home owners in their attempt to regulate house color choices. See the Rights of a Home Owner Issue.

Role 63. Single Parent on Welfare

age 18, Rivertown

Was married, spouse deserted, parents are divorced and unable to provide much help. Was a bright science student but could not finish high school. Began job training, but was forced to stop when her child became ill. Wants new opportunity for job training; needs a job. May seek out the ACLU director. As a member of a minority, feels she is being discriminated against, especially by the ban on street entertainment issue. Has been able to make ends meet by playing a piano in Pioneer Park on weekends.

Role 64. Solicitor (City Attorney)

age 45, Madisonville

Has a keen interest in municipal governance since receiving a law degree from the University of Pittsburgh. Specialized in environmental law, having taken three environmental law courses in the third year of law school. In addition to environmental concerns in Camelot, is interested in municipal charter reform and proposes to amend the Camelot Charter by adding a clause that the charter shall be reviewed in even years by a committee appointed by the council.

Qualifications: The solicitor shall be an attorney-at-law with at least three years experience who is admitted to the bar of this state.
Duties:

a. to be legal advisor to the Council and officers of the City of Camelot;
b. to draft all ordinances, resolutions, contracts, and legal documents as required by Council or other city officials;
c. to represent the City of Camelot in all legal proceedings;
d. to attend all meetings of Council unless excused by the Mayor or Council.

Role 65. Former Homeless Person

age 54, CBD

A Vietnam veteran, unskilled laborer, factory worker before he was drafted. Came home from Vietnam needing psychological counseling, but worked at the steel wheel factory until it closed in the 1970s. Has history of drug and alcohol abuse; is currently free of the abuse and has been for ten years or so. Had been homeless, but is now rehabilitated as a result of proper medical treatment and counseling. Has sought out Role 41, Attorney, to represent him on a pro bono basis (i.e., free) to oppose the Private Use of Public Space Issue because of the proposed restrictions on selling items, or begging, or "camping" in public parks. It is a violation of constitutional rights (as he sees it) to deny use of public property and the proposed ordinance will prevent anyone from sleeping wherever he/she wants. Why shouldn't one be permitted to sleep in the park if no one else is being bothered? And if the city prevents anyone from selling items on public sidewalks, the sellers will starve or have to beg. Opposes the proposed curfew ordinance.

Role 66. Part-time Worker

age 70, North Madisonville

Owns a trailer in the Celestial Trailer Park. When Social Security proved to be inadequate, took a part-time job at a fast food restaurant, serving coffee seconds, mopping up spills, picking up trash left by customers, doing whatever needed to be done. Has a bright, positive, flippant sense of reality. A no-nonsense person that others like immediately. Opposes the proposed curfew ordinance.

Role 67. Building Inspector

age 30, Rivertown

Is a graduate of Purdue University with a civil engineering degree. Is a minority group member, divorced, and lives alone. As a child, he/she experienced slum living in Chicago before the family moved to the City of Camelot. Is particularly sensitive to landlords who let their properties deteriorate. Supports other public officials in their quest for an ordinance that regulates the placement of couches in yards and porches. (See The Couches in the Yards and on the Porches Issue.)

Responsibilities: The ICC (International Code Council) certified inspector (code official) reviews the construction, maintenance, and remodeling of derelict and run-down properties.

The building inspection process is normally initiated with an application for a permit to construct or remodel a building. The inspector works with the fire department concerning fire safety of the structure and its compliance with the state, city, or county electrical, plumbing, and mechanical codes. If a deficiency is found, or if the building does not comply with the code, the building inspector is responsible for issuing orders to correct the unsafe or unlawful condition. Finally, the building inspectors keep official records detailing permit applications, fees, dates of inspections, notices, and orders issued.

Role 68. Director, Homeland Security   *age 33, CBD*

Recent graduate of Camelot State University with a major in business administration. Advocates a national security state and sees terrorism best contained with the USA Patriot Act. Supports the president's efforts to strengthen the Act. Strongly opposes the efforts of several members of the Camelot City Council to pass a municipal resolution urging that Congress repeal the USA Patriot Act.

Responsibilities: The director of Homeland Security is appointed by council and coordinates security bulletins from the state executive director of Homeland Security. Much like the state director of Homeland Security, the Camelot director coordinates local first responders, such as the police, fire, and health departments.

Role 69. Social Worker   *age 37, Madisonville*

Married; spouse works as parole officer. Child attends private boarding school. Owns small cottage on resort lake. Income barely covers monthly bills. Supports the Home for Unmarried Pregnant Teenagers Issue.

Role 70. Bartender, Mike's Bar and Grill   *age 42, River Town*

Mike's is a neighborhood bar; clientele mainly working class, but has lately been discovered by college students. House specialty is a steak sandwich. Role 70 lives in apartment above the bar, does all the ordering, and so on, except for kitchen supplies. Wants planning commission and city council to grant the special use permit to the massage therapy facility.

Role 71. Public Health Nurse   *age 60, Crown Knolls*

Divorced, has raised two daughters and seen them married. Owns a home in the northern section of the bottom third portion of Crown Knolls, in an area of transition; is concerned about whether retirement income will cover city taxes and rising expenses. Often allied with police officers in dealing with health emergencies. When the Budget Issue is considered, will support the addition of gynecologic and obstetric services.

Role 72. Chairperson of Camelot Hispanic Coalition   *age 29, Crown Knolls*

An aggressive, outspoken individual. The Hispanic community of Camelot is divided by ethnicity, age, years of residence in the United States, and attitude toward authority. Thus there is no single Hispanic point of view, although there is a shared distrust of government and politicians. Role 72's goal is to focus on issues that are important to all, or at least to many, Hispanics. Like other spokespersons for minority groups, the emphasis will be on issues that may bring jobs to Camelot, on policies that will assure equal opportunity for Hispanics to be hired, and on equal treatment by the police and the judicial system. Strongly supports the proposed curfew ordinance. Supports the Strip Mall Development Issue.

Role 73. ACLU Director   *age 41, Forest Acres*

He/she is an attorney who earns about three-fourths of his/her income by serving as executive director of the state chapter of the American Civil Liberties Union. The law practice has variety, but as one might expect, some of the cases reflect the strong concerns of the director for justice and equality under the law. In addition to the ever-present problem of assuring that due process of law is accorded defendants in criminal prosecutions, issues of freedom of speech, press, assembly, and worship, as well as issues of separation of church and state, have a potential for involving both the ACLU and its director. The ACLU also has come to the defense of persons accused of crimes where the accusation seems to be a politically motivated effort to stifle dissent or unpopular opinion. Is responsible for administering the state office operations (membership lists, dues collection and contributions, publicity, public relations, and newsletter) and for providing information to the membership as issues and cases arise. Opposes the Private Use of Public Space Issue and the proposed curfew ordinance.

Role 74. President of Camelot Chapter of AARP (American Association of Retired Persons)
age 66, College Town

A retired secondary school teacher, he/she lives in a modest three-bedroom home. Is committed to programs that appear beneficial to retirees and older members of the community who may be living on fixed incomes. Will be skeptical about the need for new growth and development; will likely oppose new taxes. Will be supportive of police issues because of sense of vulnerability as he/she gets older. Is deeply opposed to the use of taxpayer money on items such as the proposed marina. Believes that if people can afford boats, they should use their money for the marina.

Role 75. President, CANT (Camelotters Against New Taxes)
age 53, Camelot Acres

A community activist (some would say gadfly) who seems always alert to any public issue or proposal that might raise taxes. The organization he/she heads, CANT, is small, but its leader is always eager to speak at any occasion in the name of those who don't like taxes. No matter how appealing a project or program is, he/she is eager to oppose it if it might result in higher taxes. Role 75 and spouse, a lawyer, are active in conservative causes at the county and state levels.

Role 76. Freelance Artist
age 45, University Park

Works entirely at home. Is moderately successful. Sells larger canvases of landscapes and whimsical silk-screen prints of animals out of his/her residence ever since the closing of the Camelot Gallery. Is single, with a son, age twenty, and a daughter, age seventeen, both of whom are hardworking and have part-time jobs to help their family make ends meet. Has been accused of violating the zoning code because of the use of the home as a business. See the Zoning Appeals Board Issue 2. See also the Rights of a Home Owner Issue, which concerns the right to paint one's home as one chooses. Role 76 will be involved if this issue is used.

Professor Schmooz

A faculty member at Camelot State University, Professor Schmooz is the final role in Camelot. However, the role is not numbered, because it will be played by your instructor if he or she chooses to do so. Professor James R. Forrester of West Liberty State College, West Liberty, West Virginia, conceived and developed the role. Details of the role are found in the Instructor's Manual. Faculty members can obtain copies of the Instructor's Manual from the publisher.

Role Request

NAME _____

In the simulation, I prefer:

1. *An active role.* I understand that this role may well involve some time outside of class as well as public activity in class. I also realize that if I accept an active role, I must attend class regularly on simulation days. (Examples are city manager, mayor, member of council, clerk of council, the newspaper roles, the newscaster.)

2. *A semiactive role.* I understand that these roles could also involve some time outside of class, but less than that of an active role. My activities in class will not be so public, except when I am involved in a particular issue. These roles also require my presence during days of simulation. (Examples are chief of police, city planning commission, the ministers, the attorneys, the developers.)

3. *A more modest role.* I understand that these roles will not require much out-of-class time, unless I choose to be involved. There is generally much less public involvement, but I will not be anonymous. My presence is essential when there is a particular issue that involves me, but otherwise my presence is desirable but not essential to the simulation.

From the above-mentioned roles that sound interesting to you, please list as many of them as you wish:

_____
_____
_____
_____
_____
_____
_____
_____

City of Camelot Nominating Petition

The undersigned, qualified and duly registered voters of the City of Camelot, hereby nominate
_____ for the office of council member, City of Camelot, seat number_____.
(Ask your instructor whether seat numbers are to be used.)

	NAME	ADDRESS	DATE
1.	_____	_____	_____
2.	_____	_____	_____
3.	_____	_____	_____
4.	_____	_____	_____
5.	_____	_____	_____
6.	_____	_____	_____
7.	_____	_____	_____
8.	_____	_____	_____
9.	_____	_____	_____
10.	_____	_____	_____

Attestation by Petition Circulator

I hereby affirm, subject to the penalties for perjury, that the above signatures were recorded in my presence and that the names and addresses are accurate to the best of my knowledge.

Date:_____ Name: _____
                                    (Signed)

This document was received at_____O'clock_____ M _____
                                                       Clerk,* City of Camelot

Petitions must be filed with the City Clerk,* City of Camelot, not later than 5:00 p.m. of the last simulation session preceding the election.

*Your instructor, if there is no clerk.

Your Evaluation of *Camelot*

Your instructor will indicate when this form should be filled out.

1. Compared to other courses (or portions of courses) that you have taken, how would you rate the *Camelot* simulation?

2. What do you consider to be the most important thing(s) you learned from the simulation?

3. Was there anything about the simulation that you found disappointing? Explain.

4. Do you have any suggestion for improving the simulation?

5. Suppose that a friend had a choice of different sections of the Urban Politics course, or the American Government course, and one of the sections of each of those courses used *Camelot*. The friend asks you whether he or she should choose the section offering *Camelot*. What would be your advice?

6. Please indicate whether your role was:
   a. An active role, such as council member, clerk, editor, or city manager.
   b. A semiactive role, such as planning commissioner or developer.
   c. A more modest role, such as president of the LWV or the owner of the Firehouse Bookstore.
   d. A small role—just one of the interested citizens.

City of Camelot Initiative Petition

To the Clerk of Council of the City of Camelot, State of _____

   We, the undersigned, qualified and duly registered voters of the City of Camelot, respectfully propose to the electors of said city for their approval or rejection at the special or general election to be held on the _____ day of _____, 20 _____, the following Ordinance:

   "The smoking of tobacco is hereby banned at any workplace, bar, or restaurant within the borders of the City of Camelot."

	NAME	ADDRESS	DATE
1.			
2.			
3.			
4.			
5.			
6.			
7.			
8.			
9.			
10.			

Attestation by Petition Circulator

I hereby affirm, subject to the penalties for perjury, that the above signatures were recorded in my presence and that the names and addresses are accurate to the best of my knowledge.

Date:_____ Name: _____
                                                (Signed)

               Address: _____

This document was received at_____O'clock_____ M. _____
                                                         Clerk,* City of Camelot

Petitions must be filed with the City Clerk,* City of Camelot, not later than 5:00 p.m. of the last simulation session preceding the election.

*Your instructor, if there is no clerk.

Topical Bibliographies

OVERVIEW PERSPECTIVES

Boulding, Kenneth E. 1990. *Three Faces of Power.* Newbury Park, CA: Sage.

Greer, Scott. 1962. *The Emerging City.* New York: Free Press of Glencoe.

Hall, Edward T. 1966. *The Hidden Dimension.* Garden City, NY: Doubleday.

Wilson, James Q. 1970. Review. *American Political Science Review* 64 (March): 198.

PARTICIPANTS: PEOPLE AND ORGANIZATIONS

Dahl, Robert A. 1961. *Who Governs? Democracy and Power in an American City.* New Haven, CT: Yale University Press.

Ehrenhalt, Alan. 1995. *The Lost City: The Forgotten Virtues of Community in America.* New York: Basic Books.

Ehrenhalt, Alan. 1992. *The United State of Ambition: Politicians, Power, and the Pursuit of Office.* New York: Times Books.

Eisinger, Peter K. 1983. "Black Mayors and the Politics of Racial Advancement." In W.C. McReady (Ed.), *Culture Ethnicity, and Identity.* New York: Academic Press.

Jones, Bryan D. and Lynn W. Bachelor. 1993. *The Sustaining Hand: Community Leadership and Corporate Power* (2nd ed., Revised). Lawrence: University of Kansas Press.

Kelly, Rita Mae, Michelle A. Saint-Germain, and Judy A. Horn. 1991. "Female Public Officials: A Different Voice?" *The Annals of the American Academy of Political and Social Science* 515 (May): 77–87.

MacManus, Susan and Charles S. Bulloch, III. 1989. "Women on Southern City Councils: A Decade of Change." *Journal of Political Science* 17 (Spring): 32–49.

Murphy, Russell D. 1986. "The Mayoralty and the Democratic Creed." *Urban Affairs Quarterly* 22, No. 1 (Sept.): 3–23.

Putnam, Robert. 2000. *Bowling Alone: The Collapse and Revival of American Community.* New York: Simon & Schuster.

Putnam, Robert D. 1995. "Bowling Alone: America's Declining Social Capital."

Journal of Democracy 6, No. 1 (Jan.): 65–78.

Schattschneider, E. E. 1960. *The Semi-Sovereign People.* New York: Holt, Rinehart & Winston.

Thompson, Heather Ann. 2002. *Whose Detroit? Politics, Labor and Race in a Modern American City.* Ithaca: Cornell University Press.

PROCESSES

Browning, Rufus, Dale Rogers Marshall, and David H. Tabb. 1984. *Protest Is Not Enough: The Struggle of Blacks and Hispanics for Equality in Urban Politics.* Berkeley: University of California Press.

Browning, Rufus, Dale Rogers Marshall, and David H. Tabb (Eds.). 1990. *Racial Politics in American Cities.* New York: Longman.

Cobb, Roger W. and Charles Elder. 1983. *Participation in American Politics: The Dynamics of Agenda Building* (2nd ed.). Baltimore: The Johns Hopkins University Press.

Fisher, Robert, William Ury, and Bruce Patton. 1991. *Getting to Yes: Negotiating Agreement Without Giving In* (2nd ed.). Baltimore: The Johns Hopkins University Press.

Greenblatt, Alan. 2002. "Anatomy of a Merger." *Governing* (Dec.): 20–25.

Jones, Charles O. 1977. *An Introduction to the Study of Public Policy* (2nd ed.). North Scituate, MA: Duxbury Press.

Levy, John M. 1997. *Contemporary Urban Planning* (4th ed.). Englewood Cliffs, NJ: Prentice-Hall.

Logan, John R., Rachel Bridges Whaley, and Kyle Crowder. 1997. "The Character and Consequences of Growth Regimes: An Assessment of 20 Years of Research." *Urban Affairs Review* 32, No. 5 (May): 603–630.

Rosentraub, Mark S. and Paul Helmke. 1996. "Location Theory, a Growth Coalition, and a Regime in the Development of a Medium-Sized City." *Urban Affairs Review* 31, No. 4 (March): 482–507.

Shuman, Michael H. 2000. *Going Local: Creating Self-Reliant Communities in a Global Age.* New York: Routledge.

Spirou, Costas and Larry Bennett. 2003. *It's Hardly Sportin': Stadiums, Neighborhoods, and the New Chicago.* DeKalb: Northern Illinois University.

Stone, Clarence N. 1989. *Regime Politics: Governing Atlanta 1946–1988.* Lawrence: University of Kansas Press.

Stone, Clarence N. 1980. "Systemic Power in Community Decision Making: A Restatement of Stratification Theory." *American Political Science Review* 74 (Dec.): 978–990.

Svara, James H. 1987. "Mayoral Leadership in Council-Manager Cities: Preconditions versus Preconceptions." *Journal of Politics* 49, No. 1 (Feb): 207–227.

Welch, Susan and Timothy Bledsoe. 1988. *Urban Reform and Its Consequences: A Study in Representation.* Chicago: University of Chicago Press.

Wright, Deil S. 1988. *Understanding Intergovernmental Relations* (3rd ed.). Belmont, CA: Brooks/Cole.

POLICIES

Clark, Cal and B. Oliver Walter. 1991. "Urban Political Culture, Financial Stress, and City Fiscal Austerity Strategies." *Western Political Quarterly* 44 (Spring): 676–697.

Newman, Oscar. 1972. *Defensible Space: Crime Prevention through Urban Design.* New York: Macmillan.

Peterson, Paul E. 1981. *City Limits.* Chicago: The University of Chicago Press.

Peterson, Paul E. 1995. *The Price of Federalism.* New York: The Twentieth Century Fund [copyright holder]. The Brookings Institution is the publisher.

Reid, Gary J. 1988. "How Cities in California Have Responded to Fiscal Pressure Since Proposition 13." *Public Budgeting and Finance* 8 (Spring): 20–37.

Sharp, Elaine B. 1990. *Urban Politics and Administration: From Service Delivery to Economic Development.* New York: Longman.

Sharp, Elaine B. (Ed.) 1999. *Culture Wars and Local Politics.* Lawrence: University Press of Kansas.

Stone, Clarence N. (Ed.) 1998. *Changing Urban Education.* Lawrence: University Press of Kansas.

Waste, Robert J. 1998. *Independent Cities: Rethinking U.S. Urban Policy.* New York: Oxford University Press.

Wilson, William Julius. 1987. *The Truly Disadvantaged: The Inner City, the Underclass, and Public Policy.* Chicago: The University of Chicago Press.

Index

A

AARP (American Association of Retired Persons), Camelot chapter, president (Role 74), role description of, 194

ACLU director (Role 73), role description of, 193–194

Ad hoc organized interests, 51

Administration-initiated policy proposals. *See* Policy initiation, administration-initiated

Affirmative action officer (Role 31), role description of, 185

Agenda setting
  and the policy process, 57
  stages of, 58

Agendas
  council
    first day, 94
    second day, 95
  planning commission
    first day, 95
    second day, 95
  preparation of, 175, 179

A.M.E. church minister (Role 32), role description of, 186

Amendments to Camelot charter, 166

Applied Gerontological Institute, Camelot State University, director (Role 36), role description of, 186

Area descriptions. *See* Camelot, area descriptions

Art sale from the R-2 home variance request issue, 152–153

Artist, freelance (Role 76), role description of, 194

Assistant city manager (Role 9), role description of, 179–180

At large elections, consequences of, 62

Attorneys, role descriptions of
  Role 41, 187
  Role 49, 189
  Role 51, 189

B

Bartender, Mike's Bar and Grill (Role 70), role description of, 193

Basic data, Camelot, 155–156

Beauty salon owner (Role 30), role description of, 185

Beauty salon zone variance issue, 105–106

Beginning the simulation, 92

Borrowing, city, 40

Budget
    central clearance point, 56, 67
    policy initiation, 54–57
    preparation of, 55–57
    worksheet, 118–119
Budget issue, 110–119
Business and Professional Women's
        Organization, Camelot Chapter,
        president (Role 52), role description
        of, 190

C
Camelot
    area descriptions, 155–159 (see also inside
        front and back covers)
        Camelot Acres, 159
        Camelot Heights, 156–157
        Central Business District (CBD), 157
        College Town, 157
        Crown Knolls, 157–158
        Forest Acres, 158
        Madisonville, 158
        North Madisonville, 158
        River Town, 159
        South Ridge, 159–160
        University Park, 159
    basic data, 155–156
    budget issue, 110–119
    budget procedures, 110–115
    Charter
        amendments to, 166
        provisions of, 160–166
    class composition of, 155–156
    economics of, 156
    election procedures, 171–172
    ethnic composition of, 155
    industry, 155–156
    map of (see inside front and back covers)
    nominating petition, 195–196
    population of, 155
    zoning regulations, 166–169
Camelot Acres area, 159. See also inside front
        and back covers
Camelot art museum, director (Role 61),
        role description of, 191
Camelot Daily News, 92–93
Camelot Heights area, 156–157. See also
        inside front and back covers
Camelot marina project issue, 118
Camelot public library, director (Role 57),
        role description of, 190
Camelot Shores project issue, 117
Camelot State University
    location (see inside front and back covers)
    president (Role 24), role description of,
        184

Candidates, selection of, 61–62
CANT (Camelotters Against New Taxes),
        president of Camelot chapter (Role
        75), role description of, 194
Careerism in elected offices, 59–61
Carport variance request issue, 152
Central Business District (CBD) area, 157.
        See also inside front and back covers
Central clearance function, 56, 67
Chamber of Commerce of Camelot,
        executive director (Role 62), role
        description of, 191
Charter of Camelot. See Camelot, Charter
Christian Revival Movement, vice president
        (Role 56), role description of, 190
Cities
    constraints on, 24–27
    definition of, 25
    fiscal constraints on, 36–47
    government, 12–23
    housekeeping functions, 29–30
    impact of federal and state regulations,
        33–35
    legal authority of, 24–27
    police powers, 29–30
    powers of, 24–27
    revenues
        constraints on, 36–47
        sources of, 36–47
    taxes (see city revenue sources)
Citizen-initiated policy proposals. See Policy
        initiation, citizen-initiated
City area descriptions. See Camelot, area
        descriptions
City government
    access to decision makers, 65–66
    diagram, 69
    forms of, 68–78
        commission, 73
        comparison of, 75–78
        council-manager, 74
        diagrams of comparison, 69
        planning commission, the place of, 82
        strong-mayor and council, 72
        weak-mayor and council, 70
    responsiveness of decision makers, 66
    salience of issues to citizenry, 63–64
    stakes in political decisions, 64–65
City manager (Role 8)
    appointment of, 162
    duties of, 162–163, 178–179
    relations with council, 162–163, 178–179
    removal of, 163
    role description of, 178–179
    salaries of, 74
    selection of, 162–163, 178–179

City planning commission. *See* Planning commission
City revenue sources
  borrowing, 40
  gambling and lottery profits, 40–41
  income tax
    description of, 37
    enforcement problem, 44
    fairness problem, 42
  intergovernmental transfers, 39
  miscellaneous fees, 39
  problems, 41–47
    borrowing, 40
    competition, 43
    debt prohibition, 40
    earmarking, 45
    enforcement feasibility, 44
    fairness, 42
    other administrative costs, 46–47
    preemption and mandates, 45
  property tax
    administrative costs, 37
    competition problem, 43
    description of, 37
    enforcement problem, 44
    fairness problem, 42
  sales tax
    description of, 38
    enforcement problem, 44
  types of, 37–39
  user fees
    description of, 39
    enforcement problem, 44
    fairness problem, 42
City taxation problems. *See* City revenue sources, problems
City taxes. *See* City revenue sources
Class composition of Camelot, 155–156
Clerk of council (Role 18)
  duties of, 161, 182
  recording *Minutes,* 182
  role description of, 182
Coalition building, importance of, 90
College Town area, 157. *See also inside front and back covers*
Commercial zoning regulations, 166–169
Commission form of local government, 69, 73
Community
  definitions, 5–11
  functional interdependence of, 5–9
Community power, 16–23
  areas of agreement in discussion of, 16–21
  cumulative patterns and, 16–21
  dispersed patterns and, 16–21
  systemic power, 18

Comprehensive plan, 82–83
Conflict of interest
  definition of, 165–166
  penalty for violation, 165–166
Constraints
  on budget changes in the simulation, 113–115
  on cities
    fiscal, 36–47
    legal, 24–26
  on participant's behavior in simulation, 87–88
Couches in yards and on porches issue, 146–148
Council
  agendas for first and second sessions of simulation, 94–95
  Charter provisions, 161
  duties of, 161–162, 175–176
  how to run a meeting, 96–99
  parliamentary rules for, 96–99
  powers of, 161–162, 175–176
  recording *Minutes,* 182
  (Roles 1–7) role descriptions of, 176–178
  sample meeting, 94
  vacancies, filling of, 161
Councilors (Roles 1–7), 176–178
Council-manager form of local government, 69, 74
Crown Knolls area, 157–158. *See also inside front and back covers*
Culture Wars issue, 52–53
Curfew issue, 148–149

D
Daily News. See Camelot Daily News
Data Tech Corporation, president (Role 47), role description of, 188–189
Decision makers
  political recruitment, 59–61
  selection of, 61–62
Decision making
  importance of, 65
  comparison of local and federal, 66
  initiative and referendum, role in, 17
  in local government issues, 68–71
  political resources and, 14–15
  public officials and, 13–14
  responsiveness of government as a factor, 66
  salience as a factor in, 63–64
  stakes in, 64–65
  systemic power and, 18–19
  types of issues as a factor, 63–67
Democracy, definition of, 12–13

Development editor, Megabook Publishers (Role 45), role description of, 188

Developers. *See* Real estate developers

Dillon's Rule, 26

Directors of various agencies or organizations. *See name of agency or organization*

Downtown hotel plaza issue, 106–110

Drug enforcement unit issue, 115

Drug testing issue, 138–139

E

Economic organized interests, 50

Economics, in Camelot, 156

Editor and publisher, *Camelot Daily News* (Role 20)
 duties and importance of, 184
 role description of, 184

Editorial writer, *Camelot Daily News* (Role 21), role description of, 184

Elected offices
 and careerism, 60
 and professionalism, 60
 and volunteerism, 60

Elections, 177–180
 at large, 62
 incumbency, advantage of, 61–62
 nominating petition, 195–196
 nonpartisan, impact of, 61
 procedures, 171–173
 sample ballot, 173

Eminent domain
 definition of, 30
 newer uses of, 30–32

Eminent domain issue, 136–138

Ethnic composition of Camelot, 155–156

Evaluation form, 215

Evolution of community power patterns, 16–23

Executive director, Camelot Chamber of Commerce (Role 62), role description of, 191

F

Fairness in housing and employment issue, 102

Federal and state regulation, impact on cities, 33–35

Feminist Majority, head of Camelot Chapter of (Role 54), role description of, 190

Fire chief (Role 19), 183

Fire department station map, 133

Fire hose issue, 131–133

Firehouse Bookstore, owner (Role 60), role description of, 191

Football player, retired professional (Role 29), role description of, 185

Forest Acres area, 158. *See also inside front and back covers*

Former homeless person (Role 65), role description of, 192

Freelance artist (Role 76), role description of, 194

Functional interdependence, changing role of, 4–8, 10–11

G

Gambling, profits for city from, 40

Gerontological institute, director (Role 36), role description of, 186

Gynecologic and prenatal services issue, 116

H

Hair stylist (Role 30), role description of, 185

Health department, director (Role 44), role description of, 188

High school teacher (Role 58), role description of, 191

Hispanic Coalition of Camelot, chairperson (Role 72), role description of, 193

Home for unmarried pregnant teenagers issue, 127–128

Homeland Security, director of (Role 68), 193

Homeless person, former (Role 65), role description of, 192

Homeowner rights issue, 149–152

Home rule
 definition of, 26
 limits to, 26–27
 role of courts in application of, 24–27

Hotel plaza issue, 106–110

Housekeeping functions of cities, 29–30

I

Income distribution, role of local and national governments in, 66

Income tax, city. *See* City revenue sources, income tax

Incumbency, advantages of, 61–62

Influence, political
 concentration of, 16–18
 resources, importance for, 14–15

Initiative and referendum
 Charter provision for, 164
 significance for decision making, 17

Initiative petition sample form, 197

Institute for Gerontology, Camelot State University, director (Role 36), role description of, 186
Institutional organized interests, 50
Insurance agent (Role 35), role description of, 186
Interest groups. *See* Organized interests
Issues
    adult bookstore (see Massage therapy facility)
    art sale from the R-2 home variance request (ZAB issue), 152–153
    beauty salon zone variance, 105–106
    budget, 110–119
    Camelot marina project, 118
    Camelot Shores project, 117
    carport variance request (ZAB issue), 152
    couches in yards and on porches, 146–148
    curfew, 148–149
    downtown hotel plaza, 106–110
    drug enforcement unit, 115
    drug testing, 138–139
    eminent domain, 136–138
    fairness in housing and employment, 102
    fire hose, 131–133
    gynecologic and prenatal services, 116
    home for unmarried pregnant teenagers, 127–128
    homeowner rights, 149–152
    massage therapy facility, 120
    noise ordinance, 132–136
    "obscene" photographs, 121–123
    officer protection program, 102–105
    planned parenthood services, 117
    private use of public space, 143–146
    resolution of sympathy, 101
    sideyard or backyard? (ZAB issue), 153–154
    smoking ban, 120–121
    strip mall development, 123–126
    topless bar and grill, 128–131
    USA Patriot Act, 139–142
    wildflowers, 142–143
    Zoning Appeals Board issues, 152–154

J

Judge Dillon, 26
Junior high teacher (Role 43), role description of, 188

L

Lancelot PTA vice president (Role 42), role description of, 188
Land-use control, 27–29

Land-use zoning. *See* Zoning
Large business owner (Role 25), role description of, 184
League of Women Voters, president (Role 28), role description of, 185
Legal authority, of city, 24–27
Legal constraints, on cities, 24–27
Legal powers, of cities, 24–27
Local government
    access to decision makers, 65
    comparison of forms of, 68–78
    issues, 63–67
    reasons for studying, 5–11
    salience of, 63–65
    weak mayor and council, 70
    See also Cities; City government: form(s) of
Local government revenues. *See* Cities, revenue
Lotteries, profits for city from 40–41

M

Madisonville area, 158. *See also inside front and back covers*
Manager. *See* City manager
Map of Camelot. *See inside front and back covers*
Massage therapy facility issue, 120
Massage therapy operator (Role 23), role description of, 184
Mayor, 161, 175
    Charter provisions for office of, 161
    duties of, 175
    office of, 175
    selection of, 175
Minister, A.M.E. Church (Role 32), role description of, 186
Minister, First Presbyterian Church (Role 48), role description of, 189
Minutes of council meeting, 162–163, 178–179
Municipal corporation, definition of, 24–25

N

NAACP, head of local chapter (Role 50), role description of, 189
Newspaper. *See* Editor and publisher, *Camelot Daily News*
Newspaper roles, importance of, 183–184
Noise ordinance issue, 132–136
Nomination for office
    form for, 195–196
    by petition, 61
    by primary election, 61–62

Nonpartisan elections, 61
  advantage to incumbents, 61
  ballot, 67
  impact on elections, 61–62, 67
North Madisonville area, 158. *See also inside front and back covers*

O

Oath of office, 181
"Obscene" photographs issue, 121–123
Office holders, selection of, 61–62
Office protection program issue, 102–105
Ordinance, enactment of, 178–179
Organized interests
  ad hoc, 51
  culture war issues, 52
  definition of, 48
  economic, 50
  institutional, 49
Organized local community, 8–9
Owner, Firehouse bookstore (Role 60), role description of, 191
Owner, Large business (Role 25), role description of, 184
Owner, Small business (Role 26), role description of, 184–185
Owner, Topless bar and grill (Role 59), role description of, 191
Owner-operator of Camelot Adult Bookstore and Massage Therapy Facility (Role 23), role description of, 184

P

Parliamentary procedure. *See* Council: parliamentary rules for; Council: sample meeting
Part-time worker (Role 66), role description of, 192
Party organization, role of, 59–61
Performance of functions in community. *See* Functional interdependence
Personal interest. *See* Conflict of interest
Planned parenthood services issue, 117
Planning commission
  agendas for first and second sessions of simulation, 94–95
  appointment of, 164, 180
  duties of, 164, 180
  place of, 82
  powers of, 164, 169–170
  (Roles 10–16) role description of, 180–182
Planning department, director (Role 33), role description of, 186

Planning departments, 80–82
Plans of local government. *See* City government: forms of
Pluralism, 57
Pluralist theory, 57
Police Benevolent Association, president (Role 27), role description of, 185
Police chief (Role 17), role description of, 182
Police officer (Role 46), role description of, 188
Policy initiation, 54–57
  administration-initiated, 55–57
  agenda setting, 57
  budget process, 56–57
  citizen-initiated, 55
  definition of, 54
  executive dominance, 55–57
Policy process, meaning of, 1–3
Political decision making. *See* Decision making
Political parties, 59–61
Political recruitment, 59–61
Political resources, 14–19
Politics, definition of, 12
Population of Camelot, 155–156
Power. *See* Community power
Power structure, conclusions regarding, 13–14, 21–23
Powers of cities, 24–27
Presbyterian Church, minister (Role 48), role description of, 189
President. *See names of various organizations and groups*
Pressure groups. *See* Organized interests
Primary elections, 61–62
Private use of public space issue, 143–146
Professor Schmooz (no role number), role description of, 194
Property taxes, city. *See* City revenue sources, property tax
PTA, vice president (Role 42), role description of, 188
Public health department, director (Role 44), role description of, 188
Public library, director (Role 57), role description of, 190
Public health nurse (Role 71), role description of, 193

R

Real estate developers (Roles 38–40), role descriptions of, 187
Recall of elected officials, 165

Recruitment for political office, 59–61
Referendum petition, 164–165
Reporter, *Camelot Daily News* (Role 22),
    role description of, 184
Residential zoning regulations, 166–169
Resolution of sympathy issue, 101
Resolutions, approval of, 162
Resources, political, 14–15
    concentration of, 16–18
    cumulative, 16–18
    dispersed, 16–18
    significance of, 14–15
Retired professional football player (Role
    29), role description of, 185
Revenue problems
    administrative costs, 46–67
    competition, 43–44
    debt prohibition, 40
    earmarking, 45
    enforcement feasibility, 44–45
    fairness, 42–43
    grant terms and conditions, 46
    mandates, 45–46
    preemption, 45–46
    state legislature role, 36–37
Revenues, local government. *See* City
    revenue sources
Right to Life Society of Greater Camelot,
    president (Role 53), role description
    of, 190
River Town area, 159. *See also inside front and
    back covers*
Role descriptions
    AARP (American Association of Retired
        Persons), Camelot chapter director
        (Role 74), 194
    ACLU (American Civil Liberties Union),
        director (Role 73), 193–194
    affirmative action officer (Role 31),
        185
    art museum director (Role 61), 191
    artist, freelance (Role 76), 194
    assistant city manager (Role 9), 179–180
    attorneys (Roles 41, 49, and 51), 187,
        189
    bartender (Role 70), 193
    beautician (Role 30), 185
    building inspector (Role 67), 192
    Business and Professional Women's
        Organization, president, Camelot
        chapter (Role 52), 190
    Camelot Art Museum, director (Role 61),
        191
    Camelot Chamber of Commerce,
        executive director (Role 62), 191

Camelot Chapter of AARP (American
    Association of Retired Persons),
    president (Role 74), 194
Camelot public library, director (Role 57),
    190
Camelot State University, president
    (Role 24), 184
CANT (Camelotters Against New Taxes),
    president (Role 75), 194
Christian Revival Movement, vice
    president (Role 56), 190
city manager (Role 8), 178–179
clerk of council (Role 18), 182
councilors (Roles 1–7), 176–178
Data Tech Corporation, president
    (Role 47), 188–189
development editor, Megabook Publishers
    (Role 45), 188
developers (*see* Role descriptions, real
    estate developers)
directors of agencies (*see agency name*)
editor and publisher, *Camelot Daily News*
    (Role 20), 184
editorial writer, *Camelot Daily News*
    (Role 21), 184
Feminist Majority, head, Camelot Chapter
    (Role 54), 190
Fire chief (Role 19), 183
Firehouse Bookstore owner (Role 60), 191
former homeless person (Role 65), 192
freelance artist (Role 76), 194
Gerontological Studies Institute, director
    (Role 36), 186
hair stylist (Role 30), 185
health department, director (Role 44), 188
high school teacher (Role 58), 191
Hispanic Coalition, chairperson (Role 72),
    193
Homeland Security, director of (Role 68),
    193
Institute for Applied Gerontological
    Studies, director (Role 36), 186
insurance agent (Role 35), 186
junior high teacher (Role 43), 188
Lancelot PTA vice president (Role 42),
    188
League of Women Voters, president
    (Role 28), 185
massage therapy operator (Role 23), 184
mayor, description of duties and how
    selected, 175
minister, A.M.E. Church (Role 32), 186
minister, Presbyterian Church (Role 48),
    189
NAACP, chapter head (Role 50), 189

Role descriptions (*continued*)
nurse, public health (Role 71), 193
owner, large business (Role 25), 184
owner, small business (Role 26), 184–185
part-time worker (Role 66), 192
planning commissioners (Roles 10–16), 180–182
planning department, director (Role 33), 186
Police Benevolent Association, president (Role 27), 185
police chief (Role 17), 182
police officer (Role 46), 188
presidents of various institutions and groups (*see name of institution or group*)
Professor Schmooz (no role number), 194
PTA vice president (Role 42), 188
Public Health Department, director (role 44), 188
public health nurse (Role 71), 193
real estate developers (Roles 38–40), 187
reporter, *Camelot Daily News* (Role 22), 184
retired professional football player (Role 29), 185
Right to Life Society, president, Greater Camelot chapter (Role 53), 190
single parent on welfare (Role 63), 192
social worker (Role 69), 193
solicitor (city attorney) (Role 64), 192
student body president, CSU (Role 34), 186
student body vice president, CSU (Role 55), 190
topless bar and grill owner (Role 59), 191
urban welfare program of Camelot, director (Role 37), 187
vice mayor, description of duties and how selected, 161
vice presidents of various organizations (*see name of various organizations*)
Role request form, 195
Rules of order, 96–99
Running a meeting, 96

S
Sales tax. *See* City revenue sources, sales tax
Salience, importance in decision-making, 64
Sample ballot, 173
Sample nominating petition, 195–196
Selection of candidates, 61–62
Shared destiny and community, 5
Shared interests and community, 5
Shared values and community, 5

"Sideyard or backyard" issue (ZAB), 153–154
Simulation
beginning, 92
coalition building, 90
constraints, 88
definition of, 87
limits of, 88
points to keep in mind, 90
reasons for doing, 87
role request form, 195
rules governing, 88
running a meeting, 96
starting a meeting, 94
understanding the process, 89
using materials, 91
voting on a motion, issue, ordinance, or resolution, 97–99
Simulation time and real time, 93
Single parent on welfare (Role 63),192
Slate making group, 61
Small business owner (Role 26), role description of, 184–185
Smoking Ban Issue, 120–121
Social worker (Role 69), role description of, 193
South Ridge area, 159–160. *See also inside front and back covers*
Special use permit; *see* Zoning regulations, 167–169
"Spot zoning," 83
"Stakes" in the decision making process, importance of, 64
Starting a meeting, 94
Strip mall development issue, 123–127
Strong-mayor and council form of local government, 72
Structure of influence in community decision making. *See* Community power
Student body president, CSU (Role 34), role description of, 186
Student body vice president, CSU (Role 55), role description of, 190
"Sunshine law," 169–170
Systemic power and decision making, 18

T
Taxation
city (*see* City revenue sources)
increase of (in simulation), 113–114, 163
problems (*see* City revenue sources: problems)
Taxes, city. *See* City revenue sources
Time, simulated and real, 93

Topless bar and grill issue, 128–131
Topless bar and grill owner (Role 59), role description of, 191

U

University Park area, 159. *See also inside front and back covers*
Urban welfare program, director (Role 37), role description of, 187
USA Patriot Act Issue, 139–142
User fees. *See* City revenue sources, user fees
Using the simulation materials, 91

V

Vice mayor, how selected, 161
Vice president, CSU student body (Role 55), role description of, 190
Vice president, Christian Revival Movement (Role 56), role description of, 190

Vice president, Lancelot PTA (Role 42), role description of, 188
Volunteerism in elected offices, 59
Voting on a motion, issue, ordinance, or resolution, 97

W

Wildflowers issue, 142–143

Z

ZAB. *See* Zoning Appeals Board
Zoning, 79–82, 83–84
    definition of, 27–28
    discussion of, 83–84
    master plan, role of, 79–84
Zoning Appeals Board, 84
Zoning Appeals Board issues, 152–154
Zoning map. *See inside front and back covers*
Zoning regulations and land use, 167–169

Quick Reference Page

I. Constraints on Simulation Participants

1. You cannot violate the laws of the state and nation.
2. You are constrained by the city charter and city ordinances, especially the budget and zoning regulations.
3. You must remain within the bounds of realism.
4. You must remain within your role.

II. Abbreviated Index

Area descriptions of Camelot, 173–177

Budget issue, constraints on changes, 121–123

Camelot City Charter, 177–182

City Manager, duties of, 179–180, 194

Clerk of Council, duties of, 178, 197

Conflict of interest, 181–182

Council agendas, 101–102

Council proceedings, sample meeting, 100

Council Members, duties of, 178, 190–191

How to run a meeting, 103–105

Mayor, duties of, 189–190

Nomination petition, 213

Parliamentary Rules, rank order, 103–104

Planning Commission agendas 101–102

Planning Commission, explanation of, 87–88

Planning Commissioners, duties of, 180, 195

Role descriptions, 189–209

Role Request Form, 211

Sunshine Law, 184–185

Zoning Regulations, 183–184

III. Issues

Art Sale from the R–2 Home Variance Request, 168–169

Beauty Salon Zone Variance, 112–113

Budget, 118–130

Carport Variance Request, 168

Couches in the Yards and on the Porches, 161–163

Curfew, 163–164

Downtown Hotel Plaza, 113–118

Drug Testing, 155–156

Eminent Domain, 136–138

Fairness in Housing and Employment, 102

Fire Hose, 131–133

Home of Unmarried Pregnant Teenagers, 146–148

Massage Therapy Facility, 131

Noise Ordinance, 152–155

Obscene Photographs, 132–134

Officer Protection Program, 109–112

Private Use of Public Space, 158–161

Resolution of Sympathy, 108

Rights of a Homeowner, 164–167

Sideyard or Backyard?, 169–171

Smoking Ban, 120–121

Strip mall Development, 142–147

Topless Bar and Grill, 148–151

USA Patriot Act, 139–142

Wildflowers, 156–158

Don't forget: There will be a debriefing and critique session at the close of the simulation, and you will be involved in it. You may want to read pages 89–90 in order to be prepared for it.

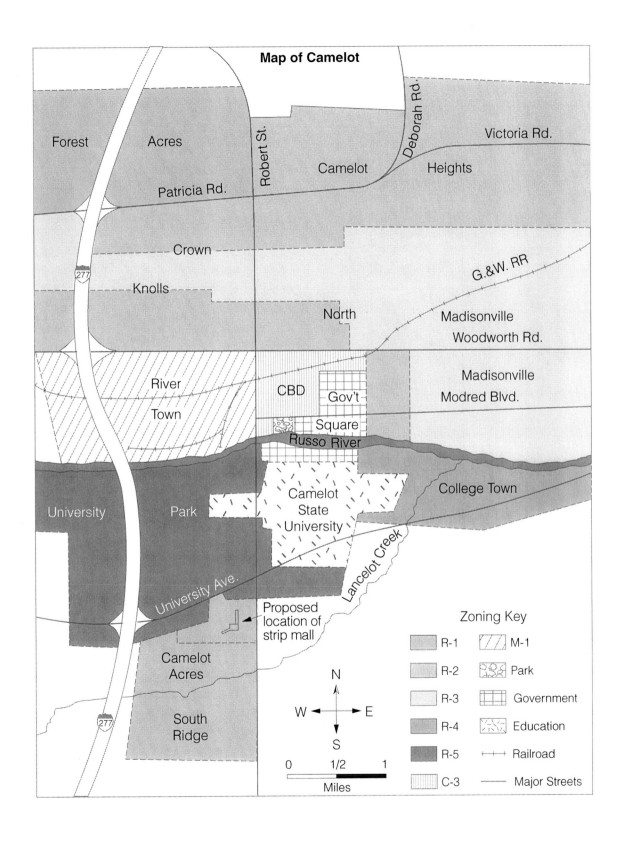

Map of Camelot

Forest   Acres

Robert St.

Deborah Rd.

Victoria Rd.

Camelot   Heights

Patricia Rd.

Crown

G.&W. RR

Knolls

North

Madisonville
Woodworth Rd.

River

Town

CBD

Gov't

Madisonville
Modred Blvd.

Square

Russo River

University   Park

Camelot
State
University

College Town

Lancelot Creek

University Ave.

Proposed
location of
strip mall

Camelot
Acres

South
Ridge

Zoning Key

R-1		M-1	
R-2		Park	
R-3		Government	
R-4		Education	
R-5		Railroad	
C-3		Major Streets	

N

W — E

S

0   1/2   1

Miles

277

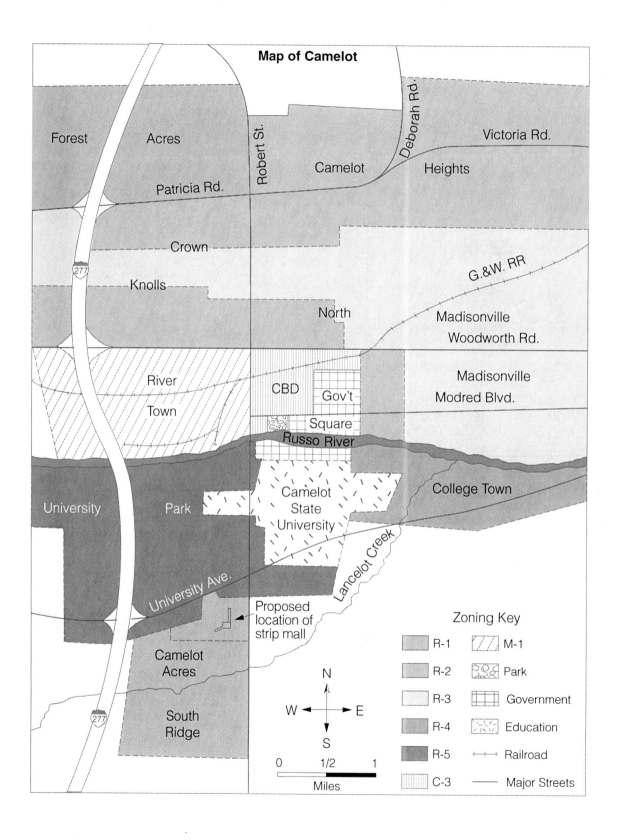

Map of Camelot

Forest Acres

Robert St.

Deborah Rd.

Victoria Rd.

Camelot Heights

Patricia Rd.

Crown Knolls

G.&W. RR

North

Madisonville Woodworth Rd.

River Town

CBD

Gov't

Madisonville Modred Blvd.

Square

Russo River

College Town

University Park

Camelot State University

Lancelot Creek

University Ave.

Proposed location of strip mall

Camelot Acres

South Ridge

277

Zoning Key

R-1		M-1	
R-2		Park	
R-3		Government	
R-4		Education	
R-5		Railroad	
C-3		Major Streets	

N
W — E
S

0   1/2   1

Miles

CPSIA information can be obtained
at www.ICGtesting.com
Printed in the USA
FFOW041551170113
717FF

9 780534 602796